W9-ACQ-171

STRUCTURAL
PRINCIPLES IN
OLD ENGLISH POETRY

STRUCTURAL PRINCIPLES IN OLD ENGLISH POETRY

NEIL D. ISAACS

THE UNIVERSITY OF TENNESSEE PRESS · KNOXVILLE

CARL A. RUDISILL LIBRARY
LENOIR RHYNE COLLEGE

829.1
Is Is
66680
July, 1969

Copyright © 1968 all rights reserved
The University of Tennessee Press
Library of Congress Catalog Number 68–17143
Manufactured in the United States of America

TO MY MOTHER AND FATHER

FOREWORD

Originally, the key phrase "Structural Principles" in the title read "The Structural Principle." At the outset, then, the book was designed to show that Old English poets were artists, sophisticated in the use of their conventions, who organized their material according to formal patterns. And although the total effect of the various chapters may now fulfill the original design, that fulfillment seems only incidental and very nearly tautological —as if I had set out to show that Old English poetry is art and that Old English makers of verse are poets. Of course they are. The only possible explanation for such an effort to substantiate the obvious would be that these obvious conclusions have not been reached or stated often enough.

From the beginning, however, the emphasis of the book has paralleled the methodology of the individual chapters. The integrity of each poem studied has been respected, and within the limitations of nature and the artifices of criticism each poem, under probing, has yielded some knowledge of its formal pattern. Thus the present title, rather than insisting on the fact of artistry, reflects the discoveries of versatility and virtuosity in the formal patterns of Old English poetry.

The critical approach of these chapters assumes that there is value in isolating formal patterns in art. The bias of a formalist critic is apparent throughout, though the formalism practiced is pragmatic rather than absolute. If art is defined as the imposition of form upon human experience, it does not necessarily follow that it is form itself which communicates; rather it is form which provides the possibility of communication. And it is the potential that counts, not the achievement (the inherent energy, not the measurable kinetic output). It is the formalist critic's job of work to illuminate the artifact by analysis, to clear the channels of communication.

But there are many ways to illuminate an artifact. Absolute formalism has anathematized most external approaches as "fallacies," including the intentional, affective, formal, influential, psychological, biographical, historical, sociological, political (or politico-economic: *read* Marxist), ideological, mythic, folklorist, ritual, and archetypal approaches. All these have one thing in common: each is an attempt to approach, interpret, or "read" an artifact in the light of *one* particular aspect of its creation, its heritage, its purpose, or its success—that is, one to the exclusion of others. No such approach can be valid or meaningful for universal application. They all proceed from a tangential position.

Yet there are times when tangential lines may be extended so as to penetrate an obscure portion of the sacred circle of art and open it up for newly enlightened scrutiny. The basic formalist principle remains unshaken: the only universally valid approach to art looks at the artifact itself. But the nature of the individual work and its ingredients will determine what other approaches are needed. The use of such additional methods in the following chapters is what qualifies the formalism as pragmatic. After all, if illumination of a work of art is the goal, any method which can successfully illuminate should be employed. In another sense, too, the general method is pragmatic: each poem is studied to discover how it works, is analyzed to see how its elements work together, and may be evaluated according to how well its elements work together and how well it works as a whole. What is meant by "work together" or "works as a whole"— to do what? No concrete absolute conclusion is possible from the relativist position which "pragmatic" implies, but the critic must discover how well the artifact works (and how

well its elements work together) to do whatever it is it has
to do.

If a work of art is allowed to limit itself in terms of what
it sets out to do, then it creates within itself its own criteria
for judgment. If a poem designed as a mnemonic device for
the number of days in each month performs that function
with universal success, it must be called an excellent poem.
One might even call it a perfect poem of its kind, if one
could not conceive of a better one of that kind. Similarly,
a poem about, say, a flea may conceivably be better of its
kind than a poem on the nature of divine love is of its kind.
This is not to say, in absolute terms, that the former is a
better poem than the latter. A flawed epic may be considered
better than a nearly perfect but trivial epigram. But such
comparative evaluations are substantially extraneous to the
work of art—and to the formalist critic, who must determine
what the artifact has to do and how well it does it. There
is room for, perhaps even a necessity for, what Wellek and
Warren call "extrinsic criticism,"[1] including the sort of
evaluative judgments suggested above and involving an ab-
solutism, with hierarchies of values and worth. But the
systems or standards must be imposed from outside the arti-
facts, even from outside the realm of art, by moralities, ethics,
and categorical imperatives. The point I want to stress here
is that until the formalist critic does his job of work on the
artifact, it cannot be placed properly on whatever scale the
extrinsic criticism is imposing.

Extrinsic criticism as I have described it inevitably becomes involved with the critic's emotional concerns. Pragmatic formalism strives, as nearly as possible, to exclude
emotional involvements. Only by approaching a pure intel-
lectuality can a critic hope to deal objectively with the objective considerations within his scope (what legislative
committees call an area of competence, meaning what the
investigator wants the witness to talk about). Yet surely

[1] René Wellek and Austin Warren, *Theory of Literature* (New York,
1956).

there is no such thing as purely intellectual art; however
"cerebral" the piece of music, however "geometric" the plas-
tic design, no aesthetic response is totally separate from an
emotional response. One might even go so far as to say that
the aesthetic response is an emotional response. In any case,
at least one of the channels of communication through which
art operates is human emotion.

How then can the critic clear the channels at the same
time that he cuts one of them off, perhaps the major one?
The answer is that we are talking about two different things.
The experience of art is significantly an emotional experience; the full experience of art requires clear channels for
all possible forms of human communication. But the experiencer is not a critic; the full experiencer is not an analyst
because he must grasp whole the whole work. The critic, on
the other hand, must reduce the possibility of error, must
attempt to *clarify* the channels of communication, that is,
explain or analyze the various workings (together) of the
elements in the artifact (the objective evidence) and account for its success, or failure, in communicating as a
whole.[2] The critic follows established laboratory procedure
by isolating the elements for investigation; it is a necessary
part of the critical process to shut off a channel before it can
be studied. When clarified, it may operate more clearly.
That is, the working of the whole may be better understood
when the rôle of each part has been analyzed; the possibilities of communication may be more complete when, each
channel having been cleared separately, the whole network
is put back together.

But the critic is also an experiencer, or to put it more
accurately the critic must nearly always have been an experiencer first. This problem, however, may be turned into
a positive advantage. If the critical analysis confirms the
aesthetic experience, if it adequately explains how the experience has been produced or communicated, it may be

---

[2] To be quite precise I would have to continue talking about the
possibilities of communicating.

said to be valid.[3] The aesthetic experience and the critical
analysis serve as checks on each other. If the analysis tends
to contradict the experience, then something is wrong. Either
the experience has been false (by which I mean that it may
have been produced by the imposition of cultural or social
biases or by the intrusion of extraneous, personal elements—
the experiencer's own individual emotions which he brings
to every experience, not those which he may be said to
share with other men) or the analysis has been false (by
which I mean that it has been thrown off either by the
critic's heavy emphasis on particular elements, by his mis-
taking certain elements for others, by his failing to recognize
certain elements, or by his failing to discern the relationships among elements). A case in point is the discussion of
Exodus in Chapter Ten. I have toward this poem an irrational bias which may be called a sentimental flaw in
critical machinery or an inherited racial characteristic or a
chauvinistic what-you-will. The demonstrable excellences of
Exodus are many, but my fondness for it exceeds what my
critical procedures can justify.

Criticism is a cumulative process and must always assume and aspire toward the ideal of a perfect audience. The
perfect audience, however, is a double impossibility. Positively, it must be aware of everything in and about a work
of art; negatively, it must not let anything extraneous intrude upon its experience of the work. That is, a hypothetical individual who is a perfect audience must assume that
every other perfect audience has the identical experience
of the artifact. Thus the theoretical possibility of a universal
response, of "one right interpretation," is established. But
the theoretical possibility is a practical impossibility, since
(1) no individual can know everything about anything and
(2) no two individuals can have identical experiences (they

---

[3] This is not to say that criticism should do no more than explain the
experience. It should help to make possible an optimum experience for
any future experiencer or re-experiencer. For this and other valuable
suggestions I am grateful to George T. Wright.

cannot eliminate the differentiae of individual personal-
ities in order to share a realm of pure reason).

It is within this ultimate paradox that the critic labors.
Working toward the ideal that he knows is impossible, he
must build on the illuminations of past critics toward an
understanding of a particular work. The scholarly apparatus
of the discipline of criticism is therefore indispensable. I
have called the critical process cumulative, but it is by no
means a linear or a spiral or even a dialectical progression
(though at times it may be all three). New knowledge sometimes eliminates old (and bad theories sometimes drive out
good); and inevitably, while new discoveries are being made,
the progression of time will obscure some of the knowledge
necessary for what I have called the full experience. This is
the ironic dimension of the critical paradox. Pragmatically,
the best criticism is that which best accounts for the workings of the elements in an artifact and therefore accounts
most completely for the possible performance of the artifact
as a whole.

The following chapters are severely limited in their approach to Old English poems. Formalistically, they search
out structural principles or patterns in the poems, but pragmatically, they employ other avenues of approach which may
have some bearing on structure. The object is to supply illumination of certain elements in the poetry as a contribu-
tion toward the cumulative progression of criticism. In part
the choice of poems has been governed by my ability to suggest something new or at least somewhat different about
them, but most of the important shorter poems have been
included. The arrangement of the chapters themselves has
an associational rationale which should be apparent at almost every turn.

Ideally my audience should have not only a general familiarity with the material but copies of the texts to follow as
we go through the poems. I have used throughout the texts

of *The Ango-Saxon Poetic Records*[4] (which will explain the absence of markings for vowel length), though the notes will contain frequent reference to other helpful editions. Several of the chapters are reworkings of previously published essays. I am grateful to the editors of *Neuphilologische Mitteilungen* for permission to reprint material in Chapters Two and Eight, *Philological Quarterly* for the first part of Chapter Six, *American Notes and Queries* for the second part of Chapter Six, and *Papers on Language and Literature* for the third part of Chapter Six.[5] I am also grateful to my friend and colleague John Tinkler, who has read all of my work with characteristically intelligent skepticism.

Thanks for the support of this project are due to the American Council of Learned Societies for a grant-in-aid, to the Graduate School of The University of Tennessee for two summer research grants, and to the Department of English, Kenneth L. Knickerbocker, Head, for released time. The greatest support, granted in many ways, is acknowledged in the dedication.

[4] George Phillip Krapp and Elliott van Kirk Dobbie, eds., 6 vols. (New York, 1931–53).

[5] "Image, Metaphor, Irony, Allusion, and Moral: The Shifting Perspective of *The Seafarer*," *NM*, LXVII (1966), 266–82; "Battlefield Tour: Brunanburg," *NM*, LXIII (1962), 236–44; "Still Waters Run *Undiop*," *PQ*, XLIV (1965), 545–49; "The Death of Edgar (and Others)," *ANQ*, IV (1965), 52–55; "Who Says What in *Advent Lyric VII?*" *PLL*, II (1966), 162–66.

CONTENTS

STRUCTURAL
PRINCIPLES IN
OLD ENGLISH POETRY

CHAPTER ONE

PROGRESSIVE IDENTIFICATIONS:
THE STRUCTURAL PRINCIPLE OF
THE DREAM OF THE ROOD

A structural principle is any artistic device that controls the ordering, arrangement, form, or formal order of a poem. When such a device is discovered, it is likely to be significant to the poem and is likely to bear important testimony to its art. Thus, this first chapter, by examining critically the structural principle of *The Dream of the Rood,* testifies to its artistry. It does not, however, pretend to be a definitive explication of the poem; and this disclaimer holds for every chapter.

The unique effectiveness of *The Dream of the Rood* sets it apart from the rest of Old English poetry, and its structural principles, too, are unique. Yet this chapter serves to initiate the entire sequence of analyses of structural principles in two ways: as a paradigm by demonstrating the possibilities of such analysis and as an introduction by finding in the intricate workings of this poem suggestions of the kinds of structural principles at work in other poems. For example, a minor aspect of this analysis considers the up-and-down movement of the poet's focus; similar devices are significant in *Brunanburh* (backwards-forwards movement) and *Maldon* (apart-and-together movement). Related to these patterns are the formal arrangements of *Daniel* and *Exodus,* in which the movement of focus is directly related to the pace of the narrative's movement. Pace and focus are also related to matters of voice, speaker, persona, and dramatic context in *Daniel* and *Exodus;* and these further matters become central to considerations of the structure of *Christ and Satan, Advent Lyric VII, The Order of the World, The Rhyming Poem,* and especially *The Wanderer.* Another group of poems shows the poets attempting, with varying success, to construct formats of shifting techniques. In *The Death of Edgar,* there is a pattern of shifting groups of euphemisms; in *Homiletic Fragment I,* a pattern of shifting metaphors with a constant tenor; in *The Metrical Epilogue to the Pastoral Care,* a pattern of shifting metaphors with a constant vehicle.[1] In *The Seafarer,* the shifting format develops through a variety of perspectives. This formal design is closest to that of *The Dream of the Rood,* in which the effect of the shifts is not only developmental but cumulative.

I call this major structural principle of *The Dream of the Rood* "progressive identifications," but part of the technique might also be described as the principle of separation-involvement. A work employing this structure invites the audience to become directly involved with its action and emotion by first separating the teller from the told. Such a process places, artificially but effectively, the artist in the position of audience; q.e.d., audience identifies with artist.[2] This placement leads to more effective and complete

[1] I. A. Richards' useful terms for metaphorical analysis appear often in succeeding chapters. He introduced them in his first lecture on "Metaphor" in *The Philosophy of Rhetoric* (New York and London, 1936), pp. 96ff. Another very helpful discussion of metaphor is Philip Wheelwright, *Metaphor and Reality* (Bloomington, 1962).

[2] This is far from the "affective fallacy"; a poet working in an oral-formulaic tradition must make use of his audience's familiarity with and acceptance of his conventions. Margaret E. Goldsmith, "The Christian Perspective in *Beowulf,*" in *Studies in Old English Literature in Honor of Arthur G. Brodeur,* ed. Stanley B. Greenfield (Eugene, Ore., 1963), pp. 75f, remarks, "*Beowulf* critics have been diffident in recognizing to the full that the stored mind of the hearer or reader is part of the poet's material. This fact, accepted as a truism by modern artists, is none the less true for Anglo-Saxon poets. . . ." But this "critical diffidence" does not seem to have persisted; in fact, contemporary critics of Old English poetry might insist that conscious poet-audience collaboration is greater and more frequent in Anglo-Saxon verse. In

identification of audience with action and emotion, especially when, in a skillful work, the teller himself seems to become involved naturally and inevitably.

Thus, because of separations, audience identifies with wedding-guest who identifies with Ancient Mariner (who identifies with Everyman—and audience); thus, audience identifies with Shelley who identifies with "traveller" who identifies with sculptor (who identifies with his statue and, ironically, with his subject King Ozymandias); thus readers can identify with Kurtz because of the careful, deliberate processes of separation and identification involving the group on the deck of the *Nellie,* Conrad himself, and Marlow. The technique has become, really, a structural commonplace, found in *Gatsby,* in Maugham's *Moon and Sixpence,* and in many contemporary novels, plays, and films. It is an essential technique of such widely disparate forms as detective fiction, the Gothic novel, and the medieval dream vision. The particular effectiveness of its use in Faulkner's *Absalom, Absalom!* is perhaps matched in English literature only in *The Dream of the Rood.*

In *The Dream of the Rood,* the poet carefully separates the dreamer-speaker from the dreamed-speaker, giving four persons (five if one chooses to separate poet from his dreamer-persona): audience, dreamer-speaker (poet), dreamed-speaker (rood), and Christ. This separation leads inevitably to total integration: when the cross is identified with Christ, the dreamer and the audience—having been brought into identity with each other and then with the cross—are also brought to a (mystical) oneness with Christ. Thus, the structure of the poem supports the apparent religious intention of the poem, the theme of the essential oneness of man and Christ, or of all men in Christ.

The first twenty-seven lines seem to be a naive dreamer's

their Introduction to *Poems in Old English* (New York, 1962), p. 19, Jackson J. Campbell and James L. Rosier note that "there is some evidence for the mixture of the secular and the religious in the audience as well as in the poetry."

straightforward description of his dream; this opening passage also sets the structural principle in motion and, further, establishes themes, devices, and language-patterns which effect the working out of that principle.[3]

The strategy of a dream-vision calls for a kind of double-objectification[4] in an opening passage which may be quite simple and brief. Because the narration reports a dream-vision, it is clear that the narration will objectify matters which might otherwise be complexly subjective or even inexpressible (unconscious = unverbalized = unobjectified). And because the matter has been placed outside to be reported straightforwardly, the poet's view seems to be objective. Naturally, the audience, since it shares the poet's "objective" view of the objectified matter, is easily taken into a close association with the dreamer-narrator.

The opening of *The Dream of the Rood* accomplishes the first identification (audience to poet) in three and a half lines, primarily with the use of two simple verbs of telling and seeing (*secgan* 1b, *gesawe* 4a). Yet even these seven verses do more, the verbs themselves initiating a pattern which—with verbs of hearing—persists through much of the poem, assisting in the progressive identifications. The poet's wish to tell (*secgan wylle*) is an invitation to the audience as direct as the initial *Hwæt*! The audience has already

---

[3] A "straight" reading of our title for this poem would apply only to this opening passage, but we may see some ambiguity in it. The poem is not only a dream about the rood, but even more importantly it is the rood's own vision.

[4] J. A. Burrow, in "An Approach to *The Dream of the Rood*," *Neophilologus*, XLIII (1959), 123–33, has noted a "double persona, strongly differentiated" and a "double focus" (p. 126) and commented that "the Cross, in its own narrative, functions doubly as a surrogate both for the dreamer and for Christ; and these two functions correspond to the double transcendental-natural image of the Cross established at the beginning of the poem" (p. 127). Burrow also recognizes that the Cross sees with the dreamer and suffers with Christ, but all his observations lead him to a conclusion opposite to mine. Far from a universal communion, Burrow finds that "the gap between the natural and the supernatural is felt as absolute" (p. 127).

accepted the invitation by the fourth line; when the dreamer says, *þuhte me þæt ic gesawe* "Methought that I saw," the audience, too, seems to see.

The dreamer says that the vision came to him in the middle of the night after men were in bed, and the use of *reordberend* "speech-bearing ones" for men is not unusual.[5] But here the choice of the figure is not incidental: the poet is deliberately emphasizing this human characteristic as part of his aesthetic plan. It fits in with his pattern of seeing, hearing, and telling and serves as a direct link to the next stage in the identifications. The word is used for "people" again in 89b. This time the rood is speaking; and when the cross speaks, it is automatically human, since people are speech-bearing ones.[6]

The imaginative mind's eye of the audience soon becomes as sharply focussed as the dreamer's vision. By 14b dreamer and audience see, without doubt, the "tree of glory" (*Geseah ic wuldres treow*), and by 18b the perception is so acute that one can see past the dazzling gold to the former strife (. . . *þurh þæt gold ongytan meahte/ . . . ærgewin*). Meanwhile another verb of seeing, *behealdan,* has been used, first (9b) to describe the angelic hosts watching the cross, and then expanded (11a) to include not only *halige gastas* "holy spirits" but also *men ofer moldan* "men

[5] Cf. *Christ* 278, 381, 1024, 1368, *Andreas* 419, *Daniel* 123, *Elene* 1282.

[6] The prosopopoeia employed in the poem has been much discussed, principally by Albert S. Cook in the Introduction to his edition (Oxford, 1905) and Margaret Schlauch, "*The Dream of the Rood* as Prosopopoeia," *Essays and Studies in Honor of Carleton Brown* (New York, 1940), pp. 23–34. Classical parallels and similarities to Old English Riddles have been found, but it is generally considered that this poem, composed with genius, goes far beyond possible sources or traditions. Burrow (p. 127) mentions "the animism implicit in prosopopoeia," and it seems to me that the personification of the rood is much more than a rhetorical device. It is no denial of the poet's genius to point out that he was employing a convention common to and important in much Old English poetry. See Neil D. Isaacs, "The Convention of Personification in *Beowulf*," in *Old English Poetry,* ed. Robert P. Creed (Providence, 1967), pp. 215–48.

over the world" and *eall þeos mære gesceaft* "all this glorious creation." The word is next used (25a) with the dreamer as subject looking upon the cross and finally *hearing* it *cry aloud* and begin to *speak words*. In the rood's narration, the process is repeated. The rood is, humanly, *speaking* and *tells* what he *saw* (*geseah* 33b, 36b, 51b) and *heard* (*Weop eal gesceaft,/cwiðdon cyninges fyll* "All creation wept, bewailed the king's fall"). Then, using the same B-type formula system[7] which included all creation as subject for *behealdon* in 11a (*ac hine þær beheoldon*), the cross says simply, *Ic þæt eall beheold* "I beheld all that" (58b). The "use of association"[8] is followed by an even more effective one which repeats a full-hypermetric-verse formula system (9b,[9] 64a). Where first the situation was dreamer describing angels watching rood, now it is rood describing the faithful watching Christ. Several aspects of the structural principle are suggested here in the three-part analogy: the association or identification of dreamer with rood, of rood with Christ, and of all living beings, mortal and immortal, with each other.

In later parts of the rood's narration, the verbs of hearing and speaking appear in lines that reveal the intimate relationship that has been built up between rood and dreamer: *Nu ðu miht gehyran hæleð min se leofa* "Now you may hear, my dear man" (78) ; *Nu ic þe hate hæleð min se leofa/þæt ðu þas gesyhðe secge mannum/onwreoh*

---

[7] John Collins Pope, in *The Rhythm of Beowulf* (New Haven, 1942), p. 224, scans it as type A with anacrusis, but a comparison with 58b shows that *heold(on)* gets only secondary accent; the alliterations are on *hine* with *halige* and *eall* with *æðelinge; ac* is metrically equivalent to *ic;* and the variation in the formula system is the shifting from measure to measure of the metrically equivalent and unimportant adverbial syllable, *þær, þæt.*

[8] The term is borrowed from the title of an exemplary article of Old English criticism—James L. Rosier, "The Uses of Association: Hands and Feasts in *Beowulf*," *PMLA*, LXXVIII (1963), 8–14.

[9] I have departed from Krapp's text here to use a generally accepted emendation for the MS reading, which is impossible. Verse 64a shows what 9b should be.

wordum "Now I command you, my dear man, that in clear words you tell this vision to men" (95–97a).[10]

The last three verbs in the pattern refer to the future: the rood talks about the words Christ will speak on the day of judgment (111); the rood tells that sinners will not know what to say (115b–116, stating an equation between faith and the ability to speak which had been implied earlier[11]); and the dreamer anticipates the time when the rood, which he had looked on before (137b), will fetch him to heaven. A further suggestion here should be noted: when Christ comes, sinners will be afraid and unable to speak in answer to Christ's words; but the rood's coming to the dreamer and speaking to him embody a test of whether the man can go on to speak of his vision, as he is instructed and as the faithful Christian should. The three-part comparison here is closely associated with another analogy which supports at least one aspect of the structural principle and accounts in part for the final passage. The rood will come to fetch the dreamer to heaven to join the community of blessed souls; Christ harrows hell to bring damned souls to heaven (that is, in both instances, faith conquers death). Again rood = Christ, and the dreamer is seen to be representative of all men.[12]

[10] Note that 95 repeats the arrangement in 78 of A-type formula system followed by an A-type formula, while 96b has the simplest of A-type formula systems (cf. 1b).

[11] Cf. l. 35.

[12] A similar comparison may appear in 21a and 110b: the dreamer's fear at the rood's coming = mankind's fear at Christ's coming. Perhaps in both cases the reason for the fear may be the overwhelming beauty of the sight. It ought to be pointed out here that although the poem deals intricately with thematic material which is doctrinal and didactic in purpose, it is lyrical in operation and effect. But cf. Claes Schaar, *Critical Studies in the Cynewulf Group* (Lund, 1949), p. 136: ". . . if there is any meaning in the word 'lyric,' then we cannot look upon the Dream of the Rood as a thoroughly lyrical poem. The emotional element is restrained . . ." Schaar's elaborate machinery of syntactical analysis contributes little to our understanding of the poem, though it seems to reaffirm the opinion that Cynewulf did not compose it.

It is important that we go back to see the initiation of the image-patterns and the structural principle in that deceptive opening passage, but it would be well to state the argument in justification of the final passage now. Every aspect of the structure we trace through the poem will have some bearing on the working of the conclusion and the effective unity of the whole poem.

The central focus of the poem is on the two inner stages of identification—dreamer with rood and rood with Christ (therefore dreamer with Christ)—but the statement which the poem ultimately makes is not a personal or individual one. It is a universal statement in which we are made to see that, through the agency of Christ and the cross, all men will be brought together in a heavenly community or communion of souls. In order to make this statement, to accomplish this totality of identifications, the poet begins with a passage designed to bring the audience into the process and ends with the harrowing-of-hell motif which, carefully suggested by parallels in theme and formulaic language, produces the desired extension of individual to universal.

The references to doomsday throughout the poem, especially the verse *anra gehwylcum* "everyone" (108a), certainly suggest that there is more than individual significance, and the general description of the harrowing of hell as parallel to or even a prototype of doomsday may suggest the essential nature of the final passage. One need not be satisfied with any general or vague suggestions, however, since an examination of language and structure affords a convincing, precise explanation.

One of the major patterns of imagery in the poem is that of light (beams, beacons, gems, gold, brightness, glory) and dark—one of the systems of formal contrast that have impressed many readers of the poem.[13] All is brightness

---

[13] E.g., Cook, p. xliii; Campbell and Rosier, p. 13; and W. F. Bolton, "Connectives in 'The Seafarer' and 'The Dream of the Rood,'" *MP* LVII (1960), 260–62.

throughout the opening passage describing the dreamer's vision. Even when the apparition flickers from gems to blood, the brilliance seems overwhelming.[14] It is important to notice the association of "glory" (*wuldres treow* 14b) with light here. We are well into the rood's narration be fore the first suggestion of darkness appears: in 46a the nails are called *deorcan*. Then the contrast appears most forcefully in the passage describing the miraculous darkness of midday:

> Þystro hæfdon
> bewrigen mid wolcnum   wealdendes hræw
> scirne sciman   sceadu forðeode
> wann under wolcnum.

> *Darkness had covered with clouds the Lord's*
> *corpse, clear brilliance; shadows went forth,*
> *dark under clouds.* (52b–55a)

The darkness surrounding the "clear brilliance" on the cross is unrelieved until the faithful carve a grave *of beorhtan stane* "from bright stone" (66b) for *þam mæran þeodne* "the glorious Lord" (69a). The brightness and glory which had begun as prime elements of the dreamer's description of his vision are now associated with Christ, but the cross tells us that they have been transferred to himself. He says that he was adorned with gold and silver (77), that the prince of glory (*wuldres ealdor* 90b) honored him so that he is *þrymfæst* "firm in glory" now (84b), that all this glorious creation (82b) will honor him now (81a), and that the dreamer should tell people about him, the *wuldres beam* "cross of glory" (97b).[15]

References to glory throughout the poem follow a pat-

---

[14] The transition from gems to blood is bridged by the word *wædum* which could apply to either or both in the way of "trappings." Similar ambiguity may appear in "treasure" since the rood could now be "adorned" with the blood of Christ.

[15] We may observe an example of the poet's metrical skill here in the verses using *w*-alliteration, 14b and 97b varying a B-type system and 90b using a simple A-type.

tern parallel to the structural principle: from dreamer's
vision to Christ to cross and inevitably including all creation. The culmination of the poem and the pattern emphasizes the point. Of the final eight instances[16] of the pattern of light imagery, six refer to glory,[17] including the last
four. And the final three (135a, 143a, 155a) employ the
same simple A-type formula system: *wuniaþ on wuldre;
wunian on wuldre; wunedon on wuldre.* Significantly,
this last occurrence, so integrally related in theme, formula,
and image-pattern to the rest of the poem, stands beyond
the point where Cook would have ended the poem,[18] almost at the end of the section which is called superfluous,
interpolated, and weak.[19]

The structural and thematic progress from individual to
universal through the stages of identification is especially
effective because of the complexity and thoroughness of the
individual identifications.[20] No single image-pattern or
theme, however dominant it may be in the poem, is allowed
to carry the structural principle by itself. Seemingly unimportant details carry some of the aesthetic burden along
with the leading voices. For example, the rood extends his
rejoicing that he is ennobled *ofer holtwudu*[21] "over [all]

---

[16] Not including *feala* 125b.

[17] L. 133b appears a normal B-type verse (another variation with
14b, 97a), which would support Pope's inclination (*Rhythm*, p. 101).

[18] Introduction, pp. liv–lv.

[19] See, e.g., Bruce Dickens and Alan S. C. Ross, eds., *The Dream of the
Rood* (London, 1954), p. 18. But many support the conclusion now,
including Kemp Malone, *A Literary History of England* (New York,
1948), p. 79.

[20] Of course, this is both rhetorically and doctrinally sound: the community is accepted as glorious only when the individual is individually
glorified. For interesting views of the combination of doctrine and
rhetoric in the poem, see H. R. Patch, "Liturgical Influence in the
Dream of the Rood," *PMLA*, XXXIV (1919), 233–57; Rosemary Woolf,
"Doctrinal Influences on 'The Dream of the Rood,'" *Medium Ævum*,
XXVII (1958), 137–53.

[21] Again, where Krapp retains the MS reading *holmwudu*, I have
employed the generally accepted emendation *holtwudu*. Krapp notes
(p. 131f) that "there seems no convincing reason for thinking that the

forestwood" (91a) to Mary who is honored *ofer eall wifa cynn* "above all womankind" (44b). The analogy is excellent: both endured the agony of bearing the Lord. Later this association is echoed when the dreamer says it is his life's hope to seek the victory-cross *ana oftor þonne ealle men* "alone more often than other men" (128). Incidentally, too, the use of *sigebeam* for cross (13a, 127a) emphasizes the cross-Christ identification when echoed in the harrowing episode: *Se sunu wæs sigorfæst* (150a). Another example may serve also to shed some light on the great metrical skill of the poet. The three verses *fægere æt foldan sceatum* (8a), *eorðan sceatas* (37a), and *feallan to foldan sceatum* (43a) aid in the identification of dreamer with rood and rood with Christ. The first and third are obviously a full-hypermetric-verse formula system, the former spoken by the dreamer of the cross, the latter by the cross of itself. The echo, the parallel, supports the identification. But Nicholson[22] has shown that several expanded verses are assimilations of two formulas, and these are prime examples.[23] Now *eorðan sceatas* is a variation of the *foldan sceatum* formula, where vowel alliteration replaces *f*-alliteration.[24] Thus, this verse, which is a description of the earth's reaction to Christ's passion, is associated formulaically with the other verses and serves to extend the identification of dreamer-rood to Christ.

The perfect blending of skillful formula variation and thematic material is revealed in another pattern which is

---

scribe miswrote *holm-* for *holt-* here." This seems a weak defense for *holmwudu*, but it may be possible to justify the unique usage here in terms of the ambiquity of *holm*, especially as similar to the ambiguity of *beam* and *beacen*.

[22] Lewis E. Nicholson, "Oral Techniques in the Composition of Expanded Anglo-Saxon Verses," *PMLA*, LXXVIII (1963), 287–92.

[23] Nicholson (p. 290) lists 43a as an example of this type of amalgamation, but curiously enough lists 8a as a simple expansion of a normal verse (p. 288).

[24] In either on-verse or off-verse. Cf. *Beowulf* 752, *Andreas* 332, *Seafarer* 61, *Genesis* 2208, *Panther* 68, *Fortunes of Men* 65, and, with double alliteration, *Riddle 88* 24.

essential to the structural principle. The dreamer, in describing his condition, says that he is "guilty with sins,
sorely wounded with defilements" (*ond ic synnum fah/
forwunded mid wommum* 13b–14a). This hints at the man-
cross equation, where *wommum* can refer both to sins of
the dreamer and to stigmata on the cross. The cross, like
Christ and saints, bleeds through scars (20a), and the
dreamer, in addition to sins, is now afflicted with sorrows
for the cross: *Eall ic wæs mid sorgum gedrefed* (20b). The
identification is made specific in action with the shift in
25–26: the dreamer is *hreowcearig* "sad with cares," but it
is the cross that cries (*hleoðrode*). And the cross, too, has
become defiled: *beswyled mid swates gange* (23a), as the
imagery of affliction and defilement promotes the association. The pattern is carried forward by means of formula
variation in the rood's speech, when he echoes the dreamer's description of himself (*Eall ic wæs mid sorgum gedrefed*
20b) with his own: *Eall ic wæs mid blode bestemed* (48b).[25]
The same expanded-verse formula system is used twice
more by the rood in describing its condition: *Sare ic wæs
mid sorgum gedrefed* (59a) and *Eall ic wæs mid strælum
forwunded* (62b). The latter variation shifts to an *st*-al-
literation,[26] with the on-verse reading *standan steame be-
drifenne* "to stand soaked with blood"—an image which
belongs to the same pattern. The whole line sums up this
particular pattern which has firmly identified dreamer
with rood, while suggesting the equation of their condition
with Christ's.

The conception of this pattern belongs to a larger thematic construction, in which affliction is prelude to an en-
nobling experience: suffering, passion, crucifixion, and

[25] Nicholson (p. 291) says, "Only the best singers are able to use their
materials so economically and to perform with such virtuosity." Although not speaking specifically of these verses, he talks about "the
complicated patterns produced by the . . . *Rood* singer."

[26] The noun of agency regularly has the alliteration in this formula
system, regardless of the half-line in which it appears.

the torment of damnation give way to spiritual elevation, martyrdom, resurrection, and translation to a state of blessedness.[27] Thus again it is apparent that the harrowing-of-hell motif is an essential culmination of the poem.[28]

Thematic material contributes in other, incidental ways to the working out of the structural principle. For example, the dreamer insists that the cross is not a gallows for the wicked: *Ne wæs ðær huru fracodes gealga* (10b). This simple contrast is expanded in the immediate context (9b–12) where, instead of a watching rabble, there is a host of angelic beholders extended to include all men and all creation. The contrast is evoked twice more, once when the rood tells how enemies *heton me heora wergas hebban* "ordered me to raise up their criminals"[29] (31b) and again when Christ is described as ascending the cross: *Gestah he on gealgan heanne* "he ascended the high gallows" (40b). Having made the distinction, the poet proceeds to erase it as he works toward his statement of universality.

A closely related device is the use of the first-person dual and plural pronouns. The rood, after speaking at length in the first- and third-person singulars of himself and Christ, brings the two together as object for the derision of the enemies (48a). Later, however, the two are separated as the body of Christ is taken down and entombed, so that *us* in 73b and 75a can refer only to the rood and the other crosses which are felled and buried together. The reference echoes the earlier Christ/cross—criminals/gallows figure. Towards the end of the poem, the dreamer, who has pointedly been speaking of himself in isolation in the first person, uses *us* to tell how Christ redeemed all mankind: *He us onlysde   ond lif forgeaf* (147). Once more the progress

[27] Bolton (p. 262) observes that "both Cross and dreamer progress from degradation to glory," while Burrow (p. 133) sees the dreamer moving "from fear and sorrow to hope."

[28] Burrow (p. 132) notes a "traditional doctrinal association between the Harrowing and the Crucifixion."

[29] Here is a perfect example of the thoroughgoing nature of the personification, which goes far beyond rhetorical prosopopoeia.

is obviously from isolation through identifications to total integration.

I have omitted up to now the use of *we* in the crux *Hwæðere we ðær greotende   gode hwile* (70). The generally accepted emendation *greotende* for MS *reotende* is easily the best solution for the lack of alliteration: the meaning is identical and no new syntactical or contextual problems are created by the change. Moreover, where the same or a similar formula system occurs in the on-verse,[30] it is regularly the noun in final position[31] which carries the alliteration in A3- or E-type verses. The closest comparison is with 24 *Hwæðre ic þær licgende   lange hwile,* which in addition to using the same full-line formula system employs as well a thematic parallel. There the dreamer sees the signs of suffering appear on the cross, but continues watching for a long while; here the cross, after watching the entombment, hearing the lamentation of the faithful, and then seeing them withdraw, goes on weeping for a good while (again, dreamer identifies with rood, and rood with Christ).

But a question remains about the passage. Although the rood has been given the ability to cry out in 26b and to speak throughout, why do the other crosses cry? An answer can be suggested by the preceding verse—*Reste he ðær mæte weorode* "He rested there with a small band" (69b)— which is generally assumed to be litotes, i.e., he was alone.[32] It seems to me rather that something else is going on. The small band consists of those left behind, the rood and neighboring crosses. As elsewhere, the individual gives way to the group as identifications are made, and as theme and structure work toward the final philosophical statement which the poem makes. This particular instance reminds one at the same time of the words of Christ to the thief[33]

---

[30] Ll. 18, 24, 57.

[31] In l. 57 an adjective used substantively.

[32] Campbell and Rosier, p. 73. The comparison with 123–24 gives a further instance of the poet's virtuosity with his materials. Cf. *Brunanburh* 34b.

[33] As Christ ennobles those crucified with him, so the cross ennobles

and of the passage in *Beowulf* where the personified weapons continue to watch while the men go off to sleep[34]— another example of the remarkable fusion of traditions.[35] One more point may be noted in the dramatic context of the *standing* crosses weeping over the *fallen* savior: the contrast of physically high and low positions—or movement—is another of the main patterns of the poem's imagery. Upward and downward movement itself seems to be one of the structural principles of the poem,[36] and it supports aspects of the thematic statement. The rood vision first appears (after all men are lying in bed) extending on high (*on lyft læden* 5a),[37] and the dreamer sees gems both down at the lap of earth (8a) and up on the shoulder-span (9a). In his narration the rood tells how he was cut down

---

his fellow crucifiers. All will be together in heaven: "Verily I say unto thee, To-day shalt thou be with me in paradise" (Luke 23:43).

[34] Ll. 1242ff. See Neil D. Isaacs, "Six *Beowulf* Cruces," *JEGP* (1963), 124f.

[35] "This delicate matter of separating or isolating the pagan from the Christian, the native English from the learned Latin, has in the past been ridden over roughshod with little attention to the successful synthesis the English made of their two major cultural traditions during the Old English period" (Campbell and Rosier, p. 1). That such a synthesis may be found, with an extraordinary degree of success, in a poem which would seem to belong exclusively to one tradition, is just one of the marvels of *The Dream of the Rood*. The fusion might also be seen in such usages as *geong hæleð* 39a, *beorn* 42a, *hilderinca* 72a, and *þegnas* 75b; Woolf notes (p. 144), "The conception of Christ as a warrior is, however, not peculiar to the Anglo-Saxon imagination." But cf. Robert E. Diamond, "Heroic Diction in *The Dream of the Rood*," *Studies in Honor of John Wilcox,* ed. A. Dayle Wallace and Woodburn O. Ross (Detroit, 1958), p. 3, where, having listed twelve usages of heroic diction, he calls such language "strangely out of place in a poem about the crucifixion of the Lord."

[36] Burrow (p. 131) finds only the "last lines of the poem . . . crowded with verbs expressing movement." For a use of backward and forward movement as structural principle, see Chapter 8 below.

[37] Another thematic parallel may exist between 3–6a and 30b–34. The latter passage relates the appearance of Christ to the cross, after enemies have humiliated and isolated him, while in the former passage it is the dreamer who is isolated from men and then has the cross appear to him.

(29a), how he was ordered to raise up criminals (31b), and how Christ hastened to ascend on him (34, 40b). He says that he did not dare to bend or break (36a, 42b–43a, 45b) or to fell the foes (38a), but stood firm (38b, 43b): *Rod wæs ic aræred* "A cross was I erected" (44a).[38] Then after Christ sends up his spirit (49b), the rood stoops to the hands of the men (59b) who raise Christ up from his torment (61a), lay him down (63a), stand by him (63b), and finally bury him (67a). After the voice of the warriors (faithful) goes up (71b), the rood and other crosses stand there weeping (70–71a) until they are felled (73b–74a) and buried (75a). He too, the rood tells the dreamer, has been resurrected and now towers under heavens (85a), just as Christ rose again (101b), rose to heaven (103a). Later the dreamer relates that his friends have died and "now live in heaven with the High Father" (134). This is the last specific image of loftiness in the pattern, but the poem winds up with a two-fold recapitulation of the downward-upward movement: the dreamer looks forward to the time when the rood will come back down to earth and take him up to heaven, just as Christ harrowed hell and raised the tormented souls to heaven.

The final verse *þær his eðel wæs* may be seen as an effective image setting forth one form of the philosophical statement of the poem. Heaven is Christ's homeland and that of the cross; through them, all will be brought to salvation; heaven is the homeland of all creation. In a poem of uncanny complexity, this beautifully simple statement is made when formulas, themes, and patterns of imagery, all guided by a structural principle, lead to the inevitable and desirable conclusion.[39]

[38] Burrow (p. 127) notes the transference or identification here: "It was Christ who could have struck down his enemies, and Christ who could have refused the ordeal . . . ."

[39] I am indebted to Robert P. Creed for his reading of this chapter. An earlier form of this essay was accepted in 1964 for publication in *Medium Ævum* but, in accordance with that journal's policy, was withdrawn in 1967 when the present volume was announced.

CHAPTER TWO

IMAGE, METAPHOR, IRONY, ALLUSION, AND MORAL: THE SHIFTING PERSPECTIVE OF *THE SEAFARER*

What does *The Seafarer* mean? For a century this question has been asked, with a variety of answers almost matched by the variety of approaches. For the most part, however, the answer has been sought by way of prior questions: who wrote it? how many? when? at how many times? over how many centuries or periods? what parts belong and what do not? what relationships with other poems may be found? how can the text be improved? is there one speaker or more? who or what is he or are they? what are the physical elements of the structural scheme? is the poem literal or allegorical? is it essentially pagan or Christian? Germanic or Celtic? original or derivative? oral or literary? artistic or trite? beautiful or banal?[1]

---

[1] Krapp and Dobbie list the principal earlier discussions of these questions. For more recent commentators, see I. L. Gordon's edition (London, 1960). The dialogue theory is reviewed and disposed of by William Witherle Lawrence, "The *Wanderer* and the *Seafarer*," *JEGP*, IV (1902), 460–80. The major supporters of allegory are O. S. Anderson, *The Seafarer: An Interpretation* (Lund, 1939), whose arguments are neatly summarized by E. Blackman, *MLR*, XXXIV (1939), 254f; G. V. Smithers, "The Meaning of *The Seafarer* and *The Wanderer*," *MÆ*, XXVI (1957), 137–53, XXVII (1959), 1–22, 99–104; and J. E. Cross, "On the Allegory in *The Seafarer*—Illustrative Notes," *MÆ*, XXVIII (1959), 104–106. For objections to Anderson, see I. L. Gordon, "Traditional Themes in *The Wanderer* and *The Seafarer*," *RES*, n.s. V (1954), 1–13; S. B. Liljegren, "Some Notes on the Old English Poem *The Seafarer*," *Studia Neophilologica*, XIV (1941–42), 145–59. For literal readings, see Dorothy Whitelock, "The Interpretation of *The Seafarer*,"

The way to approach the meaning of a poem is by a poetic analysis in which yet another question is asked: how does the poem work? And the either-or arrangement of some of the other questions ought to be abandoned. *The Seafarer*, then, may be said to mean what an analysis of its workings shows it to say, imply, and suggest. Such an approach neither closely embraces the literal readings of Whitelock and Salmon nor staunchly rejects the allegorical readings of Anderson, Smithers, and Cross. In fact, the operation of the poem as it is here viewed reflects both those meanings which might seem to be the special insights of the literalists and those interpretations which might seem to be the special discoveries of the allegorists.[2]

In the Introduction to *A Preface to Chaucer*, Professor D. W. Robertson points out that in order to appreciate medieval art one must recognize the systems of thought, the preconceptions, and the frames of reference which govern the creators and audience of that art—systems, preconceptions, and frames which may be wholly different from ours. He contrasts "a dominant medieval convention, the

---

The Early Cultures of North-West Europe (H. M. *Chadwick Memorial Studies*), ed. Sir Cyril Fox and Bruce Dickens (Cambridge, 1950), pp. 259–72; Vivian Salmon, " 'The Wanderer' and 'The Seafarer,' and the Old English Conception of the Soul," *MLR*, LV (1960), 1–10. On oral techniques in the poem, see Jackson J. Campbell, "Oral Poetry in *The Seafarer*," *Speculum*, XXXV (1960), 87–96; Wayne A. O'Neil, "Another Look at Oral Poetry in *The Seafarer*," *Speculum*, XXXV (1960), 596–600; Stanley B. Greenfield, "The Formulaic Expression of the Theme of 'Exile' in Anglo-Saxon Poetry," *Speculum*, XXX (1955), 200–206. For possible Celtic influence, see C. W. Dunleavy, *Colum's Other Isle* (Madison, 1960), pp. 82ff.

[2] Of all the commentators on *The Seafarer*, E. G. Stanley, "Old English Poetic Diction and the Interpretation of *The Wanderer*, *The Seafarer* and *The Penitent's Prayer*," *Anglia*, LXXIII (1955), 413–66, comes nearest the present reading: ". . . the poem is neither realism nor allegory. It is an imagined situation, invented to give force to the doctrine which forms the end of the poem and is its purpose" (p. 453). Stanley's article is valuable for its interesting remarks on the difficulty of separating literal and figurative in Old English poetry—how to know which is which.

tendency to think in terms of symmetrical patterns characteristically arranged with reference to an abstract hier-
archy, with a dominant modern convention, the tendency
to think in terms of opposites whose dynamic interaction
leads to a synthesis. . . . when we superimpose dynamically
interacting opposites upon medieval hierarchies . . . the
result is inevitably a distortion."[3] Although I would agree
with this thesis of Robertson's in a general way,[4] it is interesting to observe that an Old English poem may operate
on a structural principle, an aesthetic design, which relies
heavily on polarities, which, in fact, depends for its effects
on a complex system of contrasting opposites. There may
be here an explanation of the great appeal of *The Seafarer*
for modern sensibilities. Nevertheless, I hope also to provide a glimpse of the hierarchical system that underlies the
surface polarities of the poem; and here, perhaps, we may
see why the final sections of the poem are generally held
in disfavor.

Skillfully and subtly the *Seafarer*-poet goes about his
business; his purpose is philosophical, his philosophy is
traditionally Christian, and his method is ingenious. He
employs elements and techniques which we recognize as
staples of modern poetry—image, metaphor, irony, allusion—
along with that ubiquitous element of medieval Christian
poetry—the moral—to lead us inevitably through his constantly shifting perspectives to the final fixed morality of
his message. He may very well use heroic, pagan, lay, and
everyday referents as well as Christian ones, but the Christian is the fixed referent toward which he moves; which is
to say that his *rhetorike* is as skillful as his *poietike*.

The first contrast gives a name to the poem: it simply
sets up life at sea with its heavy cares as one polarity and

---

[3] (Princeton, 1962), p. 6.

[4] With one qualifying observation: the medieval physics with its four
elements, the corresponding physiology with its four humours, and the
four qualities common to both systems give some evidence of concepts
of "dynamically interacting opposites" working with or within hierarchical concepts.

the carefree life on land as the other. The poet has adopted
a first-person persona who has had much experience at sea
and can describe it with relation to himself: *be me sylfum*.
The items in this original description of life at sea are pre-
dictable and would be readily appreciated by an Anglo-
Saxon audience, despite the assertion that the man "to
whom on land a very pleasant [lot] belongs" does not really
know what it's all about (12b–13). But from the beginning
the poet moves from generalities to specifics as he builds
the descriptive contrast.

A second contrast is implicit in these opening lines, as
the details of life at sea suggest two kinds of suffering.
There is the external kind, in the image of the seafarer,
who has drawn the night-watch, at the bow of a ship which
is rolling in a heavy sea and being shaken near cliffs (6–8a)
and the image of the freezing, frost-bitten feet of the seafarer pressed numbly together as if fettered (8b–10a). Then
there is suffering within, revealed in reference to *bitre
breostceara* "bitter breast-care" (4a), . . . *þa ceare seofedun/
hat ymb heortan* "the cares abode hotly about [my] heart"
(10b–11a), and *hungor innan slat/merewerges mod* "hunger
within tore the spirit of sea-weary [me]" (11b–12a).[5] Notice
how the metaphor of frost and cold as fetters is carried
over to the cares clamping the heart, while at the same
time an incidental polarity of cold-hot is introduced.[6]

The first shift in perspective takes place in the next
lines (14–17a) and in mid-sentence. The persona begins to
discuss a concrete experience, a specific period of time
when he, "wretched with cares, inhabited the ice-cold sea
for a year (literally "winter," but by synecdoche "year";[7]

[5] Here as elsewhere and often in the translation of Old English
poetry, "my" must be supplied (as understood in the poetry). This
process is objected to by Liljegren, pp. 57f.

[6] Gordon, ed., p. 34n, calls this a "deliberate antithesis."

[7] It is always difficult, if not impossible, to say just when a metaphor
becomes petrified, loses figurative power, and becomes merely another
literalism. It seems to me that lexicographers have never been conservative enough in this regard.

the figure reinforces the previous picture of the hardships of life at sea) on the paths of exile, bereft of friendly kinsmen,[8] hung about with frosty icicles; hail flew in showers." The earlier contrasting figures—feet fettered by frost, heart and spirit in the clasp of cares and hungers—are echoed and extended in the exaggerated figure of icicles hanging about him and the immediate anticlimactic literalism of hail-showers. The latter, however, may have carried a submerged metaphor for the audience, suggesting weapons (arrows or spears) attacking the seafarer.[9]

The shifting perspective is caught in the references to *wræccan lastum* "paths of exile" and *winemægum* "friendly kinsmen." A new frame of reference, the *duguth*-society, has been subtly introduced. At first these suggestions seem metaphorical, serving to heighten the original contrast rather than introduce a new one: the easy life on land is *like* being among the friendly, protecting company of hearth-companions, secure in the hall of the lord; the hard life at sea is *like* being cast into exile from out of the duguth. Immediately, however, in the auditory imagery that follows, the vehicle of the metaphor becomes an additional tenor and we get the contrast of duguth-life-on-land with exile-at-sea. Hearing nothing but the sea resounding (18–19a), the seafarer-exile ironically evokes his former land-duguth existence by imagining the song of the swan and the gannet's and waterbird's sounds as substitutes for men's laughter (19b–21) and the mew's singing as a substitute for mead-drinking (22).[10]

The next four lines (23–26) pursue the new set of contrasts indirectly: here are personified storms, the absence of a protective kinsman, and further bird-images, with tactile and visual aspects added to the sustained auditory focus:

[8] Krapp-Dobbie, p. 295, says that this defective line "may never have been completed."

[9] See *Judith* 221 and *Elene* 117 for the formula *flana scuras*; cf. the compound *hildescurum*, *Guthlac* 1143.

[10] The ornithology of *The Seafarer* has been studied in Margaret E. Goldsmith, "*The Seafarer* and the Birds," *RES*, n.s. V (1954), 225–35.

Stormas þær stanclifu beotan,   þær him stearn oncwæð
isigfeþera;   ful oft þæt earn bigeal
urigfeþra;   ne ænig hleomæga
feasceaftig ferð   frefran meahte.

There storms beat the cliffs, where the icy-feathered
sea-swallow answered them; full oft yelled the eagle with
feathers wet with dew; not any protecting kinsman
could console [my] desolate spirit.

The passage thus evokes contrasting images without drawing
out an express relationship. At the same time, the progression toward more detailed, concrete, individualized experience continues. We are reminded of the external-internal
polarities by *feasceaftig ferð* as well as by the suggestions of
the sort of inner consolation which can come from the duguth
relationship.

The imagery tends to flatten out in the next four lines
(27–30), as the seafarer repeats the sentiment of 12b–13,
that his hardships cannot be appreciated by one who experiences the joy of life *in burgum* (a neutral term rather
than a specific reference to court or duguth, farmhouse or
townhouse). The reference to *brimlade,* however, may keep
in mind the equation of sea with the roads traveled by an
exile.

The first climax of the poem is reached in the sentence
which takes the next five verses (31–33a):

Nap nihtscua,   norþan sniwde,
hrim hrusan bond,   hægl feol on eorþan,
corna caldast.

Shadow of night grew dark; it snowed from the north;
frost bound the ground; hail, coldest of grains, fell
on earth.

The images here, precise and present, serve to bind together
in one overwhelming gesture all of the preceding impres-
sions. The dark night and the snow from the north echo
the seafarer's description of the hardships of life at sea, and
of course so does *hrim* (cf. 17a) which begins the next line.

Strategically, with apt rhetorical effect, *hrim* alone occupies a full measure of a D2 verse-type, setting the audience up for the switcheroo[11] in the second measure of the verse, where the poet now has the frost binding the ground instead of the sailor's feet (cf. 9b *gebunden*). The device is repeated immediately in 32b as *hægl,* associated earlier with the sea (17b), now is said to fall on earth. Even the verse-type (D2 with resolution of grammatical ending) is repeated. The final verse in this passage is an interesting metaphor, though not unique in Old English poetry: hail is called "coldest of grains."[12] Again the associations of sea are brought to land, ironically, as the earth bears the ocean's crop.

That there is a shift at this point in the poem has almost always been acknowledged by the commentators, but the nature of the shift and its purpose are not matters of general agreement. The first word *Forþon* is usually taken as significant to the shift,[13] but it seems to me that the rhythm of the verse (a B-type verse—*Forþon* is unaccented, incidental to the primary accent which is on the alliterating first syllable of *cnyssað* and also to the secondary accent on *nu*) tends to negate any significance.[14] Moreover, insuffi-

---

[11] Since it is customary to use technical terms from one art form to describe another, I have borrowed this precisely apt term from the technical vocabulary of vaudeville and burlesque comedy.

[12] In *The Rune Poem* 25, hail is called "whitest of grains" and cf. the Old Norse *fuþark* poem, called "A Rune Poem" by E. V. Gordon, *An Introduction to Old Norse* (Oxford, 1957), pp. 154 and 248n: "(hagall) es kaldastr korna."

[13] The *forþon* bibliography is extensive, as many commentators have thought the word crucial to their interpretations. See, e.g., W. F. Bolton, "Connectives in *The Seafarer* and *The Dream of the Rood*," *MP,* LVII (1959–60), 260–62; Marjorie Daunt, "Some Difficulties of 'The Seafarer' Reconsidered," *MLR,* XIII (1918), 474–79; Liljegren, p. 154; Whitelock, pp. 266f; and Cross, *MÆ,* XXVIII (1959), 105. But cf. Lawrence, p. 462.

[14] The word appears eight times in the poem, always in initial position in a verse (four times each in on- and off-verses), but is never accented or alliterating. Every occurrence but one (39a) is in a B-type verse, though 58a might be read as C-type. But 39a is an A3-type, and

cient attention has been given to the poetic and rhetorical significance of the accented words *cnyssað* and *nu*.

In this passage (33b–38) is introduced the idea of voluntary exile. This idea has disturbed readers: why should the seafarer voluntarily seek out the very evils and afflictions of exile at sea which he has just so feelingly described? Several presuppositions underlie the asking of such a question: (1) having adopted the persona of a seafarer, the Old English poet is required to wear that mask throughout his poem (a conception which would render the reader unable to appreciate some of the finest effects in Yeats, Eliot, Stevens, and Lowell), (2) voluntary suffering is unheard-of (Whitelock answers this objection in one way, though a glance at Krafft-Ebing would do it in another), (3) the poem has failed to erase the polarities of sea-exile-woe and land-duguth-weal (the dose of 31–33a has not taken), and (4) the poem has failed to make clear the internal-external distinction (another inoculation that has not penetrated a hard vein).

Perhaps it would be better affirmatively to account for the new perspective in the poem that comes with the idea of voluntary exile. In the first place, the shift is not drastic at all. Indeed, it seems to be the next logical step in the orderly progression of the poem. It is my feeling that the polarities *have* been effectively evoked, that the immediately preceding passage *has* suggested the breaking down of one system of polarities, and that the audience *is* prepared for another look with new understanding at the familiar material presented. "Indeed, now . . ." the passage begins, with the accent on *now*. This is a new *now*, not the present of the images of the man at sea beset with physical and

----

forþon would receive only secondary accent. In two cases, 103b and 108b, it appears in an expanded line, but all five expanded lines in *The Seafarer* (103, 106–109) consist of an expanded on-verse and a regular B-type off-verse. In fact, 103b and 108b appear to belong to the same formula-system as 27a, 39a, 58a, 72a, and perhaps 64b. In any case, the word *forþon* is insignificant in the poetry, cannot be made to sustain the structure of the poem, and need not be translated the same way each time—nor should such translation weigh heavily in interpreting the poem.

emotional troubles. The precise condition of the poet's *now* will be presented fully in later passages.

"Indeed, now thoughts beat [my] heart," says the poet, stating clearly that the action is internal, even though the verb *cnyssað* echoes the strictly external action of *cnossað* 8a.[15] The statement is stressed by further references to internal elements in *monað* modes *lust* "mind's desire urges" (36a) and *ferð* "spirit" (37a). These inner stirrings, however, prompt the poet to "try out the high seas, the tumult of the salt waves" (34b–35), to "seek a land of another nation far from here" (37b–38). Yet the suggestion of external action is not clearly literal, since it is also the poet's "spirit" that is urged to travel. The external seafaring and self-imposed exile in this passage, then, *may* be metaphorical. Perhaps they are metaphorical for death, since the language of the passage resembles circumlocutions for death found elsewhere in Old English poetry.[16]

In any case, the language here is ambiguous, as the poem moves from a straightforward explication of polarities through more complex polarities and relationships toward its final clear statement. Life at sea suggests life on land; exile suggests duguth; external conflict suggests inner turmoil; woe suggests weal. The poet evokes images and then shifts his view of them, all the while taking pains to keep the vividly presented material in the audience's mind. Thus, while reasserting the contrast of the duguth-life on land with the seafaring life, he introduces God explicitly for the first time. However good life is on land in the duguth (39–41), at sea the Lord cannot be taken for granted—His ways are mysterious, the future is in doubt (42–43).

Now a new dimension is added to the whole system of

---

[15] Stanley B. Greenfield, "Attitudes and Values in *The Seafarer*," *SP*, LI (1954), 15–19, has pointed to these words as examples of the verbal cleverness of the *Seafarer*-poet. He mentions also *gemonian* 50a and *monian* 53a, as well as what he calls puns on *dream*, *blæd*, and *duguð*. Note how the "thoughts" are personified by the action given them by the verb, a conventional device in Old English poetry; see Neil D. Isaacs, "The Convention of Personification in *Beowulf*," in *Old English Poetry*, ed. Robert P. Creed (Providence, 1967), pp. 215-48.

[16] The best examples are in *The Death of Edgar*. See Chapter 6 below.

contrasts, when to the figurations of duguth-life—the harp, the receiving of rings, and joy in woman—is added *to worulde hyht* "joy of the world" (45b), a phrase with distinct religious overtones. At this point a less skillful rhetorician would have pressed the analogy and preached explicitly the joys of the spirit as opposed to the joys of the world. But, the suggestion having been introduced, the *Sea-farer*-poet drops it for the time being. At least he drops it as a vehicle for explicit preachment. The audience, however, if it has kept up with the shifting perspectives, does not lose sight of the new view. Line 47 *ac a hafað longunge se þe on lagu fundað* "but ever has longing he who sets out to sea," reinforcing the internal-external dichotomy, suggests that it too has a spiritual-worldly analogy. And this impression too is carried forward by the audience, although the poet does not press the point.

Notice how the progression toward greater specificity is inverted in this passage. The references to duguth-life and earthly pleasures end with the very vague *owiht elles* "anything else" (46a), and the passage closes with a very general reference to seafaring: *on lagu fundað* (47b). Similarly, the next two lines (48–49), though they employ some concreteness, give a very general picture of earthly pleasure in a description of spring:

> Bearwas blostmum nimað,   byrig fægriað,
> wongas wlitigiað,   woruld onetteþ;
>
> *Groves take fruit, fortified towns become beautiful,*
> *the world hastens (is active?).*

And again these things suggest their opposites. In fact, the poet uses the verb *gemonian* "suggest" when he is explicitly directing our attention to the particular opposites. The suggestion is made *modes fusne* "to the eager mind" (50), and one may imagine the poem working so well that the audience along with the subject is eager in mind and prepared to have the coming of spring suggest going on an arduous sea-voyage. Once more there is some ambiguity as to whether the journey is a literal or figurative one: is it only the mind (*sefan*) that will make the journey? is *feor gewitan* a cir-cumlocution for "to die"? In any case, the concrete general-ization concerning the blooming of life on land in spring finds three opposites: inner turmoil, sea, and journey. Per-haps, too, the general impression of winter should be re-tained as a fourth opposite.

Then comes the much-discussed passage about the cuckoo (53–53a).[17] The image seems to make perfectly good sense when seen as part of the shifting perspectives and of an association-of-ideas pattern in which opposites are suggested. As the seasons change on land, other changes are suggested[18] and in contrasting settings. The cuckoo's call, then, is literally part of the season of rebirth and rejoicing on land, but is symbolically the reminder of the season of sadness and strife, perhaps even death, at sea.[19]

Now (55b–57) one hears another echo of an early contrast between the *esteadig secg* "grace-blessed man"[20] and those who follow the paths of exile. Perhaps the reason for re-peating this contrast now, *after* several shifts have been indicated, is that the audience is being prepared for the reversal of the original polarities and equations and the re-jection of the original definitions. The reversal is not com-pleted until the final section of the poem (beginning about

---

[17] Two recent comments attempt to justify the image in different ways: Gordon, ed., p. 8, suggests many parallels with Welsh poetry for the idea of the cuckoo as bird of lament; R. W. V. Elliott, "Form and Image in the Old English Lyrics," *EIC*, XI (1961), 8, says, ". . . the cuckoo's song changes from its merry note of spring to a harsher, hoarser call in early summer. In both poems [*Seafarer* and *Husband's Message*] the cuckoo's 'mournful' cry is a call to seafaring on the calmer and less hazardous seas of early summer." But I do not see the necessity of justifying the passage either by invoking a "tradition" or by praising "observant nature imagery."

[18] As Larry Sandberg, a former student of mine, once put it, "If spring comes, can winter be far behind?"

[19] Cf. N. F. Blake, "*The Seafarer* Lines 48–49," *N&Q*, IX (1962), 163–64.

[20] Like 9a, 56a is often inverted by the editors for metrical reasons. Both are E-type verses, but alliterating on the *second* accent. But E-

103), but it begins here at 58, when the poet repeats that
he now (*nu* 58a) has inner urgings to go to sea:

> . . . min hyge hweorfeð   ofer hreþerlocan;
> min modsefa   mid mereflode
> ofer hwæles eþel   hweorfeð wide
> eorþan sceatas,   cymeð eft to me
> gifre and grædig.

> . . . *my mind turns over [my] breast; my mind turns
> widely with the sea over the whale's home, earth's
> surface, comes back to me grim and greedy.* (58–62a)

His spirit, urging him to go, makes an imaginary flight, returning to the poet like a sea-bird with renewed appetite:

> . . . gielleþ anfloga,
> hweteð on hwælweg   hreþer unwearnum
> ofer holma gelagu;

> . . . *the lone-flyer yells, irresistibly urges mind on
> whale-road, over sea's expanse.*

It seems to me that the *anfloga* may be both his spirit which
has been soaring like a bird and also the cuckoo whose call
urges him seaward. Or perhaps there is a shifting metaphor:
in flight the spirit is a seabird; when it returns and urges
him it is *like* the cuckoo.[21] But in any case, since we have
merely a repetition of earlier statements, where is there any
suggestion of reversal? Clearly enough, it comes in the rest
of the sentence, where the reasons are stated in terms of
another contrast: this life on land is dead (*deade* 65b) and
transitory (*læne* 66a); the other has *dryhtnes dreamas* "the
Lord's joys" (65a). The detail of the earlier contrasts which

---

type verses are rhythmically identical with A-types, so that 9a and 56a
and all similar on-verses can be classified with A3-type verses as
permissible variations.

[21] Gordon, ed., p. 41, says *anfloga* "is almost certainly the cuckoo";
Salmon, *MLR*, LV, 6, says it "must refer to the soul in its bird form";
Smithers, *MÆ*, XXVIII, 22, reads "disease-bringing malign influence."
Smithers, *MÆ*, XXVI, 138, would also reject the emendation *hwælweg*
for MS *wælweg*: "clearly *wæl* 'dead body' . . . 'road taken by the dead'
or 'road to the abode of the dead.' "

evoked the joys of life, land, duguth, comfort, woman, pleasure—that is, the joys of the world—renders exceedingly moving the litotes which follows:

Ic gelyfe no
þæt him eorðwelan   ece stondeð.

I don't believe at all that to him earth-weal stands eternal. (66b–67)

The next four lines develop the idea of transience and death in earthly existence (including duguth) by listing the deprivers of life: disease, old age, and sword-hate.[22]

The strategy of the poem to this point has been engagingly effective, but the clever reversals using shifting perspective and the association of ideas by opposites have not completely accomplished the objectives. So the poet shifts perspective again and, using the same material already before the audience, now attempts a fusion of traditions. Lines 72–80a set up an equation of duguth-virtue with Christian virtue. The way to give a semblance of permanence to transient existence is by performing *fremum*[23] *on foldan* "beneficial actions on earth" (75a) and *deorum dædum* "brave deeds" (76a) against enemies or the devil. Then praise for the good man will live on, forever with the angels, bringing joy among the duguth.

Shifting perspective again, the poet begins a sustained elegiac passage (80b–102) lamenting the transience of the duguth and all earthly weal. Yet to describe the mood of the passage as lament is not quite accurate, since the Chris-

---

[22] But cf. Marjorie Rigby, "*The Seafarer, Beowulf* l. 769, and a Germanic Conceit," *N&Q*, IX (1962), 246, who finds the reversal to be merely a matter of tone, that the early passages are contemptuous, "not wistful or nostalgic," that 65–66 is "outright condemnation." The expression of what had been implicit "does not come as a surprise but as a climax to what has gone before." Most readers, however, sense the usual attitudes of elegy and ubi-sunt. See J. E. Cross, "*Ubi Sunt* Passages in Old English—Sources and Relationships," *Vetenskaps-Societetens Årsbok i Lund* (1956), pp. 25–44.

[23] O'Neil, 599n, advocates retaining MS *fremman* (cf. *Guthlac* 808a), "whose difficulty is largely imaginary."

tian notion of transience underlies it all. Whatever is sad or
appalling or depressing in this passage is the product of yet
another equation, the Christian one between individual
deaths and the decay that signifies the last days.[24]

However much like pagan elegy this passage may sound,
the fact is that for forty-five verses the poet is listing examples to show that the old ways (the ways of those who
would produce and appreciate a Germanic or perhaps Celtic
elegy) do not work. Gone are the days of gold-giving kings,
the bravery and the joys of the duguth, and earthly glory.
No nostalgia for the old ways can bring comfort at death;
but when the spirit escapes (losað 94b) the flesh-home,
it does not matter whether its life was spent in duguth or
exile, because it is able *ne swete forswelgan   ne sar gefelan*
"neither to swallow the sweet nor to sense the bitter" (95).

It is emphasized throughout the passage that what is gone
is the glory of this world (81b, 87b, 98a, 90b, 102b). This
glory is symbolized by gold, as elaborated in two customs:
first, the giving of gold to cement the retainer-lord relationship of the duguth, and second, the use of gold in pagan
burial rituals. The poet rejects the latter as a refinement
of the former: that is, the placing of gold in the grave *cannot* cement the soul-Lord relationship.[25]

By this time the poet has completed the process of reversal he began almost as soon as he initiated the pattern of
shifting perspective, the process of association of ideas by
opposites, and the sequence of attention-arresting concrete
images. The final long passage (103–122a), which harkens
back to several of the major points along the way, purports
to give the *real* definitions of weal and woe, beginning by

[24] See Smithers, *MÆ*, XXVI, 142–43, XXVII, 7; J. E. Cross, "Aspects
of Microcosm and Macrocosm in Old English Literature," *Studies in Old
English Literature in Honor of Arthur G. Brodeur*, ed. Stanley B.
Greenfield (Eugene, Ore., 1963), p. 20. Cf. N. F. Blake, pp. 163–64.

[25] As Kenneth Sisam, "*Seafarer*, Lines 97–102," *RES*, XXI (1945), 316–
17, has pointed out, this passage bears a marked resemblance to Psalm
49:6–7; but the reference to pagan burial customs makes the point more
telling here. But cf. Gordon, ed., p. 45.

establishing the reason for the seasons themselves (I take
this to be the meaning of the difficult line 103: the earth
turns—seasons change—because of the fear, the power, of
the Lord). It was God who established the earth, not only
the firm ground but all its regions (including the seas, of
course; in 61a, the *eorþan sceatas* formula has specific reference to the sea) and the heavens (104–105).

The importance of keeping faith is stressed by applying a
duguth-Christianity equation to vows. The equation is extended to include qualities of self-discipline, but the poet
breaks it down in pointing out that pagan customs are not
properly Christian at all. The crucial passage 111–115a is
one of the most difficult in the poem, not only because of
the defective lines 112–113, but also because the suggested
emendations invariably wrench the passage *out* of the specific Christian context.[26] The point is that the Christian
man must maintain his Christian charitable attitude not
only toward his friends but even toward enemies who wish
him full of fire himself or wish to burn his devoted friendly
lord on the funeral pyre: love thy neighbor and thy enemy
and return good for evil. This is perhaps the most radical
admonition in the whole poem, suggesting that religious
faiths should be kept even to the exclusion of what is expected in a comitatus relationship.[27] Yet a final gesture at
fusing traditions, or at least subsuming the old, is made in
equating *Wyrd* 115b with *meotud* 116a.

The following passage, significantly, and almost in a
single word, but surely in a single figure, ties up many of the
thematic, structural, and textural elements of the poem:

> Uton we hycgan   hwær we ham agen,
> and þonne geþencan   hu we þider cumen,
> ond we þonne eac tilien,   þæt we to moten

[26] E.g., Ferdinand Holthausen, *Anglia*, Beiblatt XIX (1908), 248; Fr.
Klaeber, "Three Textual Notes," *ES*, LXVII (1933), 341; Kemp Malone,
"On *Seafarer* 111–116," *MÆ*, VI (1937), 214–15; N. Kershaw (Chadwick),
Anglo-Saxon and Norse Poems (Cambridge, 1922), p. 27.

[27] For fuller explication of this passage, see Neil D. Isaacs, "*The Seafarer* 109–115a," *ES*, XLVIII (1967), 416–19.

in þa ecan   eadignesse,
þær is lif gelong   in lufan dryhtnes,
hyht on heofonum.

Let us think where we have a home and then think how
we come there and then consider also [how it is] that we
too will meet in the eternal blessedness, where life
belongs to God's love, joy in Heaven. (117–122a)

The key word here is *ham,* beside which is set the idea of
traveling from and returning to *ham.* Whether enjoying the
delights of land or suffering the travails of sea, human life is
a transitory voyaging, a sojourning—even *duguth*-life is
exile. Our home is in Heaven, the only real life with God.
The poem closes with a five-verse benediction (122b–124),
thanking God for the true nature of things and praying God
that He make us worthy of that Truth.

The foregoing analysis of the workings of *The Seafarer*
answers by implication some of the questions listed in the
first paragraph. Others are irrelevant to the approach employed.[28] While this analysis is by no means intended to
solve definitively all the problems of *The Seafarer,* it does
allow the poem to be viewed as a single aesthetic entity. It
sees *The Seafarer* as an artifact of rare artistic integrity,
skillfully employing a variety of poetic devices. The *Sea-*
farer-poet summons up a series of conventional images and
allusions, renders them in depth, and then by shifting perspectives relates them to the fixed point of the Christian
Truth about Life.

[28] Some very recent criticism has not been taken into account in this
chapter. John C. Pope's important essay, "Dramatic Voices in *The*
Wanderer and *The Seafarer,*" in the Magoun festschrift, is discussed
below in Chapter 3 (with an indication of why I have not revised this
chapter to include it), but it should be noted here that Pope speaks
of "shift[ing] . . . focus," pp. 185f. Robert D. Stevick, "The Text and the
Composition of *The Seafarer," PMLA,* LXXX (1965), 332–36, concludes
that the extant text of *The Seafarer* may show evidence of being an uncompleted composition. The argument is admirable for its ingenuity,
but dangerous and destructive in its implications for the possibilities of
analyzing Old English poetry.

CHAPTER THREE

ASSOCIATION AND GUILT: MOTIVE AND STRUCTURE IN *THE WANDERER*

R eading *The Wanderer*, carefully or casually, suggests what an examination of the scholarship on *The Wanderer* corroborates: it is an interesting poem with great occasion for commentary. The imagery, though familiar, is poignant. The elegiac tone, though familiar, is empathetic. The dramatic context, though familiar, is compelling. The thematic statements, though familiar, are convincing. And there are passages which, though familiar, are . . . familiar. They are strongly reminiscent of *The Seafarer*. The familiarity of the several aspects of the poem accounts for some of its power and success, but the similarity of some aspects to *The Seafarer* is what accounts for a great deal of the criticism. Whatever the parts treated, whatever the emphases, the critic eventually betrays a bias concerning *The Wanderer* which has to do with an idea about or an attitude toward *The Seafarer*.

Consider, for example, the recent argument of A. A. Prins in an article revealingly called "The Wanderer (and the Seafarer)."[1] His major point is that "the second half of *The Exile* as from l. 84 is the sequel to *The Wanderer* l. 57."[2] He begins from the general principle that "any theory attempting to explain poem-as-is is questionable since the Exeter Book is such an unreliable MS."[3] All very

---

[1] *Neophilologus*, XLVIII (1964), 237–51.

[2] P. 243.

[3] However unreliable as MS, the Exeter Book happens to be *the* MS. Any critical approach which is to be of value for readers other than the

reasonable, but the irrational bias is revealed on p. 347: "And to me *The Seafarer*, in spite of all that has been said to the contrary, ends at 64a, for here too, the seafarer never returns after those lines. No allegorical or symbolical interpretation of the first 64 lines is in my opinion tenable, and no amount of sophistication can make it so. . . . the description is too realistic for that." As if the sophistication cannot reside in the poem! As if "realistic" description rules out allegory or symbolism! Actually it is the compelling "realism," the power of a wholesale appeal to familiar and traditional material, which—in a skillful, subtle, and sophisticated way—allows the poem to employ functional symbolism and produce a kind of thematic statement which may be called allegorical.[4] And perhaps a similar statement may be made about *The Wanderer*. But there are at least three major reasons for treating *The Wanderer* wholly separately from *The Seafarer*.

For one thing, the history of the scholarship devoted to the two poems is filled with what seems a very nearly compulsive linking together of the two, a linking which has sometimes taken otherwise astute and insightful interpretations of one or the other and suddenly pulled the logic from underneath the analysis (as when the apparently flawless lucidity of a paranoiac-schizophrenic is betrayed by the diabolical mania that underlies it) and which has sometimes dictated wildly fanciful interpretations. The second reason is a matter of critical principle: it is heretical against any form of formalist orthodoxy to read a poem in the light of another poem. The presence of the two in the Exeter Book, though separated by two poems; the stubborn though fanciful hypotheses of common authorship for the two; and the demonstrable similarities of diction, theme, and allusion

---

individual critic must be based on the material we have as we have it. The creative-emendatory school of criticism leads to a total anarchy of tastes, values, judgments, and conclusions. Cf. the Stevick principle of unfinished texts cited in Chapter 2, n. 28.

    [4] Cf. the treatment of *The Seafarer* in Chapter 2.

—even if all are accepted finally, wholeheartedly, and with wholesale implications—do not make sufficient cause for abandoning this principle with regard to a formalist poetic analysis of either poem. Third, and probably most significant for me, *The Wanderer* and *The Seafarer* seem to be wholly different in more ways and in more significant ways than they are alike. This chapter, then, talks negatively about *The Wanderer* and *The Seafarer* together only in order to show the distinctions and does that only in order to show why they should be discussed (positively) separately.

While it is not my intention to make a thorough review of the sometimes fascinating complex of critical controversy on *The Wanderer* before presenting my own views, I do want to clarify some of the basic issues, touching on some of the more significant treatments and insights of recent critics, particularly where they bear on my reading. For whatever originality this essay may offer is in synthesizing the illuminating work of previous critics.[5] In surveying the criticism I am concerned primarily with discussions of the structure of *The Wanderer* which are inevitably involved in questions of dramatis personae, dramatic situation, the rôle of the poet in the poem, and the rôle of the editor in punctuating the poem. There are, of course, treatments of other critical problems both general (genre, source, etc.) and specific (readings of individual lines, words, etc.). These will be mentioned only when they have some bearing on structural problems.

But it is extremely difficult to attempt any kind of review of the scholarship on *The Wanderer* (as separate from that on *The Seafarer*) because isolating the parts of the critical treatments that apply only to the one poem frequently undercuts their premises or motivations. Let this, then, be my apology if my approach tends to be unfair to earlier commentators. The procedure will be to identify some of

[5] One has anticipated the title of this book: Thomas C. Rumble, "From *Eardstapa* to *Snottor on mode:* The Structural Principle of 'The Wanderer,'" *MLQ* XIX (1958), 225–30.

the major problems which the poem presents and to account
briefly for the major solutions.

Three times in the poem (*cwæð* 6a, *acwið* 91b, *cwæð* 111a)
direct discourse is indicated by "he said" or "he says" (amid
many other references to speech[6]), raising the problem of
speakers, speeches, and quotation marks. At three places
in the poem, first-person pronouns are employed (8–14, 19–
29a, 58–62a); every other passage employs one third person
or another. Who is this first-person persona or are there
more than one? Three "speakers" are identified in the third
person (*eardstapa* 6a, *se . . . frod in ferðe* 88a–90a and *snottor on mode* 111a): who are they? Different or same? And
who is identifying them? What is the rôle of the identifier?
In addition, other (perhaps indirect) third-person speakers
are identified: *anhaga* 1a and *Beorn* 70a. How do they fit in?

The orthodox view[7] has it that a poet introduces a speaker
whom he calls wanderer (ll. 1 and 6), the speaker delivers
a monologue (8–110), and the poet concludes (111–115) after
calling the speaker *snottor on mode*. The poet thus encloses
the speaker's speech with two uses of "he said" (*cwæð*), and
the speaker himself quotes an elegy, introduced by a generalized *acwið*. The value of such a reading lies in a degree
of formal consistency in its use of pronouns, verbs, and
speakers (poet, persona, and quoted elegist). But this view
has been challenged for five causes: (1) it relies on impressionistic common-sense rather than logic, (2) it relies on
rigorous logic rather than intelligent common-sense, (3) it
pays attention to formal characteristics of language and
structure without regard to what the language says and

[6] In 1b, 9a, 11a, 38a, 52a, 55a, 66b, 69a, 70b, and perhaps 107a and
113a.

[7] It has recently been called the "prevailing view," but it has been
challenged so often in recent years that it would seem that heterodoxy
prevails, here as elsewhere. Cf. John Collins Pope, "Dramatic Voices in
The Wanderer and *The Seafarer*," in *Franciplegius*, ed. Jess B. Bessinger,
Jr., and Robert P. Creed (New York, 1965), p. 164.

implies, (4) it pays attention to fanciful constructions of implications in the language without regard to formal characteristics of language and structure, and (5) alas it does not
conform closely enough to the commentator's own (new?)
reading of *The Seafarer*.

In 1943 Huppé overleaped the question of soliloquy or
monologue vs. dialogue[8] by suggesting that there were, in
fact, "two contrasting and complementary pagan mono-
logues [8–62a wanderer, 92–110 wiseman], framed and
bound together by the expository Christian introduction,
conclusion and 'bridge passage' [62b–87b]."[9] The subjective
judgment about the nature of the three speakers and what
they say was supported by the objective evidence of the
pronouns. Greenfield's subsequent reply accepted the evidence but turned it against the judgment, maintaining the
idea of a consistent pagan monologue (8–110) unified with
an explicit "contrast between pagan and Christian ideas" in
the introduction and conclusion.[10] Meanwhile, however,
Lumiansky had argued that *The Wanderer* is "an artistically unified dramatic monologue in which the single
speaker, the 'eardstapa,' using his own past experiences as a
case in point, examines the two lines of reasoning open to
an individual who suffers misfortune, and reports on his
attainment of peace of mind despite his misfortunes."[11] The
major difference between Greenfield and Lumiansky is the
latter's inclusion of 1–5 and 112–115 in the wanderer's
speech, a difference which produces (or is the result of) sig-

[8] The orthodox view sees a dramatic monologue. See Pope, p. 164.
But for an insistence on soliloquy see W. S. Mackie, "Notes on Old
English Poetry," *MLN*, XL (1925), 92; and Rumble, p. 229. James L.
Rosier, in "The Literal-Figurative Identity of *The Wanderer*," *PMLA*,
LXXIX (1964), 366–69, calls it an "interior monologue."

[9] Bernard F. Huppé, "The *Wanderer*: Theme and Structure," *JEGP*,
XLII (1943), 529.

[10] Stanley B. Greenfield, "*The Wanderer*: A Reconsideration of Theme
and Structure," *JEGP*, L (1951), 451–65.

[11] R. M. Lumiansky, "The Dramatic Structure of the Old English
Wanderer," *Neophilologus*, XXXIV (1950), 104–12.

nificant variation in the view of the nature of speaker and
poet as well as of the theme of the poem. I. L. Gordon,
however, spoke in 1954 of "structural weaknesses" (where
Greenfield, Lumiansky, Rumble, Huppé, and others found
ways of accounting for structural efficiency and even power),
in part because of her reading of the "face value" of the
poem: "It is this world of elegiac thought, not the real
Christian world, that supplies the poetic inspiration, and
it is the stylized elegiac genre that gives poetic shape to
these poems [*Wanderer* and *Seafarer*]."[12] In 1965, Pope
offered a new account of the structural strength of *The
Wanderer* (and *The Seafarer*), reviving the idea of two
voices, as his clever Elizabethanesque title for the poem
indicates: "The Wanderer's Lament and the Wise Man's
Meditation: Being a Double Elegy and Most Doleful Consolation in Two Voices and an Epiloque, Wherein They
that have Lost what they have Loved may Behold the Image
of their Sorrow and may Feelingly Know that All Things
Earthly Vanish into Night."[13]

Before looking at the evidence which these commentators
have interpreted with such diversity—the *swa cwæð* and
acwið, the *eardstapa* and *snottor on mode*, and the mixed
he's and *I*'s—I shall call one more witness. Sometimes the
instinctive sense which is the special province of the poet
can teach more than all the learned apparatus of the phi-
lologists; in Burton Raffel's *Wanderer*,[14] a poet's voice (is
it the *Wanderer*-poet's or Raffel's?) quotes two others: a
first-person wanderer (8–87) and a wise elegist (92–110).
There is no conflict of persons—Raffel's interpretation-
translation allows of none—because the passage 8–87 has all
been rendered in the first person. Raffel intuits that a strict

[12] "Traditional Themes in *The Wanderer* and *The Seafarer*," *RES*,
n.s. V (1954), 1–13.

[13] P. 173.

[14] In *Poems from the Old English* (Lincoln, Neb., 1964), pp. 59–62.
Raffel, my favorite poetic translator of Old English poetry, does not
neglect philological apparatus; he is frequently guided by it. The point
is that he is never bound by it.

consistency of NE pronouns is the way to capture the sense of the shifting OE persons.

Part of Lumiansky's argument had been anticipated by Mackie in 1925: "the past tense *cwæð* must refer to what precedes, and lines 1–5 should be placed within inverted commas, as the beginning of the Wanderer's soliloquy. Contrast *acwið*, present tense, referring to what follows, in line 91."[15] Accepting for a minute the principle that a preterite *swa cwæð* refers to what has already been quoted and *acwið* to what is about to be quoted, one discovers new problems in the poem. The first *swa cwæð* would then apply only to ll. 1–5, wherein the *eardstapa* talks about a third-person *anhaga*. The *acwið* would introduce the elegiac lament of 92–110, but the second *swa cwæð* would refer to the same lines or to the whole section 8–110 including those lines (and subsuming the *acwið*) or to the whole of the poem 1–110 (subsuming both the first *swa cwæð* and the *acwið*) or to some smaller segment (but including the *acwið*). The corollary to this is that if *cwæð* refers to what follows, the first *swa cwæð* can take in any or all of the rest of the poem, but the second occurrence can apply only to 112–115. Clearly, the structure does not depend on any rigid application of a *cwæð-acwið* principle of quoting; the problems the principle raises further complicate the issues of the poem. Pope exemplifies one of these problems when he points out that *cwæð* in 111 does not properly correspond to *acwið* in 91 so that *snottor on mode* cannot refer to the speaker of the closing lament, that "indefinite person [being] merely a rhetorical figment."[16]

But the principle cannot be accepted at all; linguistic and semantic evidence refutes it. Whereas *acwið* may comfortably be assumed to introduce a quotable utterance (at least sometimes), *swa cwæð* at any point in the history of the English language may refer either to what has just been said *or* to what is about to be said. Thus there is universal

[15] P. 92.
[16] P. 165.

agreement that *acwið* refers to the passage that follows, 92–110, but there is substantial disagreement about the reference of *swa cwæð* in both cases. The first instance may refer to 1–5, 8–110, 1–5 and 8–110, 8–29a, 8–57, 1–5 and 8–57, 8–62a, 1–5 and 8–62a, and many other possible combinations (which have not, so far as I know, been suggested). One's resolution of this issue necessarily depends on others, or more likely on one's reading of the whole poem. But it is closely related to the issue of who is speaking.

In reviewing Pope's analysis, one may wonder whether his subject is Old or late Middle English poetry: a great deal of the argument depends on the appropriateness of speeches to certain speakers. Thus lines 1–5 and 8–58 match the *anhaga-eardstapa* character as Pope finds him in those lines, and 59–110 match the *snottor-on-mode* character as Pope finds him in those lines. If only there were a general prologue to introduce these characters and links between their speeches to characterize them and their interaction further, and if only they were telling tales, there might be some measure for appropriateness. Pope's "consistent characterization" is consistent with his reading of the poem (and *The Seafarer*) but no more nor less consistent with the poem than the interpretations of those critics who find a more complex character speaking throughout, a character who is both *eardstapa* and *snottor on mode* or one who was *eardstapa* and has become *snottor on mode*. Perhaps, too, the poet is the (only) complex one, for in any case it is he who is quoting either a persona or a pair of personae or a persona who can quote a persona. The framework of a logical argument is weakened when the material for the premises must be isolated from the conclusion.

Thus Pope's handling of Huppé's logic (and Greenfield's) regarding the personal pronouns deftly exposes the basic fallacy of that logic: "if there are two speakers in a poem they can both use the pronoun of the first person."[17] But

[17] P. 166.

the argument may be turned on Pope's analysis: why not more than two? may not the poet use the first person? may not one first person (the poet or a persona) quote another or others in the first person? may not one first person (the poet or a persona) quote another quoting another in the first person? And the principle itself may be called in question, since the evidence of the English language shows that during every period one may refer to a first person in the third person.[18]

The point I have been trying to make is this: the evidence of the three features I have been discussing—*swa cwæð* and *acwið, eardstapa* and *snottor on mode, he*'s and *I*'s—cannot lead to a judgment, can only be employed to support a judgment already made. The judgment must be based on an understanding of the dramatic context of the poem. Pope's analysis of "dramatic voices" is unsatisfactory not only because it is finally revealed as a way of getting at the meaning and structure of *The Seafarer* but in and for itself because it fails to pursue the implications of "dramatic" or those of "voices." And along these lines Pope has chosen to ignore two of the most interesting of recent studies on the poem, Rosier's[19] and Elliott's,[20] to which this chapter must turn eventually.

The question of dramatic context is intimately involved with the question of personae, that is, the voices in the situations, and both in turn are involved with the most hotly debated question of all: is *The Wanderer* essentially Christian or pagan? The sage words of W. W. Lawrence may serve to characterize the issue and initiate the discussion: "The Christian coloring [of *Wanderer* and *Seafarer*] may be a

---

[18] I have just done so. Raffel would translate that sentence, one suspects, in the first person.

[19] See n. 8 above.

[20] Ralph W. V. Elliott, "The Wanderer's Conscience," *ES*, XXXIX (1958), 193–200.

later addition, but it is perfectly possible that it was in the poems as originally composed."[21] B. J. Timmer has called *The Wanderer* a unified whole with "purely Christian" themes—*The Wanderer* and *The Seafarer* "had better be called religious-didactic poems, probably . . . fairly old in their original elegiac form, but . . . become entirely Christian in spirit. It is impossible to separate the Christian from the heathen parts."[22] Leonard Frey sees the elements of exile and elegy turned to Christian use,[23] E. G. Stanley reaches a similar conclusion by dealing with diction and imagery (and bringing in a *third* poem),[24] and Elizabeth Suddaby finds a "blurred reflection" of Wulfstan's *Sermo De Baptismate.*[25] J. E. Cross has been somewhat equivocal on the matter, finding Christian origins for and Christian themes in certain aspects of the poem, but also placing their use in a larger tradition that embraces "epideictic oratory, the Greek *paramythia,* the Latin *consolatio,* of which Boethius's 'Golden Book' is only one example." Cross accepts as definitive the analysis by G. V. Smithers of the Christian homiletic tradition behind the elements of *The Wanderer,*[26] including the "essentially eschatological" nature of the second half; but Robertson's reading of the poem as Christian allegory[27] is probably what Cross is designating as "an ab-

[21] "The *Wanderer* and the *Seafarer,*" *JEGP*, IV (1902), 480.

[22] "Wyrd in Anglo-Saxon Prose and Poetry," *Neophilologus,* XXVI (1940), 222; and "Heathen and Christian Elements in Old English Poetry," *Neophilologus,* XXIX (1944), 180.

[23] "Exile and Elegy in Anglo-Saxon Christian Epic Poetry," *JEGP*, LXII (1963), 293–302, esp. 294–97.

[24] "Old English Poetic Diction and the Interpretation of *The Wanderer, The Seafarer* and *The Penitent's Prayer,*" *Anglia,* LXXIII (1955), 413–66.

[25] "Three Notes on Old English Texts," *MLN,* LXIX (1954), 466.

[26] "The Meaning of *The Seafarer* and *The Wanderer,*" *MÆ,* XXVI (1957), 137–53, XXVIII (1959), 1–22, 99–104. But Smithers' approach to *The Wanderer* seems often to be based on inferences drawn from his analysis of *The Seafarer.*

[27] D. W. Robertson, "Historical Criticism," *English Institute Essays* (1950), pp. 3–31, esp. pp. 18–23.

surdity," pointing out how it *differs* from *The Seafarer*.[28]
The impressionistic reading of Susie I. Tucker gets at the
Christianity of *The Wanderer* by a different route, via the
poem's ability to console "at times of loss and loneliness" for
readers, via the assertion that "Faith in security (despite all
harsh experience) standing at the centre of things is funda-
mentally the opposite of pagan belief," and via the incidental analogy with Vaughan and John Wesley.[29] Huppé,
of course, stresses the thorough-going Christianity of the
poem, while Greenfield's reconsideration shifts the emphasis only slightly; on the other hand, Lumiansky, Elliott, and
Gordon place the emphasis on traditional Germanic elements, while Rosier's special plea is for "those habits and
idioms characteristic of Old English poetic language"
(whatever traditions the commonplace themes of the poem
participate in).[30] Pope has neatly employed the elements of
this controversy to support his own thesis:

> The author of *The Wanderer*, in a more radical way than
> the author of *Beowulf*, seems deliberately to juxtapose the
> new mode and the old, to exhibit both the strength and the
> limitations of the old, and to suggest a synthesis dominated
> by the new. . . . We must beware of oversimplifying the con-
> trast between the two speakers. Both, we should assume,
> are nominally Christian, both preserve elements of old tra-
> ditions, both show some interest in the world and its values.
> But the wanderer, as a typically loyal retainer, belongs to
> the conservative aristocratic world in both life and poetry;
> the thinker, though he recognizes a native tradition of wis-
> dom, has moved into the sphere of Biblical and patristic
> learning, with some flavor of classical philosophy.[31]

Turning to the text (and setting aside the parallel issues

[28] "On the Genre of *The Wanderer*," *Neophilologus*, XLV (1961), 63–
75, esp. pp. 64 and 72; "On *The Wanderer* Lines 80–84: A Study of a
Figure and a Theme," *Vetenskaps-Societeten I Lund Årsbok 1958–1959*,
pp. 75–110.
[29] "Return to *The Wanderer*," *EIC*, VIII (1958), 229–37.
[30] P. 369.
[31] P. 171.

of *The Seafarer*), one finds only three places in 115 lines which make explicit reference to Christianity: *are gebideð,/ metudes miltse* "prays for favor, for the Lord's mercy" (1b–2a); *ælda scyppend* "the Creator of men" (85b); and *frofre to fæder on heofonum, þær us eal seo fæstnung stondeð* "[to seek] comfort from Father in heaven, where all the security stands for us" (115). At two other places, the references seem implicitly Christian: *Swa þes middangeard / ealra dogra gehwam   dreoseð ond fealleþ* "Thus this world on each of all days perishes and falls" (62b–63) and *þonne ealre þisse worulde wela   weste stondeð* "when all the riches of this world will stand waste" (74)—the last days and Judgment Day, though there may be some (Germanic) ambiguity or underlying universal concept present. At all other points in the poem, the diction and imagery are either general (referring possibly to familiar Germanic conditions or to their applications to Christian theory and morality, but referring probably to the universals that underlie both, for example, nature, mutability, transience, wisdom through experience) or specifically Germanic (referring to many aspects of Germanic society—duguth-life, Germanic architecture, the lord-retainer relationship, exile, Germanic warfare, seafaring, and even Germanic ritual). In number and power, the latter category dominates the poem. By way of contrast, *The Seafarer* has several specific references to the Christian God, many general evocations of Christian belief, and very few specific references to Germanic society or tradition (of which the only two extended ones are problematical, 97–102 and 112–115[32]).

The conclusions are inescapable. Assuming that his poem is what is extant (the only possible assumption from which a critical analysis can proceed), one must see the *Wanderer*-poet as primarily concerned with the traditional details of Germanic society; and though there is an explicitly Christian framework within which the details of the poem operate (and toward which they may ultimately turn), both the

---

[32] Cf. Neil D. Isaacs, "*The Seafarer* 109–115a," *ES,* XLVIII (1967), 416–19.

dramatic situation to be seen and the heralded voices to be
heard are clearly and loudly involved in traditions of Germanic heroic—pagan—society.

The insight of James L. Rosier is this: "Among Anglo-
Saxon poems of whatever kind or tradition *The Wanderer*
is particularly difficult to discuss pointedly because it is
intrinsically a mirror of a mind in its several states and
faculties, of memory and revery, of reason and imagination,
of perception and conception."[33] Aside from the obvious
virtues of treating the poem by and for itself and of demonstrating the necessity for such treatment, Rosier's analysis
has looked at the language of the poem and counted thirty-
five occurrences of words referring directly to the mind.[34]
In the light of such weighty evidence, one must agree that
the poem is significantly concerned with mind (though
whether "*a* mind" is, as has been seen, quite another and
not so easily demonstrated matter). But unfortunately
Rosier's analysis does not proceed from his perceptive point
of departure to an illumination of the poem; it becomes involved in terminology, confusing in procedure and purpose,
and at times even incomprehensible, at least to this reader.
His insight might have led him to clarify some of the major
issues of the poem, but it did not, I think, partly because
of his insistence on a novel approach with jargon to match,
and partly because he ignores (as does nearly everyone else
since 1958) the insight of Ralph W. V. Elliott.
    Elliott's title, "The Wanderer's Conscience," should have
been enough to put Rosier on the track: he might have been
able to integrate the idea of conscience with the idea of
mind. Elliott attempts to supply the neglected element of
motivation for the dramatic context of the wanderer:

. . . the Wanderer had every reason to be *hreo*[35] because I
believe (1) that he had made a boast, probably the custo-

[33] P. 366.
[34] P. 366n.
[35] The only notice taken of Elliott until very recently was by Cross,
in reference to this word, in 1961. But Christopher Dean, "*Weal*

mary one to fight with and for his lord unto death; (2) that
he failed to carry this out; (3) that the death of his lord plus
his own humiliation forced him into exile; and (4) that he
is now carrying his guilty secret about with him, not daring
to divulge it, torn by shame, looking for comfort where
alone he can hope to find it, in Christian faith and the very
different emphases of Christian ethics.[36]

Elliott's treatment is more suggestive than exhaustive, but
he has pointed the way. I have found his argument convincing, not only because I had independently reached a
similar conclusion,[37] but because it accounts for so much,
because it works. One need only combine the discoveries of
Rosier and Elliott and allow them to lead through the poem
to form an account of the poem as a psychological study of
a guilt-ridden mind. Such an account does not by any means
resolve the many issues touched on above, nor does it settle
conclusively the issues faced below (nor will it stand as a
final accounting), but it seems to help, to illuminate, and
to enrich readings of *The Wanderer*.

Let us assume that the active persona in *The Wanderer*
is the wanderer himself, that lines 1–7 and 111–115 constitute the only authorial intrusions in the poem, and that
the causes of the persona's exile are both the circumstance
that he is lordless and his feeling of guilt for the circumstance. How then is the whole poem to be read? Elliott,
having accounted for the dramatic context as described
above, proceeds to document the possible power of such a
situation for an Anglo-Saxon audience by discussing the
nature of the Germanic comitatus, an argument that hardly

Wundrum Heah, Wyrmlicum Fah and the Narrative Background of
The Wanderer," *MP*, LXIII (1965–66), 141–43, disputes Elliott's view
of dramatic context, imagining the speaker to be an old man who has
erected a wall around a burial mound for his lord, who fell in battle.

[36] P. 194.

[37] At one time I considered calling this chapter "A Live German Is
a Bad German."

needs to be rehearsed here again. The argument of the wanderer's speech, then, goes something like this, with appropriate commentary in brackets:

At every dawn[38] I have had to bewail [note the sense of urgency or compulsion] my cares alone now that no one is alive to whom I dare openly reveal my thoughts. I know it is considered noble for a warrior to be able to keep things to himself. [The first tension is between bewailing and stoicism. Note also that apparently the wanderer is, or was, a warrior.] No help against fate can come from *werig mod* or *hreo hyge,* so that those *dom-georne* "eager for renown" stoically keep to themselves their dreariness. I have had to do this [he too was eager for renown], though exiled, ever since I buried my lord and began to seek a new lord for understanding, consolation, and joyful entertainment. [He has been stoical but cannot be any longer. Note that his figuration of the lord-retainer relationship is two parts analyst-patient and one part ring-giver-ring-receiver.] Anyone who has been through such exile, friendless and with sorrow as his only companion, knows how bad it is. He remembers the joys of the hall, especially how his lord treated him well, and now *Wyn eal gedreas* "All joy has fallen!" Missing his lord's advice, his sleep no relief from sorrow, he re-enacts over and over in his mind the rituals of the duguth. [The use of the third person through this passage is simply a matter of projection and generalization, as the speaker assumes that anyone would react as he has; he is attempting to justify his weakness. Moreover, in focussing on the *ex post facto* weaknesses, he successfully, at least temporarily, represses the basic weakness: this is called the masking-diffusing-diluting of guilt. It is also called copping a plea.] The dreams or reveries or mirages are replaced by the harsh reality of present natural surroundings, a wintry sea, and his sorrow is heavier, renewed by memories of kinsmen and companions. He seems to see

[38] Robertson asks why the exile bewails at dawn, and, citing Gregory, he answers that dawn is a sign of the light of God's justice (p. 20), but Stanley says "the early morning is a time of terror without solace" (p. 434).

[hallucinates] them and he greets them joyfully, but they
fade away, replaced by the reality of sea birds who bring him
no familiar utterances. For one whose weary mind or spirit
has to wander like this, care is constantly renewed.[39] [Having
projected, generalized, and objectified his experience, he
has moved it further away from the guilty acts which
occasioned it. What Rosier calls the "process of ratiocination,"[40]
however circular the reasoning, is really desperate rationalization.] Indeed I can't for the world think why *my* spirit
shouldn't become sad when I think about all the life of
warriors and how they suddenly deserted the floor (of the
hall?). [I have italicized "my" because Pope has made such a
big point of the coincidence of metrical, rhetorical, and
thematic accentuation here.[41] But the accent on *eal* in the
next line is at least as pronounced,[42] and so the point is this:
"since this is *all* the grim lot of *all* warriors, why shouldn't
I be sad?" But the next line is even more revealing in the
concept of sudden desertion, which the speaker has perhaps
projected from his own act onto the fate of all men.] This is
the way the world declines every day, and a man can't become
wise until he is old and experienced enough to perceive all
this. [Now he is rationalizing his rationalizing powers!] A
wise man must be patient and not too hot-hearted (passionate)
nor too hasty of speech nor too weak a warrior nor too
heedless nor too afraid nor too rejoicing nor too greedy nor too
eager at boasting before he readily knows. [The implication is
that the persona now believes that he has learned these
things; he has derived some benefit from experience; he would
not now make a boast he didn't know he could live up to; if
he failed before, and his preoccupation with this one element

[39] The preceding passage has aroused a bibliography all its own. See,
e.g., the exchange between Sean O'Faolain and D. H. Crawford in *TLS*,
1931, 547 and 583, and the widely diverse readings of W. J. B. Owen,
MLN, LXV (1950), 161–65; D. S. Brewer, *MLN*, LXVII (1952), 398–99;
Graham Midgley, *RES* n.s. X (1959), 53–54; and Vivian Salmon, *MLR*,
LV (1960), 1–10. Again, I think Rosier and Elliott shed more light on the
obscurities, without reaching far outside the context of the poem.

[40] P. 366.

[41] P. 168.

[42] Also alliterated but carrying a full measure of a D-type verse as
opposed to an A-type.

of wisdom suggests that that was the case, blame it on his
youth and concomitant lack of wisdom.] A warrior must
wait, when he speaks a boast, until, proud-minded, he knows
whither his heart's thought will turn. [Again, and once too
often, he returns to this idea, nearly causing him to face his
guilt; but he resorts to his earlier system of rationalization and
projection, this time telescoping the process and jumping to
its conclusion:] A wise warrior has to understand the grim
truth about mutability, transience, and the inevitable destruction of all things of this world. Buildings, rulers, and men all
fall to ruin one way or another. Just as, for example, when
several have fallen in battle, the corpses suffer various fates:
one a carrion bird bore off high over the sea, another the
gray wolf divided with Death, a third a chief with sad face
buried in a grave. [I find this last clause (83b–84) the most
revealing of the speaker's tortured mind. He cannot repress the
elements of his guilt; they rise in transparent masks as
examples in his attempted generalizations/rationalizations.
Here he turns the truth inside out, imagining a sad lord
burying a loyal retainer who has fallen in battle (a child-like
fantasy); whereas he cannot escape the memory of himself as
cowardly retainer burying his fallen lord. His instance, though
sad, is idealized and sweet—he should have died and been
mourned; the truth is too horrible.] Thus the Creator of men
laid waste the earth, leaving ruins as examples of the vanity
of human activity. He [se is a difficult word, which probably
cannot be accounted for as a projected, generalized, or idealized
wiseman nor as a result of the speaker's schizoid tendencies—for
the present reading I would guess "one who," by which the
speaker means himself] reflected deeply and wisely on this
dark life, remembers much slaughter and destruction and
says . . . [I omit the nineteen-line elegy, except to note that
amid the general statements all of the concrete details refer
either to the wanderer's past as duguth-warrior or his present
as exile on a wintry sea.]

Given through 103 lines the picture of a mind driven
quite literally to distraction, it is certainly possible to conceive of that mind initiating the remarks of 1–5 and 112–
115, even projecting his guilt (and enunciating his schizo-

phrenia) one step further by the framing devices of 6–7 and
111. Thus he could again think of himself as wise in spirit
(111), repeat his object lessons about keeping faith and
living up to boasts (112–114a), and suggest that in his present misery and desolation and in the presence of his memories he has turned to God (1–7, 114b–115). The major difficulty with such an extension would be in 111b–*gesæt him
sundor æt rune*–which would then have to be read as an
ironic evocation of pagan Germanic counselors-in-action intended to show by indirection that Christian prayer is the
only efficacious meditation, Christianity the only *run,*
mystery, worth contemplating.

I say this is possible; but I would urge rather that the
notion of a gravely disturbed mind rationalizing its way to
Christian faith is both far-fetched and offensive. The poet
could, on the other hand, have created a persona and involved him in a dramatic context which allows the poet to
show by contrast the ultimate value of the Christian faith:
his audience's knowledge of and intimate feeling for the
heroic traditions allow the full impress of the situation to
take hold—and then he turns it. Keeping faith is important,
but keeping the Faith is salvation. Though the wanderer
often prays for the Lord's mercy, he cannot sensibly hope
for it (or do we have an ironic reference in *metudes miltse*
to the duguth-lord he buried?). The major difficulty in this
construction is in 111a–*snottor on mode*–which would then
have to be read as ironic: the disturbed mind of the wanderer may see itself as having attained wisdom, but everyone realizes that the true Wisdom is beyond him. The
speaker's preoccupation with aspects of the mind (Rosier's
insight again) renders this construction the more plausible.
How well such a reading suits certain contemporary tastes
will be apparent, especially the well-established preference
for showing vs. telling. But it probably overstresses some
elements of the poem while minimizing others. The perspective seems somehow awry. The insight, or combination
of insights, on which it relies must be worked back into the

framework of the whole poem, where other things are going on.

If I had a Shrevlin McCannon persona, I would have him say something like "Let me play a while now." Let us assume that the active persona is a speaker-poet, that it is he (not only his audience and certain scholars) who is familiar with the details of heroic Germanic traditions and with elements of Christian traditions, that it is he (not just some critics) who is concerned with such matters as guilt-ridden minds and elegiac laments, and that it is he who has something to say to us. The argument of the poem, then, goes like this:

A wanderer, however long his exile, often prays for the Lord's mercy. Fate is very resolute. A particular wanderer, remembering hardships and hostile slaughters, spoke thus about the death of friendly kinsmen:
"At every dawn I have had to bewail my cares alone now that no one is alive to whom I dare openly reveal my thoughts. I know it is considered noble for a warrior to be able to keep things to himself. No help against fate can come from *werig mod* or *hreo hyge,* so that those *dom-georne* "eager for renown" stoically keep to themselves their dreariness. I have had to do this, though exiled, ever since I buried my lord and began to seek a new lord for understanding, consolation, and joyful entertainment."
Anyone [anyone at all—involving audience] who has been through such exile, friendless and with sorrow as his only companion, knows how bad it is. He [the particular wanderer] remembers the joys of the hall, especially how his lord treated him well, and now *Wyn eal gedreas* "All joy has fallen!" Missing his lord's advice, his sleep no relief from sorrow, he re-enacts over and over in his mind the rituals of the duguth. The dreams or reveries or mirages are replaced by the harsh reality of present natural surroundings, a wintry sea, and his sorrow is heavier, renewed by memories of kinsmen and companions. He seems to see [hallucinates] them and he greets them joyfully, but they fade away, replaced by the

reality of sea birds who bring him no familiar utterances. For
one [anyone] whose weary mind or spirit has to wander like
this, care is constantly renewed. Indeed I [the poet-speaker,
speaking *in propria persona* for the first time] can't for *this*
world [the strongly accented alliteration emphasizes the
crucial, ironic, and anticipatory "*this* world"] think why *my*
spirit shouldn't become sad when I think about *all* the life of
warriors [again the strongly accented alliterations of *eorla* and
eal, in B- and D1-type verses, carry the crucial, anticipatory
irony] and how they suddenly deserted the floor (of the hall?
suggesting this world?). This is the way the world declines
every day, and a man can't become wise until he is old and
experienced enough to perceive all this. A wise man must be
patient and not too hot-hearted (passionate) nor too hasty of
speech nor too weak a warrior nor too heedless nor too afraid
nor too rejoicing nor too greedy nor too eager at boasting
before he readily knows. A warrior must wait, when he speaks
a boast, until, proud-minded, he knows well whither his
heart's thought will turn. [Here in 72, as perhaps also in 69b,
there may be an adumbration of the knowing and the turning
which the poet is going to state explicitly as his point.] A
wise warrior has to understand the grim truth about mutability,
transience, and the inevitable destruction of all things of
this world. Buildings, rulers, and men all fall to ruin one way
or another. Just as, for example, when several have fallen
in battle, the corpses suffer various fates: one a carrion bird
bore off high over the sea, another the gray wolf divided with
Death, a third a chief with sad face buried in a grave. [Does it
matter ultimately whether retainer buries lord or lord retainer?]
Thus the Creator of men laid waste the earth, leaving ruins
as examples of the vanity of human activity. [L. 87a *eald
enta geweorc* "old works of giants" may be an explicit reference
to the vanity of pagan ways, a bold image of what the poet
is going to offer an antidote or redemption for.] One who
reflected deeply and wisely on this dark life, remembers much
slaughter and destruction and says . . . [I omit the elegy
92–110 which the poet is quoting as if it is a familiar piece
which he has memorized, except to note how nicely it dovetails
with elements of his earlier exemplum while moving toward
the generalized conclusion.] Thus spoke a man wise in spirit,
[who] sat him apart in secret meditation. [This may simply refer

to a singer's skill or a poet's method of composing a lament,
but in any case for this reading it refers specifically to the
speaker of 92-110.] Good is he who keeps his faith, nor should
a warrior ever reveal his anger too quickly from his breast
unless he knows how to perform the remedy, as a noble quickly
can. It is well for him who seeks favor [reference back to the
first line of the poem] for himself [to seek] comfort from the
Father in heaven where all the security stands for us.

The virtues of the last reading are self-evident. It accounts for the apparent contradictions of speakers and
speeches by putting the whole poem in the mouth of a
poet-persona (the overwhelmingly dominant method of Old
English if not all medieval poetry[43]). It makes use of the
special perceptions of other readings by integrating those
perceived elements naturally within an elementary dramatic
framework. Incidentally it reworks recent insights into a
fairly consistently orthodox reading. Thus the speaker is
credited with being able to use his knowledge of Germanic
traditions to illustrate and decorate his poem and help
make his point; he is credited with being able to chart the
disturbances of a guilty mind without having to appeal to
a frame of reference embodying depth psychology or some
sophisticated epistemological system; and he is credited with
being able to turn concerns with dramatic heroic situation
and with mirroring a mind to an ultimately supra-dramatic,
supra-rational, supra-natural concern. If he seems to retain
the focus on the pagan elements, on an analysis of the drama
of his exemplum, and on universal abstractions of elegy,
mutability, transience, and the like—with very little explicit
reference to the ultimate and with virtually no preachment—that is both the material and the measure of his
success. The amount of critical energy he has evoked is testimony and tribute to that success, but I would not have the
poem seen as possessing a peculiarly modern excellence of
structure, for all the excellences it possesses.

[43] Cf. Stanley's general comments, pp. 447ff, on what Anglo-Saxon
poets were able, i.e., skilled, to do.

CHAPTER FOUR

THE EXERCISE OF ART, PART I:
THE RHYMING POEM

A useful distinction between "Classical" and "Romantic" is that the "classical work is concerned with the problem of art and the romantic work with the problem of the artist."[1] Still, both classical and romantic art are self-conscious; that is, there is always an awareness of the *activity* of art, the fact that, however natural it may seem to be, it is an *exercise,* a *function* of living which like other functions—nourishing, protecting, reproducing—is concerned with solving basic problems of life. The problems for art are those of ordering or structuring experience so that it may be expressed, communicated, and understood; so that a semblance of meaning can be produced. This awareness may be directed toward the problems of expression or the problems of expressing, toward art or the artist. In the most self-conscious art a concern with both kinds of problems is evident, a concern which in great art can syncretize the problems. *Tour de force* is a term usually applied to self-conscious art, and with sufficient pejorative connotations to preclude the juxtaposition in the last sentence of "great art" with "self-conscious art." But precisely such a juxtaposition may be seen in at least three kinds of poems using the awareness of the activity of art as a significant tool. The first includes the Classical and Neo-Classical poetry about poetry. The second includes poetry about poets, not the

[1] Neil D. Isaacs, "Faulkner with a Vengeance: *The Grass* Is Greener," *SAQ,* LX (1961), 430.

tributes of one poet to another, but such High Romantic poems as Wordsworth's "Intimations Ode," Coleridge's "Dejection," and Shelley's "Adonais." Some Provençal verse should be included here. The third includes poetry about poets *and* poetry, including a great many of the best Elizabethan sonnets and much of the best of Keats.[2]

Now the Old English *Rhyming Poem*[3] is everywhere called a *tour de force*. It is quite self-consciously concerned with fairly basic problems of art. And, though I will not claim that it is a great poem or a successful poem (or even that what I have discovered about it makes it great or successful), it is also concerned with the problem of the artist. The synthesis it offers—that both poet and poem are ultimately subject to God—actually begs the question. But the poem offers several challenges to the critic, not the least of which is the test of his methods and presuppositions. Still, one must begin with what is of foremost interest in considering the poem, the rhyming.

Rhyme, though rare, is found elsewhere in Old English poetry, the best-known example being a fifteen-line passage in *Elene*.[4] But there is nothing like the sustained, insistent rhyming of *The Rhyming Poem*. All but twenty-five of the eighty-seven lines have full rhyme between the two verses, and sixteen of the twenty-five have somewhat imperfect assonance which may be altered to account for dialectal vari-

[2] For an enlightening discussion of Keats's commitment to the subject see Mario Louis D'Avanzo, *Keats's Metaphors for the Poetic Imagination* (Durham, 1967).

[3] I have employed several variations, duly noted below, from the *ASPR* text. The poem needs re-editing because Krapp-Dobbie's conservative attitude toward the MS, while sound for most Old English poetry, may be superseded by attention to this poem's own systematic pattern.

[4] Lines 1236–1250, in which there are five lines of full rhyme, five with imperfect assonance, and four with imperfect consonance. *Elene* has other lines rhyming their two verses in 114, 115, 171, and perhaps 77 and 788. The off-verses of 615 and 616 rhyme, 50b rhymes with 51a, and 118b has internal rhyme. Most of these lines follow the pattern of rhythmic parataxis noted below, though not the syntactical parataxis.

ations or emended to regularize the otherwise consistent format. Of the remaining nine (6, 18, 36, 45, 60, 64, 69, 75, 79), four (6, 45, 69, 75) have been satisfactorily emended and two (60, 64) may stand with slightly imperfect consonance; this chapter will make some suggestions for the other three. Most are feminine rhymes (53:34, counting a reconstructed rhyme for 35b). Rhyming carries over between lines for all but thirty-two lines, perhaps thirty, since 17–18 look suspiciously corrupt and probably were originally rhymed. In fact, except for these two lines, the first twenty-six lines consist of groups of four consecutively rhyming verses. Moreover, lines 28–37 all have the rhyming unaccented syllables of weak verbal preterites, *-ade,* culminating in the nearly full rhymes of 36–37 *gearwade : hwearfade : searwade : nearwade.*[5] Additional rhyming occurs in 13 where each verse contains an extra rhyme in *scrad : -scad* within the sequence *glad : brad : lad : -glad : had : gad : rad : -bad* (13–16); in 21 with the internal rhyme *hyht : dryht;* in 57 with internal *-þrag* added to the *trag : genag* rhyme; and in the remarkable sequence 62–66a where each separate verse has an individual pair of internal rhyme-words:

flahmah fliteð,   flan man hwiteð,
borgsorg biteð,   bald ald þwiteþ,
wræcfæc wriþaþ,   wraþ að smiteþ,
singryn sidað,   searofearo glideþ,
grorntorn græfeþ,   græft . . . hafað.

No doubt the editors are justified in providing the missing word in 66b as a rhyme for *græft,* though I do not find that *hæft* (which seems the obvious choice from the context) has

---

[5] Wayne O'Neil, "Oral-Formulaic Structure in OE Elegiac Poetry" (University of Wisconsin dissertation, 1960, unpublished), p. 125, says that "the /-ade/morphemes give a perfect rime. Thus there are runs of verses like the following [30–37], all rimed . . . ." Morphemic evidence notwithstanding, *hlifade* (l. 30), for example, does not rhyme with *beacnade* (l. 31) any more than "banded" rhymes with "whistled." Even substituting phonemes, "banding" does not rhyme with "whistling" for

been suggested.[6] Naturally there is also a great deal of internal and linking assonance and incidental consonance.

Clearly, then, in most of the verses, there is more going on than simple single-rhyming within the framework of basic Anglo-Saxon alliterative form. But the poet has made his metrical problem all the more rigorous and demanding by his use of alliteration (the use of the term "initial rhyme" seems almost unavoidable here). In *every* line the alliteration between verses is augmented by an additional alliterating word in the on-verse (l. 58, the single exception, is generally emended not strictly for consistency's sake but also for sense; l. 71 has an extra alliteration in the off-verse), and with just five exceptions (34, *tr* : *t* : *t*; 40, *f* : *fr* : *f*; 43, *hr* : *hr* : *h*; 46, *br* : *bl* : *br*; 79, *h* : *hl* : *hl*) consonant clusters alliterate only with identical clusters.

The rigidity of the formal conception of *The Rhyming Poem* is evidenced also in its rhythmic arrangement. Of the eighty-five complete lines, sixty-six have the same verse-type in both half-lines, an extraordinarily high proportion. Three other pairs of lines (57–58, 59–60, 72–73) form parallel patterns where consecutive on-verses follow one verse-type and the off-verses another. The metrically deficient 9b should probably be reconstructed in such a way as to fill out a parallel pattern for 9–10. A cross pattern appears in 43–44, where in consecutive lines the on-verse of one is a rhythmic counterpart of the off-verse of the other:

Nu min hreþer is hreoh, heofsiþum sceoh,
nydbysgum neah; gewiteð nihtes in fleah.

the simple reason that the accented syllables sound completely different. There is a problem, then, in the imperfect consonance of *gearwade*: *hwearfade* (36), which I cannot resolve, having failed to discover any words like "gearfan," "gierfan," "gærfan," "gearpan," "hwearpan," "hwearwan," etc. Perhaps this was the poet's problem too.

[6] Since this was written, the suggestion *has* been made, by Ruth P. M. Lehmann, "A Lacuna in the Riming Poem of the Exeter Book," *ELN*, III (1965), 85–86. She reads, " . . . the marked one (or the grave) has captivity," but I think the paratactical structure of the whole passage calls for something like "grave-fetter holds."

Both 1–2 and 17–18 might be scanned so as to fit a cross
pattern (but 1a and 17a would then have to subordinate
one of the alliterating syllables). In four of the remaining
five lines (21, 25, 30, 39) the off-verse is a verse-type which
initiates a series of verses of the same type, in one case (30)
proceeding through the next seven lines. In 75, the off-verse
is an E-type in the midst of an eleven-line passage which has
eighteen B-type verses, including 75a (the defective verse
77b, if reconstructed, would have to be B, E, or perhaps
D2). I read both halves of 81 as hypermetric, both contrac-
tions of an A-type verse with a B-type formula-system.[7]

The rhythmic parataxis coincides frequently with syntactical parataxis. Again, in an unusually large number of lines,
the two verses have identical grammatical constructions:
thirty-seven, in four of which the on-verse in the following
line continues the sequence. In three other cases the parataxis
occurs between lines (1b–2a; 43b–44a; 46b–47a), and a
parallel pattern occurs in 52–53.

In part, the stringent demands of form have forced *The
Rhyming Poem* into the kinds of uniqueness which I have
suggested. Surely the uniqueness of its vocabulary, too (I
count forty-eight hapax legomena), is a product of the formal construct. Another result of the poet's elaborate attention to details of his metrical system is the difficulty one has
in recognizing the familiar formulas of traditional Old English poetry. Wayne O'Neil counts only eight full-verse formulas and a total of fifty-nine formulaic verses, 30 percent
of the total; he concludes that *The Rhyming Poem* "seems
clearly to be in a written rather than an oral tradition, depending upon only the most basic tools of the traditional
poetry."[8] By my count there are only five identifiable formulas in the poem (5a, 28b, 38b, 69b, 84a), but I find an
additional fifty-three formula-systems plus fifteen verses
which are variations of formulas or of verses which appear

[7] A revealing account of this kind of process is given by Lewis Nicholson, "Oral Techniques in the Composition of Expanded Anglo-Saxon
Verses," *PMLA*, LXXVIII (1963), 287–99.
[8] O'Neil, p. 75.

elsewhere (suggesting possible familiarity therewith). Thus
at least 40 percent of the verses may have reference to
traditional formulas, not too small a percentage for an oral
poem in which new principles of versifying are being added
to the old.[9] Yet I do not wish to assert that this is an oral
composition: convincing if not conclusive evidence against

[9] It would be well here to quote O'Neil's own admonition about playing a numbers game in this kind of investigation: ". . . statistics are never
final, . . . they are always tentative when the diminished returns of a
dead poetic tradition are examined. . . . in a small sample the stability
of ratios arrived at is easily upset by the entrance of new material" ("Another Look at Oral Poetry in *The Seafarer*," *Speculum*, XXXV [1960],
599). It is necessary now to point out the differences between O'Neil's
findings and my own as well as to make certain corrections and addi-
tions. The section of his dissertation Appendix devoted to *The Rhyming Poem* (pp. 206–14) marks eight formulas and forty-eight (not fifty-
one) other formulaic verses. I am counting 59a which is apparently mis-
marked and 84b which is mistakenly unmarked. I have not counted (as
O'Neil apparently and wisely does not) the twenty-four verses marked
for "measure-formulas." His list of formulas does not include 84a
scyldum biscyrede (cf. *Vainglory* 8a: *scyldum bescyredne*) and should
not include 20b (though to the supporting evidence for formula-system
should be added *Beowulf* 938b), 48a (though the system varies the basic
formula only slightly), 56a (though to the supporting evidence for formula-system should be added *Christ* 1585a), 73b (though to the supporting evidence for formula-system should be added *Psalm 57 8, Meters
of Boethius 13 70*, and *Christ and Satan* 243b), and 85b (though many
entries should be added to the supporting evidence for formula-system:
Andreas 1618b, *Guthlac* 145b, 673b, *Psalm 105 36, et al.*). Moreover, 69b,
listed as formula-system with reference to 67b, depends on *colað*, but
colað in 69b must be amended to *cealdað* to rhyme with *ealdaþ. Precepts*
69b has *ellen colað* (perhaps the formula accounts for the MS error), so
that we have either a formula with *colað* or formula-system with *cealdað*.
I would also reject 14b and 70a as formula-systems (the references are to
Seafarer 23b and *Daniel* 119b, but they are just parallel B-type verses;
rhythmic duplication must be seconded by *some* semantic duplication).
To O'Neil's catalogue of formulaic verses I would add 10a (cf. *Genesis*
1166a), 31b (cf. *Genesis* 1602b, 1891b, *Daniel* 671b), 52a (cf. *Christ* 1266b),
52b (cf. *Christ* 86a, 1104b), 74a (cf. *Guthlac* 85b, *Juliana* 377 b), 81a (cf.
Azarias 57a, *Genesis* 325b), 81b (cf. *Guthlac* 75b, 378a, 654b, 779b, *Andreas*
588b, *Christ and Satan* 49b, *Daniel* 641b, *Exodus* 269b, *Elene* 1038b,
1045b, 1061b, *Beowulf* 469b, *Maldon* 276b), 86b (cf. *Christ* 1559b), and
perhaps 75a (cf. *Phoenix* 182a). As variations of formulas I would also
add 24b (cf. *Beowulf* 1160, 3021a, *Genesis* 675b).

such an assertion is the use of oral patterns in which the *heard* effects of Old English oral poetry are superseded by the poet's metrical experiments and are retained only as *visual* effects.[10] In line 23, for example, both verses appear to be standard D2-types, but the rhyme forces them into an E-type pattern. Better examples occur when the multiple demands of rhyme, rhythm, and alliteration conflict, such as 58a, 72a, 82a, and especially 87a, *soðne god geseon,* which must naturally be scanned as a B-type verse, but where the double alliteration demands an accent on the first syllable and the rhyme an accent on the last.[11]

Two fairly obvious conclusions may be reached from an analysis of the versification of *The Rhyming Poem.* (1) There is a far greater concern with following the experimental formal system than with producing clarity of communication. This is another way of saying what every reader of the poem experiences: it is a very difficult poem, perhaps the hardest in the language. (2) The poet is deliberately calling attention to his metrical experimentation, his virtuoso performance. This is another way of saying what every commentator on the poem has said: it is indeed a *tour de force.* My study has led me past these conclusions to two others. (1) The poet's obtrusive display of technical emphasis is

There is also substantial additional supporting evidence for verses marked by O'Neil, but I must echo his own disclaimer that until a complete, accurate concordance exists this kind of investigation can never pretend to be final, however careful, thorough, and long-suffering the investigator.

[10] This accounts for the number of crowded verses which seem to be expanded verses. Pope suggests, *The Rhythm of Beowulf* (New Haven, 1942), p. 102, that only eight verses, 80–83, are actually hypermetric; I would reduce that list by half, calling 80 and 82 each a pair of crowded B-type verses.

[11] If one applies, however, the Stevick principle of unfinished composition (see Robert D. Stevick, "The Text and the Composition of *The Seafarer,*" *PMLA,* LXXX [1965], 332–36), one may suppose that the irregularities of this (or any) Old English poem are there because the poet had not gotten around to a final regularizing.

part of the thematic statement of the poem. (2) The literal
statement of the poem becomes less obscure when it is recognized that we have in it a dramatic context of a poet talking about his poetry.[12]

Anglo-Saxon poetry in general is self-consciously concerned with personae and dramatic context.[13] The *Riddles*
are the best examples of this concern, where obviously the
audience must guess who is speaking and from what situation. But *who* and *what* (or *why*) are also necessary concerns
for the audience of *The Wanderer, The Seafarer, Wulf and
Eadwacer,* and even *Precepts,* to name just a few. The history of the scholarship on these poems proves the point.
Deor has been considered to be unique in this regard, where
the persona is actually a scop and the dramatic context relates (apparently) to the fact of his being a scop.[14] But I
think we have a better example of a "poet-poem" in Old
English in *The Rhyming Poem.*

The poet is very insistent with his first-person pronouns:
they occur in no less than twenty-one verses, and in many
cases carry over as subject or object for following verses.
Generalized remarks and third-person characters (including
God) throughout the poem have some direct relationship
with the first-person speaker. The two exceptions are the
third-person referents of 51–54 and 80–83a, the *werig*
"weary [one]" and the *eadig* "lucky [one]." The former may
be seen to have an indirect relationship to the speaker, while

[12] That there is a problem of dramatic context may be suggested by
George K. Anderson's placing of the speaker in Purgatory or Hell
(*Literature of the Anglo-Saxons* [Princeton, 1949], p. 175).

[13] For a fine discussion of some of the related critical problems see the
first chapter of George T. Wright, *The Poet in the Poem* (Berkeley and
Los Angeles, 1960). "The Faces of the Poet," esp. pp. 30, 41ff, and 50. I
am grateful to Prof. Wright for his thoughtful reading of this chapter.

[14] Though *Widsith* is about a scop, it is clear that the dramatic context cannot concern a single human being. My own feeling is that
Widsith is a kind of elaborate riddle, with the solution given—*gleomen*
(136)—or perhaps suggested by metonymy—the art of poetry.

the latter is probably both a masked reference to the speaker and a convenient transition from him to the traditionally impersonal close of the poem. The point here is that the poet is calling attention to himself as speaker, as central actor, almost as vigorously as he calls attention to his metrical virtuosity. And as if to reinforce and bind these two demonstrations, he continually has reference, in the poem, to the practice of gleemanship (scopship?).

There are four direct references to scop-activities: *galdorwordum gol* "sang in lyrics (song-words)" (24a); *gellende sner* "the harpstring resounding" (25b); *sceaclas*[15] *wæron scearpe, scyl wæs hearpe,/hlude hlynede, hleopor dynede,/ sweglrad swinsade, swipe ne minsade* "harp-picks were active, sonorous was the harp, [it] rang loudly, song sounded, melody resounded strongly, didn't diminish" (27–29); and *folcum ic leopode* "I sang to the people" (40b). In 24a and 40b, the first-person persona is the subject. The inevitable result of these emphases is to read a great deal more of the poem as bearing reference to a scop. If the joys in 3a (*Glæd wæs ic gliwum*) are "joyous songs" or "songs," then the colors, colors of joys, and colors of blossoms of the succeeding verses may be metaphors for the poet's poetic abilities. No wonder, then, that "men looked at [him], feasts never failed, [and he] rejoiced in [his] life-gift" (5a–6a).[16]

If the poet is talking about his success as a scop, then some of the difficulties in ll. 11–23 may be resolved. The coming and going of travellers is the occasion for performances: apparently person-to-person diplomacy was carried on in "seasonal exchanges" (my reading for *gerscype*, i.e., *gearscype*) when the scop accompanied his lord (13–14) or helped his lord entertain a visitor (11–12, 16b–18a). His skill earned him an honored position, the protection of the

---

[15] I have gratefully accepted the emendation of MS *scealcas* to *sceaclas* offered by L. Whitbred, "Four Notes on Old English Poems," *ES*, XLIV (1963), 188.

[16] MS *feorhgiefe* has here been retained.

duguth, and wealth (15, 18b–22, 23b), at least as long as he produced and the political climate allowed (23a, 24b).[17] The central passage 30–42, which follows the direct reference to scopship in 27–29, goes beyond the suggestion that the good times allowed his art to prosper to the implication that his art was the symbol of the good times.

The transition to bad times is abruptly announced in 43 (though anticipated in 37) in reference to the poet: "Now my heart is troubled, fearful in sad conditions, near to hard necessities." It is fairly clear now that the subject of 44b–45a—"he who earlier in day was brave (or precious or valuable) leaves at night in flight"—is the poetic ability or spirit of the scop, which becomes the tenor for the metaphor of 45b–47a in the much-discussed *brondhord*. I see *brondhord* as a variation of *wordhord*, a way of talking about a scop's talent which has failed or turned bad, which has "grown stale in hearts," and which now "wanders afar."[18] It is replaced in the poet's mind by evil (47b) and grief (49b). The "weary [one]" of 51a, then, is either the failing muse of the scop or the scop himself (or both—synecdoche), and the "far journey" of 51b, contrasting with the joy-filled voyages of 11–14, marks the irrecoverable loss of the poetic skill of his youth. Perhaps *widsið* refers, as in many similar Old English euphemisms, to dying, and "the far journey begins" means

[17] *Widsith*, in one of its dimensions, suggests similar circumstances.

[18] For other readings for *brondhord*, see Joseph Bosworth, *An Anglo-Saxon Dictionary*, ed. T. Northcote Toller (Oxford, 1882–98), hereafter cited as *BTD*, *s.v. brond-hord*; Claes Schaar, " 'Brondhord' in the Old English Rhymed Poem," *ES*, XLIII (1962), 490–91; J. E. Cross, "Aspects of Microcosm and Macrocosm in Old English Literature," *Studies in Old English Literature in Honor of Arthur G. Brodeur*, ed. Stanley B. Greenfield (Eugene, Ore., 1963), pp. 13f; W. S. Mackie, "The Old English *Rhymed Poem*," *JEGP*, XXI (1922), 515 (this last reading no doubt influenced by *Andreas* 768b–769a: *brandhata nið/weoll on gewitte*). John Tinkler has supported my reading with the suggestion that *brond-hord* means "blight of treasures" (see *BTD s.v. brand* IIa); the *hord* is the word-hoard—now blighted. Such a reading, moreover, contributes to the central metaphor discussed below.

that the decline from prime has begun which will lead inevitably to death. In any case, a reference to the failing of
his poetry is made in 53–55a:

> blæd his blinniŏ,   blisse linniŏ,
> listum linneŏ,   lustum ne tinneŏ.
> Dreamas swa her gedreosaŏ. . . .

> *his glory falls, [he] is deprived of joy, is deprived of*
> *abilities, doesn't burn with joys. Thus here joys fail. . . .*

The third-person pronouns here continue and elaborate the
personification of the scop's poetic ability. One might even
render 53a "his productivity falls off," and the three words
rendered "joy" here—*bliss, lust,* and *dream*—are all more or
less implicitly associated with the *sounds* of pleasure, with
song and poetry.

These two points—the apparent concern with self and the
self-conscious use of scopship as point of reference—establish
a   basis for an analysis of the poem which leads to further
related conclusions about its structure. First, the poem is
basically a two-part (not five-part[19]) construct with two contrasting phases of the poet's career as the bifocal points.
Second, this dichotomy is supported by various sets of contrasts throughout the poem. Third, one of these is a central
metaphor in the sequence of images—reminiscent of certain
Romantic poetry—which serves to objectify the subjective
concerns of the poet (and perhaps leads to a confusion of
vehicle for tenor). Fourth, finally, the closing lines of the
poem do not form a separate section but derive from and
are implicit in the material of the poem; in fact, the conclusion may be called a synthesis for the dialectical procedure of both the vehicle and the tenor.

In the first phase, the poet-persona is at the height of his
powers; every earthly pleasure is his as a result of his superi-

---

[19] Cf. Mackie, p. 507; G. V. Smithers, "The Meaning of *The Seafarer*
and *The Wanderer*," *MÆ*, XXVIII (1959), 8; Stanley B. Greenfield, *A
Critical History of Old English Literature* (New York, 1965), pp. 222f.

ority as scop. In the second phase, his skill is gone and with it have gone all the attendant attributes of the good life. Virtually every aspect of the first phase is contrasted in the second, which begins with the shift to the present tense in 43a where it is announced by *Nu* "now" (repeated in 45b, 59a, and 83a). The first three verses (43a–44a) refer to the present condition of the poet's heart, "troubled, fearful in sad conditions, near to hard necessities," where earlier it had been joyous, secure, surrounded by creature comforts, "near to glories." Then come the contrasts already mentioned of the poet's failing genius and the generalized unpleasant journey.

The tendency toward generalization persists through the passage 55–69, in which a full depiction of the bad times is given by a montage-like technique. Throughout this passage, in several contrasts with earlier passages including similarly montage-like 24b–36, may be perceived a parallel symbolism: the poet's failure represents the general decline.[20] Joy, which dominates the earlier phase, culminating in *wæs min dream dryhtlic* "my joy was lordly" (39a), now breaks down—*Dreamas swa her gedreosað* "Thus here joys fail"—and so does the related concept of lordship—*dryhtscype gehreosað* (55). Where there were bright colors before (3b–4), now even the white becomes soiled (67a). Where time hastened, the year was productive, and the world was lively before (9b, 25a), now every hour declines as the world turns (58b–59a). Where there were the giving of life and images of arrival and staying (1a, 11a, 16b), now there are images of departure and death (56a, 61a, 66b). Strength (10b, 18b, 29b, 33a) has been replaced by weakness (57b, 60); prosperity and abundance (5b, 31b, 35a, 36) have been replaced by *borgsorg* "borrow-sorrow" (63a) and "time of misery" (which ironically "flourishes"[21] [64a]); and faith, truth, courage, and peace

---

[20] Cf. Cross, p. 11.

[21] The rhyme *wriþað : smiteþ* is slightly imperfect, but neither *writað* nor *smiðeþ* seems a desirable emendation (though the latter—"forges"— would be the less undesirable).

(24b, 31a, 34a) have been replaced by shame, hate, crime, deceit, treachery, corruption, and fiendship (56b, 57, 60, 64b, 65b, 68b; l. 37 anticipates this set of changes, and perhaps the unfathomable l. 26 belongs to this pattern of the keeping and breaking of faith). The images of the towering castle hall filled with light and song (30) and the scop in his noble seat there (15, 23b) are hollowly echoed in *steapum stapole*[22] *mispah* "it went badly with the high seat" (58a), and the images of "slaughter-spear" (61b) and "arrow-evil" (62b) may contrast with the active harp-picks of 27b, if Whitbred's emendation *sceaclas* is accepted.

At the conclusion of these generalized references with their suggestive contrasts, the poet sums up with a sequence of personal images about his impending death, a sequence which includes yet another weapon-image—*flanhred dæg* "arrow-swift day"—and culminates in the devastating (though perhaps even then trite) irony of the worm's feast and joy.[23] Here, then, is not the pointless bravado of an *ars-longa-vita-brevis* assertion—"reputation will not fall"—but a fitting conclusion to the antithetic phase of the dialectic—"reputation will not avail"—which sets up the eight-line synthetic conclusion.

The system of contrasts in the structural design and thematic strategy of *The Rhyming Poem* seems to rely on a central metaphor in which the poet's art is compared to and discussed in terms of nature. In 23a—*swylce eorþe ol* "like earth I produced"—the metaphor takes on a similetic explicitness, but throughout most of the poem it is more or less implicit or even submerged. The vegetation imagery, the

[22] The alliterative pattern requires this emendation, suggested first by Ludwig Ettmüller in 1850.

[23] Attempts to salvage l. 79 (with a rhyme that fits the context) have been unsuccessful. If *adroren* is emended to *abroten*, we need to lose the *ne* or expand it to another *nefne* (polysyndeton). Perhaps a word *(a)broten*, related to *brytian* "to profit," may be reconstructed. Surely the point is that the scop's reputation will not avail him at the worm's feast in the grave.

youth-age imagery, the seasonal imagery, and at a second remove the political-and-social-climate imagery, all are vehicles
for the single tenor of the poet's art—in its ascendancy and
in its decline. The Wordsworthian method is accompanied
by the Wordsworthian problem: what happens to poetry
when poets grow old? Moreover, there is something of the
Coleridgean paradox: a poem lamenting the poet's failures
turns out to be a high poetic accomplishment. But here is
where *The Rhyming Poem* diverges from, say, "Dejection:
An Ode," because what *The Rhyming Poem* does, essentially,
is *demonstrate* that the scop is attempting to substitute arti-
fice, technical virtuosity, and elaborate metrical exercise for
the natural poetry he says he commanded in his prime. But
The Rhyming Poem-poet, too, has attained the "years that
bring a philosophic mind," though his age has produced a
rationale even less original than Wordsworth's. Faced with
the inexorability of time—that youth and poetry and inevitably life itself will pass—his talk of the coming of *neaht*
"night" and the impending loss of inheritance and home
leads him to discuss the source of life and light (compare
the first line). For in heaven there are higher joys, true
Lordship, everlasting protection, and eternal peace.

This is not to say that the thematic statement of the poem
is finally made in the last eight lines. Surely the poem is
primarily about the scop's condition of woe after weal, but
just as surely the poet is operating in a context (and a tradition) in which the references of the last eight lines stand
as immutable points of final reference (a return to greater
weal). And the language he uses to describe the heavenly
bliss (*wynne, lisse, blisse, hyhtlice, biwerede, sibbe*) is the
language he has used throughout (cf. 4a, 8a, 12a, 20b, 24b,
37b, 39b, 76a) in describing the transitory state of earthly
bliss.

Perhaps no more need be said about the conclusion. It
is the least difficult part of the poem, the most nearly obvious, the most thoroughly conventional, and the part

where the metrics are the least obtrusive (see especially the expanded verses in 81 and 83). The poem as a whole, on the other hand, is knotty, obscure, experimental, and metrics-ridden. As a poetic exercise it is interesting—like the team juggling of "The Great Barstows"—because so many things are going on at once; as subject for a critical exercise it is interesting—like a Ximenes puzzle—because it intimidates solution; but as a poem it is successful only insofar as it makes effective comments—like *L'Avventura*—on its own failure.

CHAPTER FIVE

THE EXERCISE OF ART, PART II:
THE ORDER OF THE WORLD

L et me put the case very simply and straightforwardly: this is a poem about a poet talking to a prospective poet about poetry and then creating a sample poem which demonstrates the proper subject for poetry and makes a statement about poetry by using poetic creation as submerged point of reference for the Creator's Creation. The title "Order of the World," one of the innovations of the Krapp-Dobbie edition, is not an improvement over Grein's *Wunder der Schöpfung* "Wonders of Creation." At least "Creation" retains some of the meaningful ambiguity which functions as one of the principal controls of the poem: a poem describing the wonders of God's Creation serves as a model for demonstrating the wonders of artistic creation and the Wonders which are the proper subject for artistic creation. On the other hand, the idea of the word "Order" in the title is a good one, for the sense of order is the scop's chief impression of the miraculous Creation and the chief lesson he derives therefrom for his craft: the binding together of all things, even the most extreme polarities, is what moves the scop most (and inspires his best poetry), and the ability to take words and make them *soðe gebunden* "truly bound" (*Beowulf* 871a) is what most clearly serves as a cameo for the scop's artistic requirement, activity, and achievement. My first inclination was to combine these titles. But "The Order of Creation" is too flat, loses too much; "The Wonderful Order of Creation" sounds too much like something Robin the Boy Wonder would say ("Holy Crea-

tion, Wonderscop"); and "The Order of Wonderful Creation" is awkward and misleading. Casting about for an
alternative to combining Grein and Krapp-Dobbie, I rejected
for various (easily imaginable) reasons "Scop's Advice,"
"Scop and Gescop," "The Old Wonder-Scop," and "The
Order of the Word"; but at the risk of taking a rap for
playfulness I have settled on *Scop Talk.*

Critical opinion of the poem is unanimously low: Greenfield finds it very "loosely structured,"[1] Krapp-Dobbie says
that the various parts "do not hang together very well" and
the "autobiographical" introduction "has no immediate connection with the rest of the poem,"[2] and Anderson calls it
"disconnected and incoherent . . . wordy and rambling."[3] No
thorough analysis of the poem has ever been published; the
poem has apparently not seemed worth analyzing.[4] Three
points should be stated very bluntly: the relationships between ll. 1–37 and the rest of the poem have never been perceived; the structural principles of the poem have never
been recognized; the worth of the poem has never been discerned. When a critic says that something (sense of form,
system of structure, and the like) is not present in a work or
that it is impossible to find it, it often means merely that
he hasn't been able to see it.[5]

Again identifying the dramatic context is crucial, but here
there is no need to explore the poetry for implications. The
fully developed dramatic context of the poem is presented
in the opening thirty-seven lines, more than one third of the

[1] Stanley B. Greenfield, *A Critical History of Old English Literature*
(New York, 1965), p. 203.

[2] P. xli.

[3] George K. Anderson, *Literature of the Anglo-Saxons* (Princeton, 1949),
p. 176.

[4] The Old English Bibliography distributed at MLA in 1965 announced
as completed a book by Bernard F. Huppé, *Four Old English Poems:
Translations and Studies of Vainglory, Order of the World, Dream of
the Rood, Judith.* But I have seen no further notice about it.

[5] This argument has been presented in Neil D. Isaacs, "*Middlemarch*:
Crescendo of Obligatory Drama," *NCF*, XVIII (1963), 21f.

whole poem, a passage which Krapp-Dobbie and Greenfield call "autobiographical."

Not until the off-verse of the twenty-third line does the scop-persona speak of himself in the first person, though the poem opens with an exhortation addressed to a second-person audience and implying a first-person exhorter. Still, for the most part, the opening passage proceeds with third-person referents. This may be the reason commentators have had difficulty with the poem, for they have not identified the third-person referents with the first-person speaker and second-person hearer in a dramatic situation (even though the device of speaking about self and audience in the third person is quite familiar in Old English poetry). To spell out the necessary identifications: the audience is spoken of as *fus hæle* "eager man" (1a), *hycgende mon* "thinking man" (10b), *se þe on elne leofað, / deophydig mon* "he who [wishes to] become dear in strength (or zeal), deep-minded man" (17b–18a), *þegn modigne* "willing thane" (21b), *hygecræftig* "skilled in mind" (25a), and *monnes . . . moldhrerendra* "(of) a man . . . [of those] moving on earth" (27); the speaker as *fremdne monnan* "strange man" (1b), *wisne woðboran* "wise singer" (2a), and *felageongne* "well-travelled [one]" (3a).[6] In lines 31–36, the pronouns are first-person plural as the speaker deliberately and specifically groups himself and his audience together in a generalized community that had been suggested in 9 and 11–16. In the final line of the opening section the singer separates himself from his audience, insisting that the audience be audience—attentive to the sample poem-within-the-poem which is to follow.

This play of first, second, and third persons—along with a mixing of singular and plural and of past and present—points to the shifting of tone throughout the passage. And the identification of the mixed tones will aid in the precise identification of the characters and their rôles. Though there is some mixture of pride and humility in the speaker's

---

[6] For references to scop as traveller, cf. *Widsith* and *Rhyming Poem*.

attitude, the pride does not come from his individual accomplishment; and if *herespel* (37a) is rendered "noble lay" (*BTD*) or "glorious tale" (though Mackie simply calls it a "eulogy"[7]), the nobility or glory must reside in the subject-matter of the *spel*, not in the treatment thereof. My guess for this hapax legomenon, however, is that it means, simply, "praise-song," that is, psalm. In fact, there are many echoes of the Psalms in the language of the poem-within-the-poem.[8] But the heavy accents in l. 37, the essential alliterating syllables, fall on *Gehyr* and *hyge*: "*Listen* now to this psalm [I am going to sing] and keep your *mind* firmly attentive." Thus is heard one of the characteristic tones of the passage, that of an urgent pedagogue. It is the tone of the opening lines and of 23b–25a where it is tempered by a suggestion of futility that leads into the humility of the next passage. Yet, however often the speaker draws audience together with self in suggesting their relationship to God, he returns to the separation of the two in which he condescends, patronizes, tolerates, cajoles, exhorts, and expostulates—in which he teaches.

In his lesson plan he stresses the importance of the student's rôle in the teaching process. The learner must constantly ask questions of those who know more than he (3–7, 8–13a, 13b–16, 17–20) as well as observe the world for himself (21–22), even though there is too much for any one man to know (24–26). One can know only so much as the Lord allows (27–30), and that is likely to be little, but instead of knowledge He will grant the bliss of heaven to those who are obedient and not wanting in spirit (31–36). Similarly, obedience and attentiveness to the teacher will render the student not wanting in his craft, neither in subject-matter nor technique. Though the miraculous creation of the world puts the Creator far above mortal ken, there is yet a lesson to be derived from studying that creation, a lesson for all those who aspire to be mortal creators or artists.

[7] *EETS*, vol. 194, p. 51.
[8] Perhaps Huppé's forthcoming study of *Order of the World* will spell out in detail some such relationship.

Recognizing this lesson is possible only for those who have sufficient mental capacity. The teacher-poet is very insistent on associating poetic skill with intelligence: *wisne woðboran* "wise singer" (2a), *þurh wisdom* "through wisdom" (9a), *behabban on hreþre* "to hold (comprehend) in mind" (10a), *hycgende mon* "thinking man" (10b), *rincas rædfæste* "wise men" (13a), *a gemyndge* "ever thoughtful" (16a), *deophydig mon* "deepminded man" (18a), *in gewitte* "in the mind" (19a), *fæstnian ferðsefan* "to make his thought firm" (20a), *þencan . . . teala* "to think well (properly)" (20b), *wislice* "wisely" (22a), *hygecræftig* "thought-crafty" (25a), *in hreþre* "in mind" (28a), *to ongietanne* "in perceiving" (30a), *þinne hyge gefæstna* "keep your mind firm" (37b). But such an association is inherent in the poet's language, as a glance at some of the formulaic evidence will indicate. For example, *woðbora* appears five other times in the extant poetic corpus (*Death of Edgar* 33a, *Riddle 31* 24a, *Riddle 80* 9a, *Christ* 302b, and *Gifts of Men* 35b), twice in the formula with *wis* (first two above). For both occurrences in the *Riddles,* Baum translates "singer," and both times the contexts contain musical references.[9] In *Gifts,* in the list of fortunate men with natural talents is *woðbora / giedda giffæst* (*giedda* also appears in the *Riddle 80* passage). A better example is *hygecræftig,* which appears seven other times in the poetry (*Christ* 241b, *Riddle 1* 1b, *Daniel* 98a, *Maxims I* 3a, *Psalm 116* 1, *Psalm 118* 61 and 73). In all but the two occurrences in *Psalm 118, hygecræftig* is associated with the ability to speak, to use words,[10] and in at least one (*Maxims I* 3a) specifically with the art of poetry (the next line includes *gieddum wrixlan*).[11]

[9] Paull F. Baum, *Anglo-Saxon Riddles of the Exeter Book* (Durham, 1963), pp. 36 and 44.

[10] *Elene* includes five occurrences of *ferðsefan* but only one (316a) supports the association of wisdom with ability to use words which obtains in 20a here.

[11] The *Daniel* passage discusses Nebuchadnezzar's use of the Hebrews to advise, interpret, and prophesy for him. There may be a semantic inheritance here of the ancient association of poetry and prophecy, as perhaps also in the use of *woðboran* in *The Death of Edgar,* where,

The best evidence applies to l. 19, *bewritan in gewitte wordhordes cræft*,[12] both verses of which are formulaic:

wis on gewitte	wordhord onleac	*Andreas* 316
wis on gewitte	wordlocan onspeonn	*Andreas* 470
wis on gewitte	ond wordcwidum	*Andreas* 552
wis on gewitte	oþþe on wordcwidum	*Gifts of Men* 13

Onwend þec in gewitte,   ond þa word oncyr
þe þu unsnyttrum   ær gespræce   *Juliana* 144–145
wis on þinum gewitte   ond on þinum worde snottor!

Descent into Hell 78

The association of wisdom and the ability to use words well is clear and unanimous here, though only in the present poem does it extend specifically to the art of poetic composition—*wordhordes cræft* (19b) or *gliwes cræft(e)* (11b).[13]

On the other hand, we—like the poet's immediate audience—must remember the higher aim of intelligence, and we may be reminded of it by the connotations of *deophydig*, which generally appears along with its counterpart *deop-*

---

parallel with *cræftgleawe men*, it may refer to astrologers. John Tinkler has pointed out to me that *Psalm 116* 1 is a specific reference to the praise of God: *mid hygecræfte herigan wordum* renders Latin *laudate*.

[12] *Beowulf* 2221b reads *wyrm horda cræft* in the MS. The fact that it belongs to a formula-system may argue for retention of the MS reading, but no satisfactory explanation for the passage has ever been given. The usual emendation is *wyrmhord abræc*. It may be just as reasonable to argue that an unfamiliar verse was corrupted in the MS because of a resemblance to a familiar phrase.

[13] It may be argued that *gleow* or *gliw* has more general reference to rejoicing, but in poetic usage it appears consistently with specific reference to song or music (cf. *Rhyming Poem* 3a, *Psalm 67* 24, *Beowulf* 2105a, *Maxims I* 171a). The single exception is *Phoenix* 139a, where it seems to mean "pleasure," but the entire passage beginning at 131b fills the context with music: *hleoðres sweg / eallum songcræftum. . . . byman ne hornas, / ne hearpan hlyn, . . . ne organan. . . . Singeð swa . . . .* Incidentally, the association of wisdom and song in *Scop Talk* may evoke the suggestion of a play on *gleaw* here: "art of song" with slant suggestion of "strength of wisdom." Cf. J. Edwin Whitesell. "Intentional Ambiguities in *Beowulf*," *TSL*, XI (1966), 145–49.

hycgende in a religious context (cf. *Elene* 352, 881, *Guthlac* 1001, 1112, *Judgment Day I* 96). This double-function or double-duty of the mind is, after all, the major point in the lesson the master-poet is teaching. Echoing the cry of many a teacher of undergraduate writing, the poet says sing about what you know and seek to know what you will sing about. Look at the world, look at God's creation, and find there the only suitable subject for poetry. But you must learn your craft in order to be able to compose at all. The world is a "web of mystery" and only the poets, those who "knew how to utter proper [verse]," have been able to derive and bequeath some measure of wisdom from it; for it is only the poets who may approach the nature of the divine by mastering the art of creation. The *orgeate tacen* "the manifest sign" (8b), then, the sense of wonderful order in creation, is perceptible only to those who can order the tools of poetic creation in their minds. Thus the *dygel(ra) gesceafta* "secrets of creation" (18b) are the conventions of poetry, the only clear token— though a dim and miniscule reflection—of the miracles of divine creation.

You can know only what God allows you to know, and you must sing about that and be thankful for it. I think the *we* in 34a is ambiguous: we human beings, if we are not wanting in spirit, may attain heaven by doing God's commands; we poets, if we are not wanting in inspiration and the technical knowledge of our craft, may aspire to heaven by performing our art as God has wondrously given it to us.

Lines 38–102, beginning with the traditional *Hwæt,* constitute the poem-within-the-poem, the example which the teacher is offering to the audience in order to demonstrate (1) the proper subject-matter for poetry, (2) the reasons for such a choice, that is, the functions of poet and poetry, and (3) the significance, for the poet and his art, of the nature of the subject-matter.

It would allay some of the commentators' objections to this poem simply to enclose lines 38–89 in quotation marks and say that there is a fifty-two-line poem-within-the-poem,

with the speaker returning to his lecture in the last thirteen
lines, picking up the threads of his moral discourse, and relating his exemplum explicitly to his lesson. But it seems
to me that the last thirteen lines are part of the sample-poem,
that their statements proceed naturally from the fifty-two-
line section, and that the structure of the sample-poem
parallels in some ways (including the closing statements) the
structure of the thirty-seven-line introduction.

There is no need for *Hwæt* at the beginning of line 38,
no need to call for attention when so much of the introductory passage is a demand for attention. The word simply
signals in the most conventional way possible the beginning
of a poem.[14] The *act* of creating, which occupies only a brief
opening of the poem (38–40), gives way to the *result* and
present aspect of the creation as major subjects. The items
of creation *now* (41a) exalt the holy glory (42). Line 43,
echoed almost exactly in 82 (and echoing in turn 13b), has
a double emphasis—on joining things together and on the
fact that the joiner knew how to do so. The latter element,
on a much larger scale of course, parallels the scop's injunc-
tion to his audience that the craft must be mastered. The
former element parallels the typical description of the art
of traditional poetry, as seen in *Beowulf* 876b–874a:

> Hwilum cininges þegn,
> guma gielp-hlæden,   giedda gemindig,
> se-þe eall-fela   eald-gesægena
> worn gemunde,   word oðer fand
> soðe gebunden.   Secg eft ongann
> siþ Beowulfes   snytrum styrian
> and on spœd wrecan   spell gerade,
> wordum wrixlan.

[14] At this point I must note that composing a poem about composing
a poem with a sample composition as part of the poem has to be called
a *tour de force*. I might also suggest, indicating something of the rationale of discussing this poem together with *The Rhyming Poem*, that
some *tours de force* may be subtler or more successful than others, regardless of the artistic integrity involved.

The weaving together of things *æghwylc wiþ oþrum* "each with the others"[15] (44a) forms the basis for the passage of specifics following the second occurrence of the full-line formula (83–85):

> dæg wiþ nihte,   deop wið hean,
> lyft wið lagustream,   lond wiþ wæge,
> flod wið flode,   fisc wið yþum.

day with night, deep with high, air with water, land
with seas, flood with channel, fish with waves.

The poet is awed by the concept that all the separate entities of the created world glorify their Creator by their continued adherence to His decree, their firm bearing of their allotted natures, and their steadfast performance of their functions. His idea of the world is one of a perfectly ordered nature in which sun and stars, sea and night hasten to do the Lord's bidding, all working in harmony for the greater glory of God, all within His power and control and embrace. This sense of order is what most inspires him, and the infinite control which God exercises is what most impresses him (86–89).

The lesson for the prospective singer is obvious, though it never appears on the surface, remaining submerged in the implications of the dramatic framework: you must weave your material, your words, with the goal of bringing order to your product, exercising perfect control over your art. This point may appear to be fairly remote from the text, but a second preoccupation of the poet's vision of creation may suggest that the remoteness is illusory.

By what means does the Creator impose order upon His creation? What is "the mighty power by which is supported heaven and earth" (88b–89)? It is the power of His word. In the beginning He created *sweotule gescæfte* "clearly by

---

[15] Cf. *Meters of Boethius* II 35a, where the *æghwilc oðer* formula also occurs in a context of God ordering the world.

decree"[16] (40b) and all things had to be or do as God (the Pilot) *bibead* "ordered" (45b). What they must perform are *frean ece word* "the eternal words of the Lord" (50b), and His might is to "summon" (*laþað* 55a) all of creation. The longest individual description is devoted to the sun (cf. *Brunanburh* 13b–17a) which not only *healdeð nydbibod* "obeys the [Lord's] command" (72b) but also reflects His power by summoning another twilight (*glom oþer cigð* 71b). In the beginning, in short, was the word, and it is in his devotion to the word that the scop may partake of the nature of divine creator.

Another interesting aspect of the sample-poem is a polysemantic duguth-metaphor that operates at various points in it. This, too, may be seen to have an indirect relationship to the purpose of the sample and the structure of the whole poem. Anglo-Saxon poets frequently made use of their heroic heritage by employing heroic material metaphorically in reference to their new subject, Christianity. Perhaps the most common example is the application of concepts and language from the duguth relationship between lord and retainers to the Christian concept of the relationship between the Lord and His various creatures from angelic hosts to bare elements. Here the metaphor appears in several forms.

The dominant form proceeds from the personification of the elements of creation, such as the *heofoncondelle ond holmas* (54), who are summoned by the Lord into His own embrace; the *forðmære tungol* (69a), who passes over the sea *on heape* (69b), summoning another twilight; the *niht* (72a), who comes and obeys the Lord's command; and again the sun (73b–75), the travelling star who hastens under the bosom of earth. Taken together, all these personified retainers appear in a *þream* "throng" (41a), bear firmly their

[16] I am indebted to Mr. Patrick O'Shee for this suggestion. The evidence for this reading is not conclusive, though it is perhaps superior to Mackie's "visible creatures" or "clear creations." In at least five other places, *sweotule* is clearly adverbial: *Riddle 24* 10b, *Christ* 243a, *Wanderer* 11a, *Elene* 168a and 860a; perhaps also in *Meters of Boethius* *12* 29b and *8* 2a.

character (or the firm control) as ordered (44b–45), and stand firmly without weakening in the maintenance, protection, and power of the Lord (86–89). The Lord also takes part in the metaphor in being called *heah hordes weard* "high guardian of treasure" (39a) and perhaps also in 64–67 where the sun is called *bronda beorhtost* "brightest of brands" who carries forth light to everyone whom the *sigora soðcyning* "true King of victories" wishes to have sight (dispensing of treasure to retainers by king's messenger).

But the central figure in this form of the duguth-metaphor occurs in 47–53a:

> Swa he to worulde wlite forþ berað
> dryhtnes duguþe ond his dæda þrym,
> lixende lof in þa longan tíd,
> fremmaþ fæstlice frean ece word
> in þam frumstole þe him frea sette,
> hluttor heofenes weard, healdað georne
> mere gemære
>
> *Thus they bear forth to the world the beautiful*
> *excellence (duguth) of the Lord and the glory (host) of*
> *His works, shining praise into everlasting time;*
> *[they] perform steadfastly the eternal words of the Lord*
> *in the original seat which the Lord, the pure*
> *Guardian of heaven, set them; [they] eagerly hold the*
> *glorious bounds.*

Here the whole concept is spelled out: the Lord has established His retainers in their seats, and they are obedient to His commands, never going beyond the bounds of His control. Thus they are both the manifest form of God's excellence (*duguþ* as tenor) and the personified retainers of God's comitatus (*duguþ* as vehicle).

The form of the metaphor shifts and becomes more obvious in 90–97, where the *herga mæst, / eadigra unrim englá þreatas* "greatest of hosts, countless number of the blessed, throngs of angels" (91b–92) are called a *heorðwerud* "hearthband" (91b). This duguth is (literally and figuratively) in bliss, where there is nothing lacking, eternal feast

and joy, because they may forever look upon their King. A
final transformation of the metaphor appears in the final
passage (98–102), where all men are urged to obey their
Lord, forsake their sins, and join that heavenly duguth in
þam sellan rice "the better kingdom."

Now the relation of these duguth-metaphors to the business of the poem is implied in those elements of the metaphors that suggest the rôle a scop plays in a comitatus
situation: as contributor to and symbol of the joy of the duguth, as performer for the lord at its gatherings, as a retainer whose principal responsibility obtains in the duguth,
and possibly as a messenger or ambassador for his lord.[17]
These are the very elements that carry the metaphor at
several places.

Besides these suggestions in the sample-poem that evoke
aspects of the introductory section, there are still other and
more explicit parallels between sample-poem and introduction. One is the dictum that man must use God's gifts to do
what is allowed, however limited man's faculties (25–30 with
65b–67 and 76–81). Another is the dictum that man must
perform his proper functions in order to achieve the heavenly reward (31–36 with 86–97). The latter parallel becomes
explicit in 98–102, where the poet stoops to plain-talking
and moralizes his song, as his song had demonstrated his
earlier moralizing.

Both the sample-poem and the introduction lead to this
same point, that men (poets) may achieve heaven only by
observing their proper, assigned natures—as servants of His
Majesty the Lord. For poets, the proper subject is that very
Majesty, and they may properly treat it only by shaping it
with a semblance or an emulation of the divine control and
order—order, which is the chief manifestation of divinity in
God's creation. Thus *Scop Talk* practices its own preachment, binding together truly a thirty-seven-line dramatic-
frame introduction and a sixty-five-line poem-within-the-
poem by employing a semblance of the system of order
which is the very subject—and object-lesson—of the sample.

---

[17] See note 6 above.

CHAPTER SIX

PLUS ÇA CHANGE

STILL WATERS RUN *UNDIOP*

The structural principle of the thirty-line *Metrical Epilogue to the Pastoral Care* is essentially simple. The poem is constructed on the single metaphor of water. Campbell and Rosier note, "The metaphorical meaning of water in this poem is drawn ultimately from the story of Christ and the Samaritan woman told in John 4. Water there is the symbol of the spiritual grace of the Holy Ghost."[1] Specifically, verse 14 reads, "But whosoever drinketh of the water that I shall give him shall never thirst; but the water that I shall give him shall be in him a well of water springing up into everlasting life."[2] It should probably be noted that the close relationship of the passage and story to baptism may make the use of water something less than symbolic.[3]

Campbell and Rosier go on to say, "This spirit flows through Gregory's book for those who wish to partake, a fact which the poet . . . elaborates by adding many details to the basic metaphor."[4] It seems to me, though, that the poet, rather than elaborating the basic meaphor, is shifting the figure throughout (in a way reminiscent of the shifting perspectives of *The Seafarer*), and that more immediate sources for the figure should be noted.

[1] Jackson J. Campbell and James L. Rosier, *Poems in Old English* (New York, 1962), p. 79.

[2] All biblical references are to the King James Version.

[3] John 4 begins by comparing the number of people baptized by Jesus and John.

[4] P. 79.

The subject of the first sentence of the poem, Ðis, the first word in fact, initiates the ambiguities. The water or body of water which is consolation for men is spiritual grace, to be sure, but it is also the *Pastoral Care* itself, which both directly and indirectly is consolation.[5] In this sense the epilogue is like an envoy, and this sense seems to persist throughout the poem. Lines 9–12, for example, describe the drawing and preparation of the water by *halge and gecorene* "holy and chosen" ones, who spread praise of God over men's spirits throughout the world *ðurh halga bec* "by means of holy books." The references to Gregory and his book are unmistakable (perhaps also to Alfred and his translation). In l. 23, Gregory is specifically named as having prepared for men the doors *dryhtnes welle* "to the well of the Lord." But the metaphor is quickly shifted back to *Pastoral Care* as water, rather than the way to the water, in the final passage, which urges people (perhaps only priests, literally "retainers") to fill their vessels *her* "here." The *Pastoral Care,* then, *is* the body of water, as distilled from its original source in God, from which priests can draw in order to transmit its blessings to their flocks. But their vessels must not be leaky, lest the *scirost wætra* "brightest waters" be dispersed. The water may be thought of, then, as containing also elements of wisdom[6] and discretion.

If the figure seems to break down, it should be remembered that the principle of structure here is open rather than closed, suggestive rather than definitive. One should recognize the devices for what they are and do, rather than lament their departure from a more sophisticated or formulistic aesthetic. It should be considered enriching that the

[5] This reading is supported by the fact that the Hatton MS shows *wæter* and *scipe* clearly as separate words, allowing for a polysemantic reading: "body of water," "water-vessel," "carrier of water," "mover on water," "vessel (i.e., person, as in the Bible often) of faith," *et al.* See Vol. VI of *Early English Manuscripts in Facsimile* (Copenhagen and Baltimore, 1956), fo. 98r.

[6] Cf. 14a; Dobbie, p. 202: "spring of wisdom."

single figure can be turned to various shapes, passing through stages by subtle or straightforward shifts, allowing minds and hearts to open, turn upward, and be filled by the fluid influences.

We cannot really expect to find a single explanation—with one-for-one relationships—for the profusion of allusions to water: *wæterscipe* "body of water" (1), *wætru* "waters" (5), *fleowen* "flow" (5), *wæterscipes* "of water" (7), *hlodan* "drew" (9), *weriað* "dam" (13), *stream* "stream" (14), *tofloweð* "flow out" (15), *wæl* "well" (16), *diop and stille* "deep and still" (17), *riðum torinnan* "run in rivulets" (19), *tofloweð* "flows" (21), *to fenne werð* "comes to fen" (21), *hladað* . . . *drincan* "take in to drink" (22), *welle* "well" (24), *fætels* "vessel" (25), *kylle* "bottle" (26), *ðyrelne kylle* "leaky bottle" (27), *burnan* "stream" (28), *wætra* "waters" (29), and *drync* "drink" (30). (For the time being I have omitted all of l. 20 from this list.) Water itself may be said to signify, in various passages, faith, grace, wisdom, words, prayer, good works, and life, as well as the *Pastoral Care.* And the vessels for containing or distributing water may be the *Pastoral Care,* the hearts of the faithful, heaven, the Holy Ghost, writers of devotional books, human minds, human hearts, human mouths, words, the spirits of men (or priests, "retainers"), the willingness to learn and teach, or the attitude of prayer.

Nevertheless, the wealth of suggestions and possible analogies does not make the style "highly difficult."[7] One should be able to fathom the shifting metaphors and multiple significations without much effort, particularly with the very regular meter[8] and the straightforward, simple vocabulary. Perhaps the only puzzling passage is *nis ðæt rædlic ðing,* / *gif swa hlutor wæter,   hlud and undiop,* / *tofloweð æfter feldum   oð hit to fenne werð* "that is no wise thing, if water

---

[7] Dobbie, p. cxii.
[8] For only two lines must one resort to extra-metric anacrusis in order to find regular measures.

so pure, loud and shallow flows over fields until it comes to fen" or "becomes like fen" (19b–21).

Following as it does a passage recommending that the water be dammed up in minds, imprisoned by lips, kept alive deep and still in hearts, this passage would seem to continue the Christian expression of the Germanic (and Senecan) ideal of keeping things to oneself, together with the corollary evil and folly of letting things spill out and come to nothing. The direct contrast of *hlud and undiop* with *diop and stille* supports this reading. But certain problems of context and syntax remain. For one thing, the express function of the whole *Pastoral Care* is instruction in the ways of *dispensing* the "water," so the admonition to keep faith or grace or wisdom bottled up rather than watering it down for everybody seems out of place. The figure can be accounted for, however, by seeing that it *is* a figure throughout. The poet is not talking about metaphorical water literally running. The running over fields is metaphorical for wastefulness, and coming to fen is metaphorical for coming to nought.

More puzzling is the use of *undiop* in l. 20. If *hlud* and *undiop* are not adverbs referring to the manner in which the water flows when allowed to "run in rivulets," then they are adjectives belonging to a series with "pure" modifying "water." *Swa* modifies all three. In that case, "so loud" and "so shallow" do not seem properly to characterize the water which is also "so pure." Other readings of *hlud* are easy to find, so that the water becomes "resonant" or "resounding";[9] but this makes *undiop* even more of a problem, since one would expect the "sounding" quality of the pure water to be a product of its depth or quantity (that is, the roar of an ocean or cataract as opposed to the babbling of a brook).

My first inclination was to read *undiop* as "exceedingly deep, deep beyond measure of depth" (by analogy with

[9] Cf. Henry Sweet, ed. and tr., *King Alfred's West-Saxon Version of Gregory's Pastoral Care* (*EETS*, vols. 45, 50), p. 468: "murmuring."

unrim), but two other occurrences of the word make "shallow" clearly called for. In one, a chronicler describes a *crucethus* (a torture-box) as *scort and nareu and undep*.[10] In the other, the translator of Gregory's *Pastoral Care* uses *undiope mod*[11] to translate *cordi angusto.*

The latter passage occurs very near the end of the *Pastoral Care* and also talks about overflowing, suggesting that Dobbie may have been hasty in finding "nothing in the metrical epilogue to connect it inescapably with the *Pastoral Care,* except perhaps the mention of Gregory."[12] Gregory— in explicating the question, "Who then is that faithful and wise steward, whom his lord shall make ruler over his household, to give them their portion of wheat in good season?"[13]—says, "What is expressed here by a measure of wheat is the properly measured word, that it may not be wasted on a heart too limited in its capacity to hold it."[14] The incidental metaphor, perhaps already petrified, of wheat as water may have suggested to the poet of the epilogue a connecting of *undiope* and *oferflowe,* though he shifts the adjective from container to liquid.

Other parts of the *Pastoral Care* may also illuminate the metrical epilogue, for Gregory makes use of water metaphors quite freely. One passage makes use of the scientific principle of water seeking its own level:

> For the human mind behaves after the manner of water: when enclosed, it collects itself to the higher levels, because it seeks again the height from which it came down. But when released, it loses itself, in that it scatters itself to no

[10] G. N. Garmonsway, *The Anglo-Saxon Chronicle* (London, 1954), p. 264.

[11] Sweet, p. 459.

[12] P. cxii. But I wonder whether Dobbie finds the reference to Gregory merely a possible connection or believes that there may be other links.

[13] Luke 12:42; cf. Matthew 24:45. The King James Version reads "meat" for "wheat" in both places.

[14] St. Gregory the Great, *Pastoral Care,* tr. Henry Davis (Westminster, Md., 1955), p. 231. All quotations from Gregory are taken from this translation.

purpose through the lowest levels; indeed, all the superfluous words wasted when it relaxes its censorship of silence,
are so many streams carrying the mind away from itself.[15]

Interestingly enough, the Old English version of the passage bears significant dictional resemblances to the epilogue: *toflewð, wierð . . . to fenne,* and *riðum torinne.*[16]
A subsequent passage[17] reveals that the epilogue may be
closer to the suggestiveness of Gregory than to the translation of Alfred. Gregory is demonstrating the possibility of
multiple uses of water as a metaphor by referring to Proverbs 17:14 ("The beginning of strife is as when one letteth
out water") and 18:4 ("The words of a man's mouth are as
deep waters, and the wellspring of wisdom as a flowing
brook"). This becomes the single-minded and slightly confused "The wise Solomon said that a very deep pool is
weired in the wise man's mind, and very little of what is
useless flows out."[18] This discrepancy alone could account
for the problem raised by *diop* and *undiop* in the epilogue.

A resolution of that problem, at least as regards the
practice of faith, is offered by Gregory himself in his commentary on yet another water metaphor, the cistern and foun-
tains figure of Proverbs 5:15–18. The basic reference is to
"the relations of husband to wife, [but] Gregory applies
the passage to the pastor's preaching."[19] Inverting a traditional Germanic maxim and blithely offering *non sequitur*
as solution for paradox, Gregory says, "We, then, divide
the waters in the streets and yet keep them to ourselves,
when we diffuse our preaching far and wide, but have no
intention whatever of winning the praises of men."[20]

The poet of the epilogue does not seem to have reference to this explication of Gregory's, except in the general
extension of water imagery to containers. But the crucial

[15] Davis, p. 132.   [18] Sweet, pp. 278f.
[16] Sweet, pp. 276f.   [19] Davis, p. 261
[17] Davis, p. 133.   [20] Davis, p. 176; cf. Sweet, pp. 372ff.

passage does not perpetuate an earlier error of the translator. The water is pure, but some waste it. Instead of remaining still in men's hearts, it is released in folly and becomes loud and shallow. The rivulets are loud and shallow as opposed to the still, deep, living well, though both are made up of the so-pure water. Seen as parts of an extended metaphor, the adjectives themselves may be recognized as metaphorical, and the whole passage, as part of a structural principle involving a chorus of alternating tenors for one metaphorical vehicle, may be seen as an integral part of an excellently constructed poem.

THE DEATH OF EDGAR (AND OTHERS)

975 was a bad year in England; if one is to judge from the versified entry for that year in the Chronicles,[21] it was a bad year not only for the people but also for the poetry. The critical condemnation of this poem is unanimous, but—without attempting to resuscitate the poem as being more than the work of a pedestrian versifier (what else can one call the man who devotes his longest sentence, twelve verses out of the seventy-four in the whole poem, to naming the death-day?)—I would like to point out that the poem does have the semblance of an artistic concept behind it. Unlike the *Metrical Epilogue,* the tenor remains constant while the vehicles constantly shift: the poem consists of a series of ways and images for expressing death. In fact, the poem should probably have some such title as "975, Year of Death."

Many circumlocutions for death and dying were avail-

---

[21] The full poem appears only in the Parker and Abingdon Chronicles.

able to the Anglo-Saxon poet,[22] and the poetic chronicler makes use of several in a poem which amounts to an exercise in varying expressions for popping or kicking off. The poet has two basic ways of talking about the big sleep: describing metaphorically the swan-song or exit-line and describing, realistically or even symbolically, the reaction to the passing of the deceased. *The Death of Edgar* is structured by arranging alternating groups of these types of expressions.

The first group (1–10a) contains four circumlocutions for going to glory or Abraham's bosom, this time concerned with the passing of Edgar: *geendode eorðan dreamas* "ended earthly joys"; *ceas . . . oðer leoht* "chose other light," that is, "glory"; *þis wace forlet,/ lif þis læne* "left behind this weak, this transitory life"; and *gewat/ . . . of life* "departed from life." The language of the first and third is contradictory, while the second is noncommittal and the fourth is as nearly prosaic as possible. One would be hard put to find sophistication here, either in artful pattern or irony.

The second group (10b–12) has a single image which emphasizes the fact that Edgar has crossed over the river or the great divide. It is the direct result that the scepter has passed to his son Edward, *cild unweaxen* "child not fully grown." The implication is that Edgar's demise is untimely since his son is not yet ready to take his place as *eorla ealdor* "chief of chiefs, earls, nobles"—again I would see no irony in the phrase; it is merely a stock expression for king.

The third section (13–15) again has but a single image, expressing how Bishop Cyneweard has had his last gasp, reward, horizon, or round-up. The metaphor is quite simple and, apparently, deceptive: Cyneweard *of Brytene gewat*

---

[22] For a list of euphemisms available for a twentieth-century writer, see Louise Pound, "American Euphemisms for Dying, Death and Burial," *American Speech*, XI (1936), 195–202, reprinted as a separate pamphlet in Bobbs-Merrill Reprint Series in Language and Linguistics, no. 75 (Indianapolis, n.d.).

"went from Britain."[23] Still, this brief passage contains descriptions of the bishop which have implications for the complete picture of his giving up the ghost. Cyneweard was *tirfæst* "glory-firm," which is reminiscent of the earlier "chose other glory" and also implies that his spirit is with the angels. He is described, moreover, as *goda,/ þurh gecynde cræft* "good through innate strength," which reinforces the suggestion that his goodness and strength live on.[24]

But the fourth group (16–23) relates the grim reactions to Cyneweard's being six feet under or full fathom five. Here the effects of the good bishop's cashing in his chips depict a concomitant spiritual death. Praise of the Lord was brought low (17b–18a) among the Mercians, and many wise servants of God were dispersed (18b–19a). The loss of Cyneweard inspired *gnornung micel* "great mourning," but God—who is called *mærða fruma* "chief or source of glories," a phrase which echoes and combines the former references to earthly and heavenly glories—became *to swiðe forsewen* "too severely despised." The meaning of 23b *þa man his riht tobræc* is not clear; but it seems to be "when one broke His law," implying a period of lawlessness and sin when God was held in despite because the man most filled with the spirit of His love had bought it or caught it while sinners went unpunished.

The fifth group (24–28) describes what appears to be the exiling of Oslac. Three different words for home or homeland are used in this five-line passage: *earde,* from which Oslac was driven; *eðel,* the home of whales, over which he was driven; and *hama,* of which he was bereft. But if "departing from Britain" is a circumlocution for conking out, then even more obviously "being driven over the sea, bereft of dwelling places on earth" is a circumlocution for biting or kissing the dust. It is surprising that questions have been raised concerning what happened to Cyneweard, but not to

---

[23] See Dobbie, p. 151; Klaeber, *MLN,* XX (1905), 32. But cf. Charles Plummer, *Two of the Saxon Chronicles Parallel* (Oxford, 1899), II, 163.

[24] Klaeber, p. 32, takes *þurh gecynde cræft* as describing how Cyneweard *of Brytene gewat,* i.e., he died from natural causes.

Oslac. Perhaps Oslac is referred to in some historical document after 975, but I have not found any such mention.[25] Perhaps the concrete descriptions of the sea suggest too clearly the imagery of an actual banishment over "gannet's bathing place," but a metaphor is all the more effective for being concrete in its double-imagery. Besides, Old English poetry is filled with metaphorical language in which eternal rest and going west are associated with imagery of home, homeland, and sea.[26] Moreover, in *The Death of Edgar* we have ample evidence from context and structure that Oslac is no longer with us or caput. The poem moves through six sections, the first, third, and fifth telling how Edgar, Cyneweard, or Oslac has breathed his last, the second, fourth, and sixth telling what has happened now that Edgar, Cyneweard, or Oslac is pushing up daisies. The sixth section (29–35a) shows two cosmic reactions to the violent end of the wise old warrior, two examples of the implied cause-and-effect relationship of events coincidental in time. First, there is the appearance of a new star or comet in place,[27] in general a sign of a significant event, but specifically a commemoration of a translation from one sphere of existence to another.[28] Second, there

[25] Cf. Jackson J. Campbell and James L. Rosier, *Poems in Old English*, p. 76: "We have no other information about Bishop Cyneweard of Wells after this time." Even if Cyneweard and Oslac turned up alive later on, however, the poetic exercise under discussion would still render the translations given here valid.

[26] E.g., *Dream of the Rood* 119–121, 131b–134a, 154b–156, *Fortunes of Men* 26b, *Wanderer* 52–57, 81b–82a, *Seafarer* 38, 52, 63–66a, *et passim*.

[27] L. 30a: *steorra on staðole*. Dictionaries and glossaries frequently list "firmament" as a secondary meaning for *staðol*, but John Tinkler, "A Critical Commentary on the Vocabulary and Syntax of the Old English Version in the *Paris Psalter*" (Stanford University Dissertation, 1964, unpublished, but to be published by Mouton), pp. 156f, has suggested that the *st — — — on staðole* formula means simply ". . . in place" or "firmly." Cf. *Beowulf* 926, where *stapole* should probably be emended.

[28] Cf. J. E. Cross, "Aspects of Microcosm and Macrocosm in Old English Literature," *Studies in Old English Literature in Honor of Arthur G. Brodeur*, ed. Stanley B. Greenfield (Eugene, Ore., 1963), pp. 20ff.

is famine throughout the world, a product of *waldendes wracu* "the Lord's vengeance."

My suggestion is that the specific cause of the visitations celestial and terrestrial is the murder of Oslac, although the famine may have been brought on by the spiritual decay implied throughout the poem. This implication, as conveyed in this passage, leads the poem to the general statement with which it closes (35b–37). The coda is anticlimactic and simple-mindedly optimistic, though possibly ironic: God made up for everything (all the deaths and the results of death) by afterwards giving *blisse gehwæm / egbuendra þurh eorðan westm* "bliss to each island-dweller through earth's bounty." The irony would be in the suggestion that compensation for the ills of this world comes in joys of this world. Perhaps this is the only possible hope in a year of spiritual, physical, and poetic decay such as 975: wait till next year. Nevertheless, one can at least recognize if not respect the aesthetic sensibility of a chronicler who attempted to present a series of events in poetic fashion, with whatever linguistic wit he could muster, governed by a unifying structural concept.[29]

WHO SAYS WHAT IN *ADVENT LYRIC VII*?

Campbell's edition of *The Advent Lyrics of the Exeter Book*, in many ways a model edition for Old English poetry, follows the usual assignment of the dialogue in *Advent Lyric VII* (*Christ*, ll. 164–213).[30] It is the same arrangement as that of Thorpe, Grein, Assmann,

[29] Material for this and the previous section of Chapter 6 was included in a paper read at the South Atlantic Modern Language Association meetings in Greeneville, S.C., November, 1964: "Water and Death: Structural Principles in Two Old English Lyrics."

[30] Jackson J. Campbell, *The Advent Lyrics of the Exeter Book* (Princeton, 1959), pp. 58–61.

Gollancz, Cook, and Krapp and Dobbie;[31] but it is not the only one. Cosijn proposed another, which was followed by Holthausen and Zupitza and Schipper, and S. B. Hemingway a third.[32] This discussion will suggest other possible arrangements.

All but three of the hundred verses in this lyric are dialogue, and there has been general agreement on the assignment of seventy-five verses of dialogue. The last passage of thirty-four verses is a single speech, Mary's report of the Annunciation to Joseph; it is separately introduced (*þa seo fæmne onwrah/ rhytgeryno, ond þus reordade* 195b–196) and stands outside any controversy. Further, there is no question about 185b–195a; they must be assigned to Joseph, who speaks therein of taking a pure virgin from the temple only to find her changed *þurh nothwylces* and then voices his problem about whether he should speak out.[33] And the poem opens with seven verses that can only be Mary's: "O my Joseph, son of Jacob,/ descendant of David the great king,/ now must you sever a firm affection,/ reject my love?" (Campbell's translation). The differences of opinion, then, are all centered in 167b–185a, quoted here without any editorial punctuation:

> Ic lungre eam
> deope gedrefed   dome bereafod
> forðon ic worn for þe   worde hæbbe

[31] Benjamin Thorpe, *Codex Exoniensis* (London, 1842); Christian W. M. Grein, *Bibliothek der angelsächsischen Poesie* (Göttingen, 1857–58); Bruno Assmann, *Bibliothek der angelsächsischen Poesie*, 3. Band (Leipzig, 1898); Israel Gollancz, *Cynewulf's Christ* (London, 1892); Albert S. Cook, *The Christ of Cynewulf* (Boston, 1900).

[32] P. J. Cosijn, "Anglosaxonica IV," Paul und Braune's *Beiträge*, XXIII (1898), 109f; Ferdinand Holthausen, reviewing Cook, *Literaturblatt*, XXI (1900), 372; J. Zupitza and J. Schipper, *Alt- und mittelenglisches Übungsbuch*, 11th ed. (Wien and Leipzig, 1915); Samuel B. Hemingway, "Cynewulf's *Christ*, ll. 173b–176a," *MLN*, XXII (1907), 62–63.

[33] Cook, "A Remote Analogue to the Miracle Play," *JEGP*, IV (1902), 426, points out that "Joseph's hesitation as between speech and silence . . . is found in Pseudo-Chrysostom and Pseudo-Augustine."

sidra sorga   ond sarcwida   170
hearmes gehyred   ond me hosp sprecað
tornworda fela   ic tearas sceal
geotan geomormod   god eaþe mæg
gehælan hygesorge   heortan minre
afrefran feasceaftne   eala fæmne geong   175
mægð maria   hwæt bemurnest ðu
cleopast cearigende   ne ic culpan in þe
incan ænigne   æfre onfunde
womma geworhtra   ond þu þa word sprecest
swa þu sylfa sie   synna gehwylcre   180
firena gefylled   ic to fela hæbbe
þæs byrdscypes   bealwa onfongen
hu mæg ic ladigan   laþan spræce
oþþe ondsware   ænige findan
wraþum towiþere   185

The standard arrangement gives 167b–176a to Joseph,
176b–181a to Mary, and 181b–185a to Joseph as part of
the speech which continues through 195a. Cosijn assigns
167b–175a to Mary as part of her opening speech and 175b–
185a to Joseph as part of his only speech in the poem.
Hemingway would have Joseph speak 167b–173a, Mary
speak 173b–175a, and Joseph speak 175b–185a as part of his
long speech.

It is not difficult to see why Hemingway's reading has
gained no support. He sees the whole segment as governed
by a mood of despair, thereby explaining why Joseph ex-
claims "eala fæmne geong" and therewith placing that
exclamation at the beginning of a speech. But his "solution" depends on the bold emendation of minre 174b to
ðinre, and though it gives to Mary a passage "manifestly
inappropriate as coming from Joseph," it fails to face some
of the larger problems of the poem.

Cosijn's objection to the traditional arrangement is based
entirely on what he calls the "unmöglich" placing of eala
fæmne geong,/ mægð Maria at the end of a speech.[34] Cook

34 P. 110.

agrees that such placing "is extremely rare, if not unex-
ampled" but argues the weight of "objections on the other
side."[35] Campbell makes a stronger case: "[Joseph's] closing cry . . . expresses his tortured reluctance to believe
what his reason tells him must be his beloved's dishonor."[36]
It seems to me that these words (like the rest), as part of a
dialogue, should be assigned to the person who in context
is more likely to speak them, whether they occur at the
beginning of a speech or not.

A good argument which might be adduced in support of
Cosijn's arrangement would explain *sarcwida* 170b and
tornworda 172a as the hostile words of Joseph's declaration
to Mary that he must "put her away privily." This is the
source of her affliction; because of them *she* must weep
(*Ic tearas sceal / geotan geomormod* 172b–173a). The succeeding statement that God may easily relieve her wretched-
ness is a reference (strangely the only one in the poem—
though the traditional arrangement allows for *none*) to the
possible appearance of an angel of God to explain the Annunciation to Joseph.

Further, it is Joseph who seems to have been finding
fault with Mary, not vice versa. Cook, assigning 177b–179a
to Mary, finds a parallel in Germanus, where she says to
Joseph, "Thou art righteous and blameless,"[37] but there
are marked differences in the implications of word and
tone as well as in context. Joseph here is overwhelmed by
the enormity of any possibility of sin in Mary; he is pre-
occupied with his earlier image of her in perfect innocence,
and he defensively says he hasn't ever found any sign of
guilt in her before, but now (notice the tense shift from
178 to 179) he confuses her grief with the possibility of
guilt. (Notice also the polysemantic suggestions in the word
gefylled, suggestions which are valid only if Joseph uses
the word.)

[35] *Christ*, p. 98.
[36] P. 23.
[37] "Analogue," p. 426.

Cook fancies "a charming *naïveté* on the part of Mary" in this passage,[38] and Campbell suggests "that she has missed the words *for þé* . . . and indeed has missed the point of his entire speech. She thinks he is bemoaning some sin of his own."[39] But it is Joseph who fails to understand. Joseph's humanity is easy for Mary to comprehend; it is the divinity in Mary that is difficult for Joseph to comprehend. Yet Cosijn's arrangement falls into an inconsistency which seems to be based on an assumption shared with Cook and Campbell. Cosijn, ascribing the hostile words 183–185a to outsiders, assumes as Cook and Campbell do that there has been gossip.[40] But there can have been no rumors, or Joseph's whole problem would be non-existent, the whole speech (185b–195a) pointless. For he fears what people *might* say if they knew, and his course of action is designed to prevent any such knowledge. I suggest that these lines (183–185a) are Mary's, that the "enemies" include (or *are*) the hateful words spoken by Joseph, and that she seeks a way to reject his announced purpose with its implications and imputations. Thus, she has picked up and developed the figure of 167b–172a where words are personified as hostile.

The focus of *Advent Lyric VII* is not on a troubled Joseph; it is not a psychological study of a confused man weeping, grieving, and trying to rationalize a right way out of *his* affliction. The focus is on Mary grieving, weeping, and finding a way to make things clear to Joseph and right with him. Of course the audience is concerned with Joseph, as Mary herself is, but such concern is secondary to the major purposes of the poem and the larger context of the group of poems.

Here, then, with a synopsis of the dialogue, is a new suggested assignment of lines, requiring no emendations:

164–167a   MARY: *Must you [really] now reject me and my love?*

[38] *Christ*, p. 98.   [39] P. 23.
[40] See Campbell, p. 23, and Cook, *Christ*, p. 98.

167b–172a JOSEPH: *I am afflicted by the hostile words I have*
           heard before you.
           (Or Mary. It is easier to explain these words as
           Mary's, but I rather like the notion of Joseph
           afflicted and insulted by what he has had to say
           and the idea of Mary adopting his conceit.)
172b–175a MARY: *I must weep. God may easily relieve my woe.*
175b–176a   *O young girl, Mary the virgin.*
           (Either the end of Mary's lamentation or the
           beginning of Joseph's rationalization. I prefer
           the former despite its *unmöglich* occurrence at the
           end of a speech.)
176b–181a JOSEPH: *Why lament? I never found fault in you*
           before. But now you are speaking as if you
           were guilty of every sin.
181b–182a *I have received too much evil on account*
           of this pregnancy.
           (Appropriate to either, continuing Joseph's
           tone or establishing Mary's new tone.)
183–185a MARY: *How may I refute the hateful talk or find*
           any answer against the hostile ones?
185b–195a JOSEPH: *I took a virgin. She is now changed by I*
           don't know what. Shall I speak out or
           keep silent?
195b–196 Then the girl revealed the true mystery.
197–213   Mary narrates the true mystery of the Annunciation.

Pope has objected to the usual assignment of speeches in
Advent Lyric VII, not because the speeches are inappropriate to the speakers, but because the rapid shifting itself
is very unusual.[41] Yet a poetic tradition that allows for
shifts in perspectives (as in *The Seafarer*) or metaphorical
tenors (as in the *Metrical Epilogue*) or metaphorical vehicles (as in *The Death of Edgar*) and is often concerned
with mixing voices (as in *The Dream of the Rood, The*

---

[41] John C. Pope, "Dramatic Voices in *The Wanderer* and *The Seafarer*," *Franciplegius*, ed. Jess B. Bessinger, Jr., and Robert P. Creed
(New York, 1965), p. 187.

Wanderer, and *Christ and Satan*) can surely tolerate a compressed fusion of the structural design in rapidly shifting voices.

THE OLD ENGLISH *TASTE OF HONEY*

The common metaphor of the taste of honey has given rise to such ironic expressions about life as a bittersweet, earthy play and a coy, brassy band arrangement. But the Old English poem deals directly with the contradictions of life without bitterness or brass or irony of any kind. A version of the common metaphor—along with related figures of bees, lips, and tongues—is the central organizing feature of the poem, forming the basis for both its structure and its thematic statement.

Krapp's title for this poem from the *Vercelli Book* is *Homiletic Fragment I,* distinguishing it from a fragment in the *Exeter Book,* while Grein's title, *Be manna lease,* is sometimes used and sometimes translated. This may lead to such confusion as may be found in George K. Anderson's *Literature of the Anglo-Saxons,* where on p. 174, under the title *The Failings of Man,* it is called a "counterblast at man's wickedness" which is much more interesting than *Vainglory,* and on p. 347, under the title *Homiletic Fragment I,* it is called "a dreary series of didactic verses, forty-seven in number, on the hypocrisy of men, with 'honey in the mouth' and 'a venemous tail behind'; 'like bees they sting,' though they give forth a 'honey-taste' in their promises. And so the world wags; let us try to do better." There is apparently no connection recognized between the "two" poems.

Critical comment on the poem is virtually non-existent, though it has been recognized that there is some influence from Psalm 28. Grein (followed by Anderson, who sees vv. 3-4 of the psalm as the basis of the poem[42]) found the whole poem to be a paraphrase of the psalm, concluding that very little is missing from the beginning since the fragment picks up at the third verse of the psalm.[43] Greenfield merely indicates that "Near its beginning it paraphrases verse 3 of Psalm 28."[44] Actually only lines 9-15a closely parallel the passage from Psalm 28, and this section, introduced by *Forðan se witiga cwæð* "Indeed the wiseman says," should be enclosed in quotation marks as Krapp has it. In fact, *witiga* should be rendered here as "prophet" or more accurately "psalmist." The reference to scriptural authority merely supports the thematic development of the poem, while incidentally employing a metaphor related to the central one. It is impossible to draw from this reference to the *witiga* any valid conclusions about what or how much is missing from the fragment.[45] If the poem as it exists appears to be as nearly complete a structure as its statement warrants, we may give the poet due benefit of the doubt and suppose that not much is missing. But the psalm has nothing to do with that judgment.

The central metaphor of the poem, from which my title is derived, occurs in the hapax legomenon *hunig-smæccas* (28b). Although it sounds like the name of a packaged breakfast food, *hunigsmæccas* sustains the structure of this forty-seven-line (but only ninety-two-verse—1a not being extant and l. 8 being deficient) fragment. The taste of honey is what lying men have in their promises—the fair words, smooth peace-words, with which they pledge faith, artfully deceiving with their tongue, while in their inner minds they are thinking treacherously and wound-

[42] *Literature of the Anglo-Saxons* (Princeton, 1949), p. 175.

[43] See *Sprachschatz*, p. 872; cf. Krapp, p. xxxix.

[44] *A Critical History of Old English Literature* (New York, 1965), p. 203.

[45] I am indebted for this and other suggestions to Mr. Henry Herlong, who has pointed out to me the differences in the dramatic contexts of the whole poem and the whole psalm.

ing secretly by devil's craft (24–30). The metaphor has been
set up by the simile which precedes (18b–22a): "They (that
is, sinful ones [9b] or lie-workers [11b]) are singularly like
the bees [who] carry both together, [have] delicious food
and have a poisonous tail behind, honey in the mouth,
pleasant feast." The three intervening verses—*Hwilum
wundiaþ | sare mid stinge, þonne se sæl cymeð* "Some-
times they wound sorely with sting, when the time comes"
(22b–23)—seem to echo a passage from Boethius.[46]

Looking back through the first thirty-four verses, one
finds several other anticipations of the central metaphor.
The coming of sorrow (1b) into men's joy (2b) is the
broadly generalized statement of the situation which is
imaged forth in the metaphor: the obverse of sweetness is
inevitably a sting. This is followed by a concrete statement of the particular situation upon which the tenor of
the metaphor is based:

> Eorl oðerne   mid æfþancum
> ond mid teonwordum   tæleð behindan,
> spreceð fægere beforan,   ond þæt facen swa þeah
> hafað in his heortan   hord unclæne. (3–6)

> *One noble slanders behind (backbites) another with
> insults and with abuses, speaks fairly (or fair
> [words]) before, and nevertheless has that deceit in
> his heart, an unclean hoard.*

This passage sets up several echoes for subsequent parts of
the poem: *tæleð behindan* for *tægel . . . on hindan* (20b–
21a); *spreceð fægere* for *fæger word* (17b) and *fægerum
wordum* (26a); *þæt facen* for *mid facne* (17a) and *facenlice*
(26b); and *hafað in his heortan* for *hafað on hindan* (21a)
and *hafað on gehatum* (28a).

After the pronouncement that God sees all this evil
comes the paraphrased excerpt from Psalm 28, a plea to
spare the speaker the company of liars and hypocrites while
he is alive and the punishment that attends members of

[46] Cf. *Meters of Boethius 18* 5–11.

CARL A. RUDISILL LIBRARY
LENOIR RHYNE COLLEGE

that company after death. The particular phrasing (or paraphrasing) of the passage has three interesting aspects. First, *ligewyrhtum* (11b), in addition to the literal "lie-workers" or "lie-smiths," suggests "flame-workers"[47] (implying that the labors of falseness are rewarded with the wages of hell-fire) and also the devil.[48] Second, the *smeðe spræce* (12) anticipates the *smeðne sybcwide* (29a), an appositive for *hunigsmæccas*, thus directly associating the *witiga*'s quotation with the central metaphor. Third, the last verse of the quotation, *wære mid welerum,* because of its formulaic nature, evokes several possible connotations; but it remains, as far as I can determine, a unique figure in Old English poetry.

The seven other occurrences of the C-type formula-system — — —*wélèrum* are all found in the sometimes tortured versifying of the *Paris Psalter*. In *Psalm 118* 13 the occasion is part of a fervent prayer of praise and alone among the seven carries no pejorative connotations. Twice in *Psalm 58* (vv. 7 and 12) the reference is to heathens or sinners who have "swords in their lips" and whose lips are involved in cursing and lying. In *105* 25 the reference is to Moses, angered by his people's reversions and speaking unadvisedly. In *139* 3 the reference may be general or perhaps to Saul as the enemy of David, but in any case angry lips are associated with lying tongue, with poisonous adder and serpent (*ætrene wyrmas,* cf. *ætterne tægel* 20b[49]), and with *torncwidum* "distressing words" or "offensive speeches" (cf. *teonwordum* "abuses" 4a). In *140* 4 the reference is to lips as the last guard against the escaping of evil words and therefore a defense against losing wisdom and falling into evil ways. This occurrence is interesting in respect to the *Taste of Honey* passage because it is followed by the prayer

---

[47] I am indebted for this and other suggestions to Mr. Stephen Cox.

[48] Grein, *s.v. wyrhta,* lists as compounds *firen-, lyge-, mán-,* and *un-rihtwyrhta.*

[49] The two occurrences of *ætterne ord* in *Maldon* (47, 146) take on added power if it is seen that the basic formula-system refers not to weapons but to poison-bearing creatures.

ne on heora gecorenesse   became æfre which in the King
James Version has become "and let me not eat of their
[men that work iniquity] dainties."

Closest of all to the present context is the occurrence
in *Psalm 65* 13 in which the reference is to the speaker's
(David's) vows. He is now pledging or repledging to perform the services which previously his lips and mouth had
spoken when he was in trouble. Implied is the distinction
between what is merely said and what is actually done
(without regard to the apparent paradox that he is only
saying it again). The occurrence in *The Taste of Honey*
takes that implication, expands it into a new dimension
of distinctions, and renders it quite explicit. The formula-
system is used here to indicate people who "promise fidel-
ity faithfully with their lips" but who think something
else (*swa hyra hyht ne gæð* "their thought doesn't go so").
The earliest instance of the word "lip-service" recorded in
the OED is 1644 (*Direct. Publ. Worship* Pref. 2), though
there is a suggestion of lip-service versus heartfelt belief in
1558 (E.P. tr. *Cranmer's Confut. Unwrit. Verities* Pref. A
iiij: "We were lippe gospellers from the mouth outeward
and no farther" [*s.v. lip* 6 a (b)]). But it is clear from *The
Taste of Honey* and perhaps from *Psalm 65* that similar
associations of "lip" came into English more than half a
millennium earlier. When taken together with the metaphor of honey-taste, "lip-service" may be felt as richer in
connotations and more meaningful. In any case, the rest
of the poem makes them both more meaningful.

Between the paraphrase of part of Psalm 28 and the
simile which sets up the metaphor proper comes a transitional passage of three lines (15b–18a), serving as a recapitulation of the motifs already established: the ugliness
and corruption that have come into minds (though the
subjects are singular, the sense is generalized plural) and
stained and filled them with evil are opposed to the fair-
seeming exteriors as evidenced in the words. Line 17 cap-
sulizes the oppositions in *facne* and *fæger* (just as line 5
had *fægere* and *facen*; the opposition of the two is repeated

finally, within the simile, in line 26 as *fægerum* and *facen-lice*), while 16b *sare geblonden* stresses the sense of mixture or confusion. (Rather than "mingled with affliction," I read *sare* as adverbial: "severely" or "sorely confused"; so also 31b *mane geblonden* "evilly" or "cruelly confused." Cf. the use of the *sare* – – – formula-system in 23a.) One of the implications brought home in this passage is that the situation is unnatural: the evil is introduced from outside; the deceit is an invasion of the natural state; the contradictions of seeming and being are the result of corruption.

The – – – *geblonden* formula-system is repeated in the first line following the statement of the metaphor, as the final seventeen lines of the poem begin their four-stage process of extending the metaphor toward the pious conclusion. The first stage, including the linking formula-system, simply expands the scope of the discussion from individual men to the world at large—this world, the *mid-dangeard*—which is similarly confused (31–32a).[50]

The second stage (32b–36a) introduces the cause of the effects which have been described. It is "the old one," the devil, who is bringing deceit, affliction, and treachery to the world and to men. He is responsible for the confusions—*miltse mid mane* "mercy with evil" and *nið mid geneahe* "strife with abundance"—in the world, by implication also for the confusion within the hypocrites and liars. Moreover, the strength of his persuasiveness (34b) suggests in two ways that his weapon is the taste of honey: he is responsible for the sweetness of temptations (the "dainties"), and he is the arch-hypocrite whose lips smack of sweet but empty and false speeches and promises.

The third stage (36b–42) includes both the introduction of a new system of polarities and a negative statement relating to the central metaphor. The new polarities oppose

[50] This instance might be added to the list of examples in J. E. Cross, "Aspects of Microcosm and Macrocosm in Old English Literature," *Studies in Old English Literature in Honor of Arthur G. Brodeur*, ed. Stanley B. Greenfield (Eugene, Ore., 1963), pp. 1–22.

gastlice lufe "spiritual love" and the true and peaceful joys to *hyht* and *woruld wynsume* "pleasure" and "world-joys." Whoever chooses the latter is "neither wise, clever, [nor] soul-crafty in soul-advice." He has succumbed, as the argument of the poem has it, to the taste of honey; he is the devil's victim.

The final stage (43–47) extends (but in a sense narrows) the basic metaphor by making an explicit statement of the lesson of the metaphor. There is something far more attractive than the taste of honey—the *heofones leoht* "light of heaven"— and "now that we know [the remedy] let us think on and hope for the better." Let us seek "comfort for [our] souls up among the angels when God wishes to make an end of [our] life on earth": it is soul-comfort that counts (and lasts), not the concept of creature-comfort implied in the "taste of honey."

This opposition of spiritual love and earthly pleasure may seem quite remote from the earlier oppositions of lying and faith, appearance and reality, and sweetness and stinging. But the controlling metaphor quite naturally expands and supports the shifting statement by the means suggested —dictional echoes, connotative values, formula-systems, and especially the power of the metaphor itself.

Not that a metaphor based on bees is especially original. Boethius, as noted, made use of the same two capacities of the bee, honey-making and stinging.[51] In another source very familiar to Old English poets, bees are used in a different metaphor: Psalms 118:12,[52] referring probably to the enemies of David, says, "They encompassed me about like bees; they are quenched as the fire of thorns . . . ." The juxtaposed swarming bees and unquenchable fire (the Authorized Version has a very awkward translation here) as

[51] See note 5 above. Chaucer's rendering of this passage, Book III, Metrum 7, has shifted the emphasis somewhat; in Book III, Metrum 1, he has "Honey is the more swete, if mouthes han first tasted savours that ben wykke."

[52] The *Paris Psalter*, like most medieval texts, numbers it 117.

the enemies of the righteous form strong suggestions of devil and Hell. It may be that the Old English *Taste of Honey* retains the association, and that the bee, with the honey-smacks on his lips, is a type of the devil. But the point to stress in conclusion does not deal with any possible originality in the conception of the metaphor: the only claim to be made for the poem is that it is interesting for using such a concept as a basis for a strong structural scheme. Nor is the use of metaphor as unifying structural principle unique (compare the treatment of *The Metrical Epilogue to The Pastoral Care* in this chapter), but as far as my reading has taken me I have found no other Old English poem employing a metaphor-based structure in the same way—controlling the development, the thematic statement, and especially the flavor of the poem.

CHAPTER SEVEN

STRUCTURE AND EXCELLENCE: *DEOR* AND THE CRITICS

A critic may ask a number of questions about a poem: what is the correct text? what does it literally say? what does it suggest? what does it mean? how does it mean? what are its genre, structure, techniques, motifs, influences, provenience, *race, moment, milieu?* To this list we must now add—how nearly finished is it? A wise colleague has suggested that once these questions are answered, the most important one remains: So WHAT?[1] Such a question presupposes satisfactory answers to the other questions and implies three large problems of its own: (1) the interrelationship of the separate categories and what that means for the poem as a whole, (2) the question of how good the poem is, and (3) the significance of the poem as poem (implying, ultimately, the question of the significance of poetry).

This essay begins with a question of its own: wherein lies the excellence of *Deor?* Yet such a question presupposes the excellence of the poem, and I am not prepared to make such a presupposition. The basic question, then, is—whence cometh the presupposition of excellence for *Deor?* It comes in the recognition of a formal structure, strophe and refrain, an easily recognizable form. The critics' unconscious assumption is that such a form automatically promotes excellence in poetry, an assumption produced by the super-

[1] For these and other words of wisdom I am grateful to Marvin Spevack, now director of the English Seminar at the University of Muenster.

imposition of standards from one culture or aesthetic upon another.

Careful analysis may uncover the structural principles in some Old English poems, such as the principle of progressive identifications in *The Dream of the Rood,* or the shifting-perspective design of *The Seafarer,* or the fluid-metaphor plan of *The Metrical Epilogue to the Pastoral Care.* But such forms are neither apparent to the modern reader nor analogous with forms he appreciates (which is the same thing) nor do they carry with them a presumption of excellence (which is also pretty much the same thing).

The critics have tended to proceed from this first to a second presupposition—that strophe-cum-refrain form in Old English operates the way Modern English strophe-cum-refrain form operates. Even if we had more than *Deor* and *Wulf and Eadwacer* and a charm or two to go on, this would be a dangerous assumption. But on the basis of the existing evidence, *any* determination of the parts that strophe and refrain play in the Old English poetic aesthetic is dangerous guess-play.

Deor has sections punctuated by a single line repeated six times. So WHAT? The critics have answered this big question by showing how well the thematic material is supported by the superstructure of strophe and refrain. The consistency of each interpretation supported by the form is striking; equally striking is the lack of agreement in interpretation of theme. The only areas of agreement are the excellence of the poem and the fine way the form supports whatever the theme is. Yet these are the very areas which cannot logically produce objective evidence. Perhaps that is the secret of Deor's charm: after all, if unheard melodies are sweeter, unknown allusions are likely to be more stimulating.

There are two major camps on the methodology of form-supports-theme in *Deor:* (1) logical progression from stanza to stanza[2] and (2) independent stanzas linked only by theme

---

[2] F. Norman leads this camp. See " 'Deor': A Criticism and an Interpretation," *MLR,* XXXII (1937), 374–81; "*Deor* and Modern Scandi-

but with some associational progression.[3] Again, both camps
should be challenged on logical grounds. Both have made
assumptions based on an understanding of the theme as
suggested by the refrain, *viz.* that it refers to the passing
of evils. Therefore each stanza is interpreted as a specific
evil which passed, either a series of related evils or a series
of independent evils. But, as Frankis suggests in the course
of his ingenious construction of a Deor character and story,[4]
three of the sections *may* be construed as the passing of
good. In fact, when one sees that each section has *two* figures involved, one may construct at least four possible statements of meaning for the refrain, that is, four significantly
different statements of the general theme:

1. evil passes, good will come;
2. good passes, evil will come;
3. what's good for one is evil for another, and vice versa;
4. all things pass—wait till next year.

I am not offering any of these as a statement of the theme
of *Deor.* A case could be made for each. They are equally
valid or invalid. They are also equally trite. Surely such a
theme (whichever of them one chooses to prove) does not
in itself make for an excellent poem. What one must do is
invent the excellence of the examples that carry the theme,
an excellence suggested by such things as the richness of
the allusions, the "charm and simplicity of expression,"
the "lyric sweep of the whole," the concreteness and vivid-
ness of the deftly drawn vignettes, the "singing quality,"
the moving quality of the personal portrait at the end, "the
parallelism and contrast," the "clarity and elegance," the
"greatness of the . . . structural achievement . . . a series of

navian Ballads," *London Mediæval Studies,* I (1938), part 1; "Problems
in the Dating of *Deor* and its Allusions," *Franciplegius,* ed., Jess B. Bessinger, Jr., and Robert P. Creed (New York, 1965), pp. 205–13.

[3] The champion of this camp is Kemp Malone. See his *Deor* (3d ed.,
London, 1961); "Mæðhild," *ELH,* III (1936), 253–56; "On *Deor* 14–17,"
MP, XL (1942), 1–18; "The Tale of Geat and Mæðhild," *ES,* XIX (1937),
193–99; "An Anglo-Latin Version of the Hjaðningavíg," *Speculum,*
XXXIX (1964), 35–44.

[4] P. J. Frankis, "*Deor* and *Wulf and Eadwacer:* Some Conjectures,"
MÆ, XXXI (1962), 161–75.

strictly independent parts [made] into a closely knit whole,"
producing "one of the . . . most interesting and provocative
of the Old English verse remains," a "fine little poem of
folk philosophy."⁵ I submit that these are inventions based
on the principle that stanzas and refrains make good Old
English poetry.

A Cheyenne proverb says, "If you build your wikiup from
the top, it may look handsome as you ride into camp, but
later you may lie on damp buffalo-skins." The muddy lands
given us by Deor's (and Heorrenda's) lord would not tempt
a Cheyenne, who would lie and rely on solid ground and
then only if he knows it well enough.

Then what can one safely say about what *Deor* actually
says? The first section or stanza (1–6) discusses Weland's
hardships including what Niðhad did to him. It is not quite
certain exactly what Niðhad did to him, though icono-
graphical evidence suggests that the smith was hamstrung.⁶
The vengeance (*wræc*) Weland experiences may be his revenge on Niðhad, Niðhad's revenge on him, or something
else unknown to us. (Line seven is the first occurrence of the
refrain, which will be discussed at its last occurrence.)

The second section (8–12) says that the murder of Beadohild's brothers was less grievous to her than her discovery
of her pregnancy, and that she didn't know what she should
do about that. "That" presumably refers to her pregnancy,
though conceivably it could refer to her brothers' murder
or even to her guilt feelings concerning her self-centered
emotions. Moreover, there are at least three possible meanings for the first seven verses of this stanza: (1) she felt bad

⁵ From the voluminous bibliography on *Deor* I have culled, out of
context to be sure, these words of praise from W. W. Lawrence, "The
Song of Deor," *MP*, IX (1911), 23–45; Morton W. Bloomfield, "The
Form of *Deor*," *PMLA*, LXXIX (1964), 534–41; Malone, *MP*, XL (1942),
2; L. Whitbread, "The Third Section of *Deor*," *MP*, XXXVIII (1941),
371–84; and J. J. Campbell and J. L. Rosier, *Poems in Old English*
(New York, 1962), p. 69.

⁶ See L. Whitbread, "The Binding of Weland," *MÆ*, XXV (1956),
13–19.

about her brothers' death, worse about her pregnancy—the
meaning inferred from reconstructions of the story of Weland and Beadohild; (2) Beadohild was unhappy about her
pregnancy but happy about her brothers' death—a meaning
suggested by the frequent coincidence of litotes with comparative constructions in Old English; and (3) she was even
more joyful about her brothers' death than about her pregnancy—applying the litotes to both parts of the comparative
structure.[7]

The third section (14–16) deals with loss of sleep because
of a love—which may or may not be tragic or sorrowful—
between someone whose name or part of whose name may or
may not be Hild and someone who may be Geat or a Geat
or someone or something else. Lines 18-19 tell that Theo-
doric, presumably either the Goth king or the Frankish
king, ruled for thirty years a certain stronghold, the identity
of which is unknown, the various theories depending on
which version of whose story one draws on. The poet adds—
it must seem ironic to the modern reader—that whatever the
three preceding verses refer to was well known to many.

The fifth stanza, like the first a six-line section (21–26),
says that Eormanric was a Goth king, a "fierce" one at that,
and that many warriors wished for the kingdom, presumably Eormanric's, to be overcome.

Lines 28–41 constitute one or two—perhaps three—sections, though not interrupted by the refrain. The first three
lines reveal a sorrowful man thinking how hard life is—an
endless portion of hardships. The next four lines shift both
the thematic statement and the attitude, saying that grace
and glory are bestowed on many a man, a portion of griefs
to some. Moreover, it is a wise lord who does the distributing. This is usually taken to mean God, though it ought to
be remembered that Anglo-Saxon scops frequently relied

[7] F. Norman, in a letter to me, says, "Surely, the fact that Beaduhild
gave birth to Widia—though this is later than the original Widia figure
—is sufficient cause for rejoicing? Illegitimacy was not all that trouble-
some in Germanic days."

on their audience's familiarity with the metaphor which likens earthly and heavenly lords. (Incidentally, if *dryhten* here in 32 is God, perhaps *hlaford* in 39 may also be God.) Another possibility is that ll. 28–30 constitute an *if*-clause subordinate to the next four lines.[8]

Line 35 is a formula which announces a shift to a first-person persona. He was the scop of the lord of the Heodings and had a title (Deor), an excellent position, a devoted lord, and an estate. Subsequently, however, a song-skilled man named Heorrenda replaced him, at least in the estate.

The poem closes with the sixth occurrence of the refrain. "It passed over with respect to that, so it can or will with respect to this." The application to the last section would seem to be that Deor's good times passed (replaced by Heorrenda's good times), and that his bad times will pass too (perhaps along with Heorrenda's good times). Can the refrain be applied similarly to the earlier sections? That is, does each section describe a reversal of a situation and look forward to another reversal? The fourth and fifth sections may, since they deal with long but finally terminated reigns and look forward to the end of the succeeding regimes. And the first, with the suggestions of vengeance, may anticipate a second reversal. But it is difficult to construct an analogous situation for the second and third stanzas.

Well, then, can the second genitive of respect in each of the first five sections anticipate the present situation of Deor, revealed in the final section, which is thus assured and reassured of its temporary nature? If this is the case, then the sequence of ideas goes something like this:

1. that vengeance or bad situation passed, so can or will this, whatever it is;

2. that situation, whatever it is, passed, so can or will this, whatever it is;

3. same as 2;

4. that regime passed, so can or will this, whatever it is;

[8] Edward B. Irving, Jr., pointed out this possibility to me, crediting the suggestion to John C. Pope.

5. same as 4;
6. like the men who sat and brooded and wished in 5, one sits and broods;
7. then he thinks that a wise lord distributes good and evil lots;
8. I had a good lot, was succeeded by Heorrenda—that passed (the good lot) and so will this (the evil lot, which may now be associated with vengeance, misery, sorrow, and political situations).

That is not a bad system of organization for a poem, but a serious problem is that its efficacy depends on the audience's familiarity not only with the figures alluded to in sections 1–5, but also with the individual situation described in the final parts. We must then assume, as Frankis does, that Deor and Heorrenda, the scops of the Heodings, were famous legendary figures.

Let me try the refrain one more way, though I have not begun to exhaust the possibilities. The first genitive of respect in every instance refers to the situation just described, a situation known to have been temporary, though perhaps of long duration. The last situation is not known to the general audience, so the poet *tells* that it was temporary. There is no consistency as to the nature of the transitory situations—there is a mixture of good and evil lots. The second genitive of respect in each refrain refers to a current situation involving both singer and audience. It may be *any* current situation. We may have here, after all, a little poem of folk philosophy *or* a charm-like piece of consolation for any difficult set of circumstances *or* even a begging poem with imagined circumstances (though this is far from the line of reasoning employed by Lawrence or Huppé[9] or Bloomfield or Eliason[10]).

I say we may have, but it seems impossible to tell. The rationale of Deor's organization cannot be fathomed by

[9] Bernard F. Huppé, *Doctrine and Poetry* (New York, 1959), p. 236.
[10] Norman E. Eliason, "Two Old English Scop Poems," *PMLA*, LXXXI (1966), 185–92.

whatever hypothetical reconstruction is placed on the facts we have, though such approaches are likely to be far more rewarding than any approach which proceeds from a presumption of excellence based on a modern fancy for stanzas and refrains.[11]

A NEGATIVE NOTE ON *WULF AND EADWACER*

Many of the points I have made about *Deor* are applicable to *Wulf and Eadwacer* as well; but my rumblings have mostly been pre-empted by Alain Renoir in his "*Wulf and Eadwacer*: A Noninterpretation."[12] Yet Renoir has not gone far enough. That is, his noninterpretation is not non-interpretative enough. Though he carefully avoids assertions based on any assumption which is not founded on textual evidence, he nevertheless manages to imply an interpretation of the poem; and I insist that *any* single interpretation of this poem must make assumptions not supported by evidence from the text. Rejecting many of the extra-textual and illogical assumptions of earlier scholars, Renoir has succumbed to others.

Wulf and Eadwacer is a puzzle (many have even called it a Riddle), and it might be helpful to approach it as one would a logic problem. Logic can demonstrate not only the invalidity of some readings but also the potential falseness of some appealing and valid readings. In setting up some guidelines for an approach to *Wulf and Eadwacer,* then, I would offer the following observations.

1. The dual pronouns *Uncerne* (16) and *uncer* (19) must

[11] A version of this essay was presented to the Old English group at MLA in 1965. Professor Eliason presented some of the material from his article on the same program. Afterwards he suggested to me that a presumption of excellence for *Deor* could be made on the basis of its inclusion in an expensive production like the Exeter Book.

[12] *Franciplegius,* pp. 147–63.

refer to the speaker and one other person; but, if there are
three (or more) characters involved in the dramatic context
of the poem, there can be no absolute assurance that both
duals refer to the *same* pair. As a corollary, there can be no
assurance that *þine* (13, 14) and *þu* (16) necessarily refer to
two different second persons.

2. The plural pronouns *us* (3, 8), used by a poet who repeats dual usage, *probably* indicate a "we" of more than
two people in the refrain. Yet most, without questioning
why *unc* is not used, assume the referent to be the speaker
and *one* other character.[13]

3. What is generally called a refrain consists of the three
verses of lines 2 and 3 repeated as lines 7 and 8. While it is
handy to call this a refrain, one should avoid concluding
that it does what a refrain is generally expected to do. Too
little is known about the use of such repetitions in Old English poetry (see the preceding comments on *Deor*). They
may be purely repetitive or incremental or ironically varia-
tional *aut al.*

a. The last verse of the refrain—*Ungelic(e) is us* "it is
different with us"—does not necessarily refer back to what
has been described. It may introduce what follows. And
there is no guarantee that it has an identical function both
times; one may refer back, the other look forward.

b. The whole refrain is not necessarily a single unit. The
first two verses may refer back, the third look forward.
Moreover, if the three verses perform as a unit one time,
they do not necessarily do so again.

c. It is impossible to tell the object of the "difference."
For instance, if *Ungelic is us* (3) refers back to *willað hy*
hine aþecgan, gif he on þreat cymeð (2), the difference with
"us" may put "us" in the place of "they" or of "him"—or
the difference may be in the expected treatment suggested

[13] E.g., Kemp Malone, "Two English *Frauenlieder,*" *Studies in Old*
English Literature in Honor of Arthur G. Brodeur, ed. Stanley B. Greenfield (Eugene, Ore., 1963), p. 108: ". . . but not with Eadwacer and his
wife: 'It is otherwise with us.' "

by *apecgan* or in the possible condition suggested by *preat*. Besides, the difference suggested in l. 3 may be of an entirely different kind from that suggested in l. 8.

4. Since *apecgan* (2, 7) is subject to opposite interpretations—"receive" in the sense "take care of, assume protection of" or "take in" in the sense "devour, consume"—one's interpretation of the whole poem dictates how one thinks "they" will treat "him." But it is possible to suppose that the ambiguity was knowingly employed by a poet who might want to suggest "protect" in one case and "destroy" in another or both at once.[14]

5. As Burton Raffel's translation[15] indicates, *willað hy hine apecgan* may be a question: "Will they receive (or consume) him, if he comes . . . ?" But it could be declarative once, interrogative another time.

6. One possible (I think the probable) meaning of *preat* (2, 7) is "troop, band." The military imagery of 5, 6, and 11 supports such a reading, and a possible addition is a rendering of *lac* (1) as "battle": "it is with my people as if one gives them battle." Since the battle (or "gift," the usual rendering) is figurative, perhaps the *preat* is too.

7. Since it is not absolutely certain that *eadwacer* (16) is a proper name, all the possibilities for a compound noun (a hapax legomenon) ought to be examined for literal or figurative appropriateness: "ease-watcher," "easy-watcher," "easy-waker," "again-watcher," "again-waker," "barrenness-watcher," and so forth.

8. In the last sentence it is barely possible that the clause *þætte næfre gesomnad wæs* refers, not to *giedd*, but to *mon*. Whereas "One easily tears apart what was never joined, our song together" is neatly and suggestively paradoxical, it doesn't have the literal clarity of "One who (or "that which": the confusion of genders is not altogether unheard of) was never together (that is, one who has never known or

[14] Cf. J. Edwin Whitesell, "Intentional Ambiguities in *Beowulf*," *TSL*, XI (1966), 145–49.

[15] *Poems from the Old English* (Lincoln, Neb., 1964), p. 64.

shared our togetherness) will easily tear apart our song together."

All this is not to say that there should be no interpreting *Wulf and Eadwacer*. These suggestions are offered merely to make clear some of the obstacles to consistent and valid readings of the poem. Many are culled, but few are cogent. The text is so cryptic that pure logic can only be destructive. Thus, no valid interpretation (one that stands up under logical, objective scrutiny) can be *finally* accepted or rejected. On the other hand, continued efforts at interpretation should be encouraged, because they provide a concrete framework, however tentative, within which the emotional appeal of the poem may be seen to operate.

CHAPTER EIGHT

BATTLEFIELD TOUR: BRUNANBURH

The first nine verses of *The Battle of Brunanburh*[1] introduce the three major thematic elements of the poem. The very first line names and describes King Æthelstan, and the poem is clearly, at least on one level, a panegyric of him. Second, we are led to believe that the poem will tell about a battle, and we are not disappointed, although the battle is related in a manner rather unusual for Old English poetry. Third, a philosophical concept is introduced, the heroic idea that life-long glory (*ealdorlangne tir*) is won by victory in battle.

Moreover, and perhaps more important, the first steps are taken in establishing the structural principle of the poem. This structural principle gives controlling unity both to the various themes and to the artistic concepts which make up the complex of the poem.

The word *Her* which opens the poem appears to have at least three purposes. Customarily in the Chronicle, it appears next after the year and means "In this year." But the Chronicle is not customarily composed of heroic poetry, and *Her* seems to be used like the word summoning attention at the beginning of an oral performance; it is the poetic chronicler's equivalent of the *Beowulf*-poet's *Hwæt*. But the word does, in fact, mean "in this place" and not strictly "in this place in the annual roster," because the sense of

---

[1] The edition of Alastair Campbell (1938) is a useful supplement to Dobbie's.

place is all-important to the poem. The poet means, from the first, to focus the attention of his audience on the place where the battle was fought.[2] He is using the pointing finger of the tour-guide and begins immediately to describe what should be seen at this historic site.[3] It is here, right here on this field, that the mighty King Æthelstan won his fame. Exactly where? Why, *ymbe Brunanburh* "around Bruna's stronghold,"[4] the poetic guide says, before the first sentence has ended. But another important indication of the emphasis on place has been given even earlier. In the second line Æthelstan is called *beorna beahgifa* "ring-giver of warriors" and the ambiguity is effective. The phrase may mean that he is the one among the warriors who gives rings. But it also may mean that he is one who gives rings *to* warriors—a king. The picture of a warrior-king outstanding among warrior-kings is stressed in the description of Æthelstan as a generous king who distributes gifts to his retainers. This is a kind of double-exposure (or montage effect), with the image of a king in battle superimposed upon the image of a king distributing gifts around his board. The device is not only impressive by

[2] The actual location of Brunanburh has been the subject of extensive study and hypothesis. See the thorough discussion in Campbell's edition. The best support for a particular place is J. McN. Dodgson's for Bromborough in Wirral, "The Background of Brunanburh," *Saga-Book of the Viking Society for Northern Research,* Vol. XIV (1956–57), 303–16. Cf. A. H. Smith, "The Site of the Battle of Brunanburh," *London Mediæval Studies,* I (1937), 58. The argument for Bromborough is quite logical and, if only history and literature were governed by logic, would be completely acceptable. As it is, we must content ourselves with Dobbie's conclusion, pp. xxxixf: "The Battle of Brunanburh was fought, we may assume, somewhere along the west coast of England, roughly in the area between Chester and Dumfries, but the available evidence does not enable us to determine the exact place."

[3] Cf. Dobbie's note, pp. 146f, on the use of *Her* and its relationship to meter.

[4] This is the rendering of Francis P. Magoun, Jr.: see *Zeitschrift für deutsches Altertum,* LXXVII (1940), 65–66. But see Kemp Malone, *MLN,* XLII (1927), 238–39, for the reading "Brown's castle." This problem, too, is discussed in detail by Campbell.

itself, but has a functional purpose as well. It is used to keep the focus on the field while bringing in expositional material.

The next passage advances the action of the poem on several levels. The first descriptions of the battle itself are given. The king and his brother along with their sword-companions (*hamora lafan* "those left by hammers," that is, "products of the forge") won glory by splitting the shield-wall, hacking at the battle-shields made of linden wood. These are general and conventional descriptions of battle, to be sure, but the images are vivid because every sword and shield is individualized by the simple device of describing its origins.[5] This device also enables the poet to move back for expositional material while he retains the focus on what is going on at Brunanburh.

He does the same thing with the king and his brother, going back to their noble origins (*geæpele . . . from cneomægum*), while the philosophical element is re-introduced in the obligation of nobility to protect land, treasure, and home (*land ealgodon, / hord and hamas*). On still another level, the personification of the weapons, already suggested in the idea of their accompanying the men into battle, is re-emphasized by linking warriors and weapons with identical device, approach, and purpose.

Now, having focussed attention on the battlefield itself, at least having set it around Bruna's stronghold, the poet begins to mention items and points of interest. He strews corpses around (*Hettend crungun*) and once again moves backward to tell the enemy's origins; but there is also the suggestion of moving forward when he says that those who

[5] Some interesting remarks on a similar device are made by R. E. Kaske, "Weohstan's Sword," *MLN*, LXXV (1960), 465ff. He does not carry the argument through to the realization that the *Beowulf*-poet is both characterizing, individualizing, the sword and also making some points about a hero by comparing and contrasting a fellow warrior-creature, the sword itself. All weapons are so treated in *Beowulf*. See Neil D. Isaacs, "The Convention of Personification in *Beowulf*," in *Old English Poetry*, ed. Robert P. Creed (Providence, 1967), pp. 215–48.

fell were *fæge* "doomed to death." He pictures the ground as *dænnede / secga swate:* a possible meaning for the verb is "stained" as it seems likely that the poet-guide is here pointing out the strange discoloration of the field from the "blood of warriors."[6]

In a sequence of images describing the sun, the poet relates the fact that the battle lasted all day. First it is a glorious star (*mære tungol*) just coming up in the *morgentid,* then it is *godes condel beorht* gliding high overhead (*glad ofer grundas*), and finally it sinks *to setle* "to its seat." The last is a submerged metaphor in which the sun and God are likened to a loyal retainer and his lord: the word *setl* is regularly used in heroic poetry, even in compounds, to denote a seat in the hall of a ruler. Moreover, in most of the formulas in which it appears, it is a seat taken after the performance of a conventional or courteous service, and usually at the behest of the lord.[7] Nor is the figure gratuitous poetizing. It retains the focus on the field in physical terms, and, by using as points of comparison the proper conduct and relationship of liege and lord, it returns to the essential subject-matter of the poem.

But it is not enough for the poet that he has told about the dead warriors; he must relate the cause as well as the effect (which is another way of describing the backward and forward movement from the focal point of the field): many

---

[6] Dobbie remarks, p. 147, "The interpretation of this word has caused much controversy." A discussion follows of the various suggestions which had been offered.

[7] See *Beowulf* 2013, 1786, 1782, 1232, 2019. Cf. *Beowulf* 1289, 5, 1087, *Juliana* 687. The same metaphor appears in *Genesis* 1514, where it is a small part of a metaphor underlying the whole poem. Fuller explication of this passage in *Brunanburh* may be found in Neil D. Isaacs, "The Battle of Brunanburh 13b–17a," *N&Q,* n.s. X (1963), 247–48. The interpretation I have proposed, as Fred C. Robinson has suggested to me, is supported by the MS reading *þære sunnan þegn* in *Phoenix* 288. Usually emended, this phrase has been defended and explained by N. F. Blake, "Some Problems of Interpretation and Translation in the OE *Phoenix,*" *Anglia,* LXXX (1962), 50–62. See pp. 60f.

were shot over shields, killed by spears *(garum ageted . . .
ofer scild scoten)*. Others, fleeing, were cut down from behind by swords *(heowan herefleman hindan pearle)*. Nor is
it sufficient to call the swords sharp; a word must be used
which captures the picture of how they got that way—*mylenscearpan.* The image of the bodies on the ground is particularized
by listing some of the fallen. They include five *cyningas
giunge* "young kings" from the invading forces, seven *eorlas
Anlafes* "of Anlaf's chiefs" among a countless number
(unrim) of slain troops, the kinsmen of Constantinus, and
finally his son, young and inexperienced *(giungne æt guðe)*.
Having extolled the West Saxon nobility in terms of its
lineage, the poet delights in describing the cutting off of the
enemy lineage.

In the process of presenting these images, the backward
and forward movement from the field takes over completely,
and many scenes before and after the battle are clearly
imaged forth. The description of the arrival of the invaders
in the bosom of a ship *(on lides bosme   land gesohtun)* with
its connotations of security[8] and eagerness for fighting is
particularly effective in comparison with the description of
the departure of a much smaller band as the ship presses
out to sea *(cread cnear on flot . . . on fealene flod)* with its
suggestions of fear, darkness, and foreboding. The ships
themselves along with the vikings appear to be dreary survivors of spears: *Gewitan him þa Norþmen nægledcnear-
rum,/dreorig daraða laf.* Here *secan* is used to express their
eagerness to escape, and ironically to stress the reluctance
with which they are returning home as losers.

The most impressive aspect of this central portion of the
poem is the way the picture of the battle itself is conjured
up. It is done entirely by indirection, and yet the result is a
clear and dramatic evocation of the fighting. The poet pro-

---

[8] The use of *æra gebland* for "sea" does not appear to destroy the
suggested feeling. Cf. *Elene* 239. The mixing of waves makes the sea,
rough or not.

jects far forward to the defeated warriors' return to their
homelands, where they have neither cause to boast (*hreman
. . . þorfte*) nor grounds to laugh (*hlehhan . . . þorftun*)
about the battle they were fortunate to escape alive. From
this vantage point the poet can look back to the battlefield
where doomed men were put to sleep by swords (*sweordum
aswefede*); where the son of Constantinus was ground to
pieces in wounds (*wundun forgrunden*); where there was
hand-to-hand fighting (*hondplegan*) and joining of swords
(*mæca gemanan*) and clashing of swords (*bilgeslehtes*) and
conflict of banners (*cumbolgehnastes*) and meeting of spears
(*garmittinge*) and meeting of warriors (*gumena gemotes*)
and conflict of weapons (*wæpengewrixles*).

Now, having firmly projected the image of the defeated
men, the old one, the gray warrior (*har hilderinc*), and the
other dreary, ashamed survivors (*dreorig daraða . . . æwisc-
mode*), the poet goes back to the field again to point out the
contrast of the victorious leaders. Æthelstan and his brother
Edmund return home exultant and happy to boast of their
victory (*wiges hremige*). Again the verb *sohton* connotes
eagerness, and again the importance of family and homeland is stressed.

But the attention of poet and reader remains focussed on
the field where the traditional beasts of battle[9] appear in
order to complete what warriors and weapons had begun.
The verse *Letan him behindan,* which serves as a transition
from the victors to the spoils which remain, is very important in the context of the structural principle. They,
that is, the brothers, *left behind them* the scavengers to
divide the corpses. Primarily, they were leaving the corpses
behind, knowing the scavengers would be there, and perhaps exulting in this aspect of the victory as well. But
artistically, the poet (along with the brothers) is leaving
both corpses and scavengers behind on the field for the
audience. After all, that is where the reader is, and the poet

[9] See Magoun, "The Theme of the Beasts of Battle," *NM,* LVI (1955),
81–90.

stands there with him, pointing out the sights and relating
causes and effects, historical background and significances.
And how clearly we see these beasts, the dark raven with
his dusky coat and horny beak (*saluwigpadan* . . . *hyrned-
nebban*), the eagle with his gray coat and white tail-feathers
(*hasewanpadan*, / *earn æftan hwit*), the greedy war-hawk
(*grædigne guðhafoc*), and the other gray beast, the wolf of
the forests (*græge deor*, / *wulf on wealde*). They are all conventional accouterments of the Anglo-Saxon battlefield scene,
but this traditional quality does not reduce the sharpness or
effectiveness of the imagery. Rather, it has the opposite result. For in poetry from an oral tradition, formulas and
themes impart a denotative meaning elicited by a particular
context; but beyond that they supply a host of connotative
meanings evoked from the common store of suggestions, emotional and intellectual, which the particular formulas and
themes hold in the hearts and minds of audience and poet.
This theme of the beasts of battle should suggest other uses
of the same theme and thereby render the sense of the particular context at once more universal and more concrete.

The poem closes with what at first seems to be an eight-
and-a-half-line digression, telling of the greater battle of
another invasion, the successful one of the Angles and
Saxons, and including the incidental image in which books
are personified as *ealde uðwitan* "old scholars."[10] This final
section should be seen, however, as rounding out the whole,
tying up the loose ends, leaving only the now complete
image of the battlefield around Bruna's stronghold.

Primarily, in this passage the poet is pointing up the
size of the slaughter by referring directly to the greatest
slaughter his audience would ever have heard of. This is
precisely the way an oral-formulaic poet operates. He must
fill his tales with allusions and suggestions, but must not do
so in an abstruse, tangential, diffusive, or digressive way.

---

[10] The possible ambiguity of *uðwitan* as meaning books as well as
men may be present in *Menologium* 166 and especially in *Elene* 473.

When he wishes to illuminate the battle between the West
Saxons and the invading Scottish-Norwegian forces by
referring to that between the Welsh and the invading
Angles and Saxons, he does not speak of the former in
terms alluding to the latter. Rather he speaks directly of
the latter, building up the image of the former all the while.
This technique also holds for the conventional allusiveness
of words. For example, speaking of a weapon as a warrior,
or the sun as first a candle and then a loyal retainer, is a
direct accretion of detail for the visual image of the weapon
or the sun. Simply, the more we are told about how something
looks or acts, the more clearly we visualize and recognize it.
And if we have something we know well to compare it to,
so much the better for our visualization and recognition.

In the final passage, the poet as panegyrist also is praising
Æthelstan for being in the tradition of his great Germanic
ancestors. Incidentally, he is tying up the smithy-war motif
in *wigsmiþas* "battle-smiths." It had appeared in *hamora
lafan* (6b), *mylenscearpan* (24a), and *forgrunden* (43b).

Moreover, he is effectively summing up the philosophical
concept he began with—that the West Saxons and their
rulers have won life-long glory by defending their homeland. There is, first, the reminder that their ancestors came
not only seeking a homeland, but also eager for glory. They
acquired both homeland and glory by victory in battle over
the Welsh. But there is the obiter dictum that what is first
won by the invading triumph must be retained or re-
affirmed or re-won by successful and continued defense of
that homeland and that glory.[11]

Finally, as artist, the poet is applying the last brushstrokes
to his canvas. Casually, almost by-the-bye, a unifying symbolism has been introduced. The word *eard* "homeland"
in the last half-line of the poem gives added meaning to the

---

[11] Is it also a slap at the Welsh, some of whom took part in this in-
vasion-uprising against the West Saxon leadership?

word *Her* "here" with which the poem begins.[12] What has
happened "here," in the field around Bruna's stronghold,
which has been described so vividly, is meaningful for the
entire "homeland," Britain, which can see its own glory
in this picture.

It is just possible that this symbolic quality dictated the
use of the particular structural principle used to unify the
many diverse elements in the poem. In any case, the depiction of the battlefield occupies the central portion of the
canvas of the poem. The poet works both backward and
forward from it, producing images which tell the causes and
antecedents and including images which tell the effects.
Thus, the many conventional or traditional elements, the
thematic concepts, and the artistic devices are tightly organized into a richly meaningful but singleminded poem.[13]

[12] The last word of the poem, *begeatan,* is used curiously in Old
English poetry. It may mean merely "happened" or "befell," referring
to something bad which came to someone (*Beowulf* 1146, 2130, *Seafarer* 6). But where a person is its subject, it suggests a hard-won attainment (*Beowulf* 2249, *Andreas* 378, 480, *Christ* 1689, *Elene* 1152).

[13] This is substantially the paper read for English 1 at the 1960 MLA
meeting. I am grateful to Robert P. Creed of SUNY at Stony Brook,
Marvin Spevack of the University of Muenster, and Malvin Zirker of
the University of Indiana, all of whom read it at various stages and
made valuable suggestions.

CHAPTER NINE

THE ONE-MAN BAND
OF *CHRIST AND SATAN*

It is harder to discern structural principles in a long narrative poem than in a short lyric poem: the lyric may be seen whole, may be held before the eye of the critic for his steady observation and analytical scrutiny. An analytical microscope holds the poem on a single slide for the objective, formalist approach. A long narrative poem (or epic or novel or motion picture), on the other hand, presents obvious difficulties for the structural analyst. Some aspects of structure will be immediately apparent, such as a formal division into books, chapters, cantos, fits, episodes and the like; but in most cases these divisions are artificial, are necessarily present for the very reason that essential elements of the structure of the whole cannot easily be observed. Only the shorter units may be seen whole, and both the relationships among the units and the structural principles that support the whole without regard for artificial divisions must be discerned without benefit of laboratory procedures of isolation and magnification. The critic must turn the wrong end of the telescope upon the work; but if his eye is keen, he may still be able to distinguish the details of structure. The problems involved should act as a challenge rather than a deterrent for the critic. Yet some, failing to discern unifying elements in a long Anglo-Saxon poem, proceed to divide it up into shorter poems.[1]

In the 729-line *Christ and Satan*, the central organizing

---

[1] Or into three disunified divisions, as Wülker (1894) arranged *Christ and Satan*.

structural principle is not to be found in the arrangement
of episodes in the narrative, nor in the formal system of
contrasts between the title figures, nor in the dramatic progression of thematic material. It is not even to be found in
the artifices employed for purposes of transition between
the episodic, characterizational, thematic, and dramatic
motifs (though in fact all of these elements are involved in
the overall structural design). The structural principle of
Christ and Satan may be found in the pattern of the speeches
by the seven separate voices, distinct from his own, which
the narrator uses.

The climax of the poem is the confrontation of the title
characters in the temptation scene, a climax not only of the
dramatic (and extra-chronological) arrangement of the material, but also of the poet's principal technique—the quoting of speeches. Here within fifty lines there are at least
four speeches, two each by Christ and Satan, in an exchange
of dialogue quite unusual for Old English poetry.[2] Moreover, it is likely that at least one full speech, perhaps two,
and portions of one or two more are missing.

This climactic scene is introduced so abruptly that it has
led commentators to suppose the beginning of a separate
poem at this point. But the abruptness is illusory. The
transition, though compact, is nonetheless effective when
the audience has recognized the structural devices that lead
up to it. The shift to the temptation scene occurs in three
lines, 663–665:

> Þæt is se drihten,   seðe deað for us
> geþrowode,   þeoden engla.
> Swylce he fæste   feowertig daga

> *That is the Lord, prince of angels, who*
> *suffered death for us. Likewise he fasted*
> *forty days. . . .*

[2] *Advent Lyric VII* is an exceptional case, so exceptional indeed that
Pope says, ". . . I do not myself believe in the rapid interchange of
speeches ascribed to Joseph and Mary in our editions," in "Dramatic
Voices in *The Wanderer* and *The Seafarer*," *Franciplegius*, ed. Jess B.
Bessinger, Jr., and Robert P. Creed (New York, 1965), p. 187.

The word *swylce* "likewise" is the key to the double-locked transition here: (1) He suffered death for us (a reference back to Christ's passion and crucifixion, which though they chronologically should *follow* the temptation are treated here earlier as part of the dramatic progression *toward* the temptation) and He likewise endured the fast and the temptation for us; (2) He inspired the apostles in a glorious forty days on earth (which, though it chronologically occurs *after* the crucifixion, harrowing, and resurrection, forms part of the thematic progression *toward* the temptation climax), and He likewise spent forty days in the desert, fasting and ultimately enduring Satan's temptation.

Satan comes to Him and tempts Him. The poet calls the tempter the one "who had been thrown out of heaven so that he plunged into hell" (667b–668). Then the narrator *describes* the placing of stones in Christ's lap and says that Satan *bæd him for hungre hlafas wyrcan,* but the only direct quotation is *"gif þu swa micle mihte hæbbe"* (672). Christ's reply is quoted directly but is broken off at 675, before the familiar "not by bread alone" is heard. Then, in 676–678, there is a confusing passage which may be part of a different speech by Christ, or, more likely, part of the poet's reaction to Christ's answer to Satan's *second* temptation. I think that there is here, as Krapp says,[3] a considerable gap, which probably included the rest of Christ's first reply, Satan's second temptation of leaping from the Temple (with appropriate speech), and Christ's second reply (the poet following the order of Matthew 4:3-10 rather than Luke 4:2-13).

At any rate the poem proceeds with Satan's offer of power over all the world, though, except for the suggestion in *Foh hider to me* (685b), he misses the opportunity to develop metaphorically the parallel of a formal oath of duguth fealty. Perhaps this is a deliberate omission since the theme of power (earthly, political power) is what is being stressed, a theme which has been developing throughout the poem.

[3] *ASPR*, I, 246.

And Christ's answer, in the poet's design, includes powerful ironic reference to that theme. Christ refers to Satan's political power as being—not the kingdom of God (692b), but— the den of torment, and after saying that Satan can offer no hope to his people and uttering the familiar "Get thee behind me!" (*Cer ðe on bæcling!* 697b), He orders Satan to measure the extent of his political dominion with his hands.

The short conclusion of the poem (710-729) follows Satan back to hell where the enormity of his punishment is impressed upon him. The description includes the elements of darkness, fire, prison, and noise which have become so familiar throughout the poem; and now he must measure it all with his hands. He has been ordered to measure it within two hours (708), but it seems to him now so vast—a hundred thousand miles (720)—that of course there will never be any two hours in which he can fulfill his sentence. As he gazes around him, the *egsan gryre / deofla mænego* (725b-726a) rises up, and the final line is lamented by the chorus of the damned—*La, þus beo nu on yfele! Noldæs ær teala!*—a fitting conclusion for Satan to hear, and, by the double focus which I shall suggest is a principal device of the poet, a fitting lesson for the audience to hear.

Gollancz objects to the abruptness of the conclusion and finds a one-line curtain speech to be untenable, positing therefore an uncompleted manuscript.[4] The whole passage seems to me just right as a conclusion, with the line (717) just before the lacuna suggesting the (dramatic) finality of this particular confrontation. And I especially like the last choric utterance: the poet cannot resist having that distinct voice heard again, and he fittingly closes with a parting shot of his favorite (and trademark?) technique. Incidentally the lacuna between 717 and 718 is probably no more than a two-line break, and probably involves no separate sentence.

What has been described as the dramatic and thematic

---

[4] Sir Israel Gollancz, *The Cædmon Manuscript* (Oxford, 1927), pp. xcix n2, xcix f.

confrontation of Christ and Satan, though for a chronological narrative[5] it would have to come early in the poem, is actually the fourth confrontation of the title characters in the poem. The first is the expulsion from heaven, the second is the harrowing of hell, and the third is judgment day (though Satan's part in this future action is only implicit). In a sense, the temptation of Adam as described by Eve is another anticipatory confrontation.

The poem opens with a treatment of various aspects of the first confrontation, the war in heaven and its effects;[6] and the opening passage introduces most of the devices, thematic and technical, which serve to unify the structure of the poem. The poet's initial statement concerns the power of God, which became clear to men through the wonders of creation (as if, anachronistically, men were able to see the creation). But he shifts almost immediately from the Lord (*meotod* 2a) as creator to Christ (*godes agen bearn* 10b) as creator.

At the end of the recital of God's omnipotent and omniscient performances, one's attention is drawn to Adam and Satan:

Adam ærest, and þæt æðele cyn,
engla ordfruman, þæt þe eft forwarð.

First Adam and that noble race, the angel chief,
who afterward fell. (20–21)

This is the first example in the poem of what I call double focus. Surely an essential technique of poets working in an oral tradition is the use of allusions and apparent digressions in which the image of the specific subject is developed and sharpened by references to other well-known figures

[5] I have been using the noun *narrative*, but the genre of *Christ and Satan* is not so easily labeled—qualifying adjectives like *dramatic, episodic*, and *homiletic* would have to be incorporated for any precise ascription of genre.

[6] The interesting possibility that Milton was familiar with the Junius MS has aroused much conjecture. See, especially, Stephanie von Gajšek, *Milton und Cædmon* (Vienna, 1911).

and situations from the tradition's common stock. In this
case, the double focus is more complex: the angel chief who
fell is Satan, but Adam too subsequently fell. This scene, as
described by Eve later in the poem, anticipates ironically
the climactic confrontation of Christ and Satan. The phrase
þæt æðele cyn is somewhat confusing, since with similar
ambiguity it may refer to mankind as the noble descendants
of Adam or to the angels as a noble race whose chief led
them, or a part of them, to their fall. The confusion is com-
pounded at lines 365–367:

> Wæs þæt encgelcyn   ær genemned,
> Lucifer haten,   leohtberende,
> on geardagum   in godes rice.

Of the commentators on this passage, only Krapp[7] refers
back to ll. 20–21, but he concludes that the awkwardness of
syntax favors the view of Gollancz and Thorpe that there
is a gap in the manuscript.[8] Clubb's suggestion of synecdoche[9] might well be applied to both passages, but there
are two other possibilities which ought to be considered.
One is that cyn be translated "progeny," a rendering that
retains an ambiguity as to number which may be the point
of the original. The other is that the poet in these two
places is deliberately setting up or playing on the interchange of multiple voices and soloist which he uses in his
dramatic structure: Satan's speeches often use first-person
plural pronouns and the chorus of the damned sometimes
uses first-person singular, at least once actually shifting to
Satan and back without any announced transition. There is
no close resemblance here to the first-person singular employed by a Greek chorus, but the device does suggest the
cinematographic technique of closing in and panning out—
isolating individual units while keeping crowd effects.

[7] P. 239.
[8] Gollancz, p. civ; Benjamin Thorpe, Cædmon's Metrical Paraphrase
of Parts of the Holy Scriptures, in Anglo-Saxon (London, 1832), p. 287n.
[9] Merrel D. Clubb, Christ and Satan, an Old English Poem (New Haven,
1925), pp. 96f.

By line 22 we are focussed singly on the damned in hell with prominence given to the theme of pride, the dominant deadly sin which caused the fall. But even with the focus on hell we remember heaven because the surging flame is contrasted with the lost light in heaven. (The polar contrasts in the imagery are dominated by light/dark, though hot/cold, noise/song, and others may be found fairly frequently.) Moreover, the assertion that the fallen angels *in helle ham staðeledon* "established a home in hell" is an oblique or ironic reference to the traditional motif in which heaven is called the proper home for all.

Before the first voice, that of the old one himself, is heard at 36b, the poet says *God ana wat / hu he þæt scyldige werud forscrifen hefde* "God alone knew how He had condemned that guilty host" (32b–33). This combination of omnipotence and omniscience is what dominates the opening passage with its associations of God and Christ, of Adam and the angels, and of the angels and Satan.

Satan's first speech, introduced by the narrator in five verses, includes in its twenty-nine verses (36b–50) a description of the conditions in hell and a lament for the contrasting elements in heaven irrevocably lost to the damned. The *ðeostræ ham* is an ironic reminder of the *hehseld* of heaven,[10] the *bættran ham;* and the wretched sounds of the devil's voice as described (and then perhaps imitated) by the poet ironically evoke a reminiscence of heavenly song. Sound imagery forms an integral part not only of the heaven/hell contrast but also of the dramatic episodes in the poem. Moreover, the poet frequently calls attention to the sound of the speakers' voices (which may be an indication of his preoccupation with the sounds of his own voice).

[10] It is surprising, not to say disappointing, that the poet makes no use of the similarity of *hel* and *heal* for slant suggestions or additional connotations. But he is scrupulous, in talking about "hell," to use only *seld* (nine times), *sel(e)* (six times), *bold* (twice), and *hof* (once) for "hall." Similarly he avoids the potential effects of formula-systems (used with success in *The Dream of the Rood;* cf. Chapter 1 above) for "stained with . . ." and "wounded with . . ." in 127a, 155b, 156a, 179b, 185b.

Suggestions of imprisonment vis-a-vis freedom (lying in chains vs. standing about the Lord) and of the importance of obedience in what amounts to a submerged duguth-metaphor (cf. *heleð ymb hehseld* 47a) are also in evidence here; but perhaps more significant are the shift from *we* (37, 41, 44) to *ic* (48) and *me* (49) without apparent shift in point of view and Satan's acknowledgment that he is suffering *for oferhygdum* "because of [his] pride" (50a). The first speech of the chorus of *begnornende* fiends follows a simple two-line introduction. Its twelve lines are full of recriminations addressed directly to Satan's loathsome face (*Atol . . . onseon* 61a). They blame him, especially his pride, concluding with the interesting accusation that Satan told them that *his* son was the lord of mankind. This arrant and arrogant presumption may be the clearest conceivable cameo of Satan's pride.

The following passage (65–80) of recapitulation is framed by comments on the sound of the chorus's voice which has just been heard and a description of the sound of Satan's voice which is to follow. Where sorrow marks the former, the latter is more vividly and vigorously described in terms of sparks, fire, and poison followed by the litotes *ne bið swelc fæger dream* "it is not such a pleasant joy" (19b). This verse employs both the standard kind of general irony by understatement and also a more specific irony by evoking the sounds of a (heavenly) feast as contrast for the lament of the devil. Between these framing and transitional passages, the poet recapitulates the motifs of Christ's power and original triumph over Satan, the sin of pride, and the light/dark contrast of heaven and hell. In addition he introduces a new element of contrast, the wandering of the damned (*hworfon* 71, *hwearfedon* 72) as opposed to the abiding of the blessed (e.g., standing about the hall 47). This element of wandering, brought in so unobtrusively here, begins to become significant in Satan's next speech as it is associated first with exile and then expanded to involve the journeys of demons to human lands.

This is Satan's longest single speech in the poem (81–124), and it develops rather fully his motivations for rebellion. As he sees it, what he wanted was *agan me burga gewald* "to have for myself power over cities" (86b: the fortified places of heaven? or earth? or both?) and *eall to æhte* "[to have] everything as possessions" (87a). He confesses to lust for power and greed for universal possessions (both of which are sins of *superbia* rather than *luxuria* or *avaritia;* that is, what Satan desires is the power and possessions that belong properly to Christ[11]). References to the theme of power and possession are also found in this speech at lines 100, 106, and 116.

Besides additional acknowledgments of pride and a number of allusions (97–104) to the dragons and serpents familiarly associated with the fiends of hell, the speech contains several references to homes—no home, dark home, wretched home, home in captivity vs. home in glory, and so forth. Satan's preoccupation with homes is probably related to the concept of wandering and exile, expressly noted here for the first time in *wadan wræclæstas* (120a). Particularly significant in the development of the homeland theme is Satan's announcement, toward the climax in the temptation scene (111–112), that he and his host (*and eower ma*) will visit other (human) lands. The announcement, although apparently innocent (it seems to say merely that Satan and company are not bound by hell's territory, but from time to time will wander in flight elsewhere), ominously adumbrates the loss of Eden, the tempting of Christ, and even the passion and resurrection.

The four-line bridge to Satan's next speech, with its images of fire, cave, and venom, makes hell sound like Grendel's lair: *fyrleoma stod / geond þæt atole scræf attre geblonden* (127b–128); and Satan's new plaint refers to the elastic nature of his *sele* "hall." Though later in the poem

---

[11] An interesting treatment of another dramatic figuration of pride may be found in Eric W. Stockton, "The Deadliest Sin in *The Pardoner's Tale,*" *TSL*, VI (1961), 47–59.

he laments that it is a hundred thousand miles to the gate, he now moans that he is too big to hide in it. He complains of the geographical, topographical, and especially meteorological conditions: it is hot, cold, windy. The hall and home motifs are repeated along with the contrasts of light and sound and there is the Arnoldian (or Laocoönian) image of naked men contending with serpents (134b–135a). Satan laments that he ever knew glory (hell is so much the worse by contrast: Satan's reasoning thus follows the psychology of one technique of the poet). He also laments that although there are souls which he may lead home to hell (an ironic anticipation of Christ's harrowing of hell and subsequent leading of souls home to heaven), they are only those whom God will not have. And he must listen to the constant moaning of his *hellescealcas*[12] while the blessed sing psalms of praise, the sound of glory, for the Lord.

The following bridge, another four-liner (159-162), has two figures worth noticing. The first calls Satan *firna herde* "shepherd of sins," evoking a secondary focus on Christ for the ironic contrast with Satan. The second works a variation on the sparks, fire, and poison of Satan's earlier speech (78–79a). The three separate elements of the earlier description are now combined in a double-metaphor: *Word spearcum fleah / attre gelicost* (161b–162a). The speech thus introduced may be called the climax of the sequence of Satan's "lyrics." It is an elegiac passage (163–188) opening with nine consecutive *Eala – – –* verses. The burden is *ubi sunt*, but it is ironic *ubi sunt*: the theoretical answer to the rhetorical question "where are . . ." is not "gone forever with the passage of time" but "just where everything always has been and always will be." The themes of power/possession and obedience/loyalty (as in corrupt vs. proper duguth-society) and of exile (176, 180, 187) appear in this lament, but perhaps its most moving passage is the one

[12] Perhaps there is an ironic slant suggestion of "hall-servants" here. Cf. similar suggestions in J. Edwin Whitesell, "Intentional Ambiguities in *Beowulf*," *TSL*, XI (1966), 145–49.

where Satan says that he cannot reach toward heaven with his hand, look toward heaven with his eyes, or ever hear the sounds of heaven with his ears. The narrator's next section (189–227) is no mere bridge between speeches. It is explicit preachment based on the dramatic material so far presented: do not provoke Christ, since He will punish men with hell for pride; choose God—Christ—who revealed His power by driving the multitude to hell; remember truth and law and the rewards of heaven. Though there can be little doubt that such passages weaken the poem, the poet has undertaken to integrate his preachment with the artistic dramatic material of his poem. Thus he repeats thematic elements, such as the two references to pride (*for oferhygdum* 196a, 226a); he echoes images, such as the shining countenance of the angels (222b, cf. the horrible face of Satan 61a); and he abandons his distant-narrator position for a first-person reference, in which he seems to be saying that he himself heard further lamentation from hell: *Ða get ic furðor gefregen feond ondetan* (224).

The next fifty-one lines are complicated by an apparent, but unannounced, alternation of speeches between Satan and the chorus of the damned. The shifts are suggested by the changes in pronoun number and by the appropriateness of the statements, but of course in oral delivery the scop has other ways of indicating change of speaker (ways sure to be employed by a performer who puts such great store in his ventriloquism as the *Christ and Satan*-poet does). The assignment of all these speeches can be only tentative (especially where the poet may be employing subtle devices similar to the cinematographer's cutting and fading in and out, close-up and pan, montage, and super-imposition), but I think it should be as follows.

1. The chorus (we) regrets the lost joys of heaven, especially the songs and sounds of glory (including the trumpet, *beman stefne*—an anticipation of judgment day?), and describes the nobility of Christ (228–244).
2. Satan picks up the cue by discussing his envy of Christ,

and then he rehearses the speech in which he incited the
angels to rebellion (245–252a; the quote-within-the-quote runs
248–252a).

   3. The chorus recognizes the speech, calling it the *idel
gylp* "useless boast" which persuaded them to reject
Christ for Satan and led them into exile. Having felt His
anger, they acknowledge the power of Christ and describe
their punishment, which includes being surrounded by fire:
even those who journey to the land of men take their
hell-torment with them (252b–264). The last sentence
(261b–264) is the most nearly ambivalent in the whole
passage. Its pronoun reference is neutral, its statement is
equally appropriate to chorus and Satan, and it might even
be assigned to the narrator himself; but I have given it to
the chorus because it provides a good cue for Satan's
succeeding speech.

   4. Satan says that they may journey to middle-earth, but
they will never reach *eadige of eorþan* "the blessed of earth"
(ambiguity: they'll never get back to heaven and they
can't touch good men). Still, with his hands (cf. 168a—a
B-type formula-system) he may lead the heathens to hell
(repeating the motif of his leading the rebellious angels and
again ironically anticipating the harrowing). He ends
by describing his grief, but the most significant part of the
speech is the repeated threat that some of the adversaries of
God will wander through the world of men stirring
up strife (265–278).

There follows an extended passage in the poet's own
voice (279–384), broken only by a five-verse quotation from
Christ (306–308a). The concern with voices is emphasized
when the poet attributes God's anger to their evil speeches
(*womcwidum* 281b). For the most part, the narrator has
turned preacher here, urging his audience to purge evil
thoughts, to remember God's strength, and to prepare a
grene stræte (286b) up among the angels. The focus shifts
from heaven abruptly to hell and back to heaven again,
with the descriptions recapitulating the familiar motifs
and contrasts. Of interest are the poet's confession of his
inability to describe the light of heaven (348–352), his shift-

ing (or mixing) of metaphors when he explains that the fragrant blossoms of heaven are the words of God (356b–357), and the addition of the gnashing of teeth to the sound-contrasts (*gristbitungc* 333a, *toða geheaw* 338b). Double focus is provided in several places, such as the application of duguth-metaphor to Satan and his band (324ff; the usual application to Christ, as echoed frequently throughout the Anglo-Saxon poetic corpus, could not escape the audience's attention even if there were no such reference in the immediate poem or passage). The citation from Christ

> soðfæste men,   sunnan gelice,
> fægre gefrætwod   in heora fæder rice
> scinað in sceldbyrig
>
> *Truth-firm men, like suns, fairly adorned,*
> *shine in the shield-town of their father's kingdom*

is an example of another kind of double focus, where the figure describing heaven in terms of threefold protections of earth (fort, shield, father) includes a figure describing earthly men in terms of heavenly bodies.

When the focus returns to heaven (at 344), the action shifts back to the rebellion. An element of the description of hell—darkness—is incorporated with the theme of pride as Satan thinks to establish a *hehseld* co-equal with God's: *swearte geþohte* (371b). The image is all the more striking, coming as it does in the midst of a passage filled with the light of heaven (including the etymologically interesting reference to Lucifer). Once again the expulsion, accomplished through *nergendes nið* "the wrath of the Saviour" (376a), is told; and there is an addition to the image-pattern of 61 and 222, contrasting the faces of the divine and damned, in 376b–378a:

> and no seoððan
> þæt hi mosten in þone ecan   andwlitan seon
> buton ende
>
> *and never thereafter might they look upon*
> *the eternal face . . .*

I have not translated *buton ende* above because I want to note the ambiguity: it may mean both "without end," i.e., "forever," and "except at the end," i.e., "until judgment day."[13]

Almost at the end (378b) of this long passage between speeches, the poet becomes truly a narrator again, taking the audience quickly along into a new episode, the harrowing of hell. The Lord's wrath accomplishing the expulsion gives way naturally to His battering down the gates of hell. At the same time, the bliss of those who are saved, the terror of those who are damned, and the reference to Christ as *deman* "judge" all make the harrowing episode a prefiguration of judgment. The episode is fully developed, of course, by means of a speech. This one (385–397) is spoken by the chorus of the damned, who describe the harrowing in terms of great light and noise, of terror and unpreparedness, and finally of the separation of the redeemed souls and the damned.

The military overtones of *storm* (385b), strengthened by the image of Christ as a feudal general—*þegen mid þreate* "the thane with the troop" (386a)—are recapitulated in the poet's next passage (398–407) in which the harrowing is portrayed as a battle between Christ and Satan. The verses *hæfde drihten seolf / feond oferfohten* "the Lord Himself had overcome the fiend in fighting" (402b–403a) anticipate the temptation, of course, but the focus is kept on the battlefield (as in *Brunanburh*), where at dawn *seo fæhðe* is still apparent. One almost expects the carrion creatures to appear, but instead there is a different kind of division of bodies, or rather souls. Christ leads the blessed ones, the race of Adam, to heaven; but Eve cannot look into glory yet until she speaks (or, to put it another way, the poet cannot let pass a reference to Adam without assigning a speech to a new voice).

---

[13] It has been suggested to me that there is a possible third meaning, a scatological reference to what they *can* look upon; but I reject this notion.

In Eve's description of the temptation and fall, she and Adam parallel the fallen angels: promised by Satan the rule of heaven (413), they disobeyed God and were sent to hell. In describing the harrowing, she suggests that amid the horror and awesomeness there was great joy that Christ would invade hell on behalf of those lost souls, and she also relates that a thane of the Saviour came home to hell around three nights ago. Gollancz[14] is sure that this refers to Judas, therefore dating the harrowing on Easter Sunday morning. But the poet relies too heavily on orderings other than chronological for one to put much faith in this reasoning. While the suggestion of Judas is undeniably present, it seems to me more important to recognize in

swylce him wuldorcyning
for onmædlan   eorre geworden

likewise the King of glory became angry
with him for his pride (426b–427)

a reference to Satan's fall and in Eve's account a further acknowledgment of her guilt. She has pleaded to be saved with *minre mægðe* (her and Adam's children? all the human souls saved?), but it is not until she identifies another familial relationship that she is released. The poet describes her (435–436) reaching out to Christ and praying *þurh Marian had,* and her final speech (437–440) reminds Him that He was born on earth of her daughter.

With that reminder Eve is freed to go up, but the damned are thrust farther down with Satan. The poet rehearses the torments of hell, to which is added a new dimension, death —*deaðes scuwan* 453b, *hinsiðgryre* 454b—a dimension which seems to bring hell into the perspective of a damned human condition on earth; then he shifts abruptly (455) to the triumphal entry into heaven of Christ leading *Abrahames cynn.* The thematic association which accounts for the transition occurs in 460: *Hæfde þa drihten seolf deað ofer-*

[14] P. ci n.

wunnen "the Lord Himself had overcome death" (cf. 402b–
403a). The heavenly welcome is very like the celebration
of a military victory, which the brief recapitulation of the
harrowing reminds that it is. And in introducing the speech
of Christ to the company of souls, the poet calls them His
fyrde "army" (468a). With Christ's speech (469b–511) the pace begins to mount
approaching the climax. Images, themes, motifs, episodes,
and allusions are paraded through in double time. The
shifts come faster than before and the rationale of transitions is not always so easy to fathom; from the long view
the poet seems to have only the singleminded purpose of
building toward the temptation scene. (The following account tries to keep pace with the movement by hurrying
along touching only the high spots.) Christ addresses Adam
and Eve and all their children. He talks of their fall
through the devil's agency, of their punishment, and of
His unique power to redeem them. This leads Him naturally to talk about His birth on earth and His passion,
crucifixion, and resurrection; that is, he rehearses his first
redemption of them—which chronologically prefigures this
one. (Perhaps the intimate association of the harrowing
with crucifixion and resurrection is symbolic: the harrowing is a concretized dramatic symbol of the meaning of
crucifixion and resurrection.)

Harrowing and resurrection are fused ambiguously in
the narrator's next segment (512–534), where he gives
Christ's speech when He *of deaðe aras* (514b). Even when
he goes on to say that no iron-bound stone could stay Him,
the double focus continues: *on þæm fæstenne* (519a) refers
both to the "sepulcher" from which He rose and the
"prison" which hell has been compared to; the old familiar images of the resurrection are blended with the newly
familiar images of the harrowing. The blurred secondary
image of the saved souls being summoned to heaven fades
now beneath the sharp picture of Peter and the other dis-
ciples being summoned to Galilee, though the contiguous

fact of summoning, the thanks paid the Lord by those summoned, and Peter's reference to *laðne bend* (537b) sustain
the hell-motifs in the background.

The heathens, says Peter, will pay for laying on bonds
(echo of hell, anticipation of judgment day). The heathen
hands (538a) give way to the hands of Didimus (doubting
Thomas, 542a), and the proof of Lordship in the bleeding
of Christ's wounds leads the poet back to the passion and
its beauty, from which he preaches eternal thanks to Christ
for leading all men home to heaven from bonds (resurrection, harrowing, judgment day). In quick succession now
come the forty days before the ascension; the ascension
(with appropriate music); the promise of the descent of
the Holy Spirit (Pentecost); Pentecost fading into a glimpse
of the Last Supper;[15] a brief take of Judas in hell with
Satan, fading into the scene in heaven of Christ sitting at
God's right hand and distributing help and salvation (like
rings to loyal retainers).

An exhortation to obey Christ leads into a description
of the *third time* when Christ will have interceded for men,
that is, on judgment day, projected by the poet in terms of
sounds: the voice of Christ, the trumpets of the archangels,
and the cries of the living and the dead. It will be not only
the longest day (Darryl Zanuck's film presented a visual
analogy) but also the greatest din: *þæt bið daga lengust,
and dinna mæst* (605). The final division into good and evil
will take place then, the righteous will go to heaven (God's
welcome is quoted 616–618), and the accursed, judged by
Christ through His strength, will be sent straight to hell
(God's decree is quoted 626–627). There they must forever
endure torment, bondage, cold, and—perhaps worst of all—
deofles spellunge (636b). The poet offers yet another recom-
mendation for obedience, suggesting that the rewards of
heaven be kept in mind—the *geat gylden* (647) and the
eternal *leoht* (648) and *swegle* (646). A brief quotation
from the chorus of the blessed (656–658)—who praise God,

[15] Gollancz, p. c, calls this "a somewhat strange sequence of thought."

the Protector, the Judge, and the Creator, for leading His
children to this blessed home—is followed by a report of
þegnas around the Prince, praising Him with much song.
This leads to identification of the Prince as Christ and a
quick shift into the temptation scene (with which this discussion began).

Thus, by a somewhat tortuous route, the poem leads to
the central and climactic action of the temptation scene, a
scene which brings the major motifs, the dramatic and
thematic material, together in a meaningful way. Most
important for this study, the scene serves as a climax for
the structural principle of using as many distinct voices as
possible. I have called this the "one-man band" technique
because the effect, it seems to me, is admiration for the
many different sounds the poet can make rather than appreciation of the orchestrated unity of the whole. Whereas
the *Beowulf*-poet uses a dozen-odd voices in sustaining and
organizing the narrative, building the drama, developing
the thematic statements, and enriching his poem with variations of pace and tone and with depths of subtlety and
nuance (which our sensibilities are still groping to grasp),
he does not call attention to the device. The *Christ and
Satan*-poet, on the other hand, using eight voices to organ-
ize his material, emphasizes his ventriloquism in such a
way as to suggest that he is using his material to sustain
his act. This is why his poem, which upon analysis reveals
fairly substantial artistic endeavor, has seemed to be a
loose collection of biblical episode and moral application.
The one-man band is remembered for the novelty of the
performance, never for the artistry with which his medley
of tunes was integrated.

CHAPTER TEN

OTHER VOICES, OTHER DOOMS

DANIEL AND THE CHANGE OF PACE

The *Daniel*-poet almost always seems to be in a great hurry. The few exceptions are all set-pieces: the hymn of Azarias, the hymn of the trio in the fiery furnace, and Daniel's dream- and handwriting-analyses. Unlike the poet of *Christ and Satan,* he does not seem to take every advantage to show off his versatile ventriloquism. Rather, he avoids a multiplicity of voices even when his material offers ample opportunities. Except for some brief, perfunctory snatches of conversation *(deofolwitgan* "magicians" and Nebuchadnezzar, 130–133, 136–144; Nebuchadnezzar and a *ræswa* "counselor," 411b–415, 416b–429; Nebuchadnezzar, 472–485; and Nebuchadnezzar again, 608–611), only the set-pieces are direct quotations. But the *Daniel*-poet is apparently not at all concerned with demonstrating his technical virtuosity. Though the critic may point to the use of several techniques, none can be seen as structuring the whole poem. Every device the poet employs and every element of the traditional material he chooses is rendered insignificant in its own right as the poet turns everything to his singleminded purpose of stating, restating, and exemplifying his theme.

Identifying the theme of *Daniel* is no difficult matter, and identifying its genre, although a somewhat more complicated problem, may be accomplished without difficulty at the same time. *Daniel* is an *episodic-narrative exemplum* on the *sin of pride* and the *virtue of humble obedience.* It has its lyric elements such as the two hymns, but they too—

like the bits of narrative filler with their telescoping of time, the more fully developed episodes such as Daniel's dream-analyses, the occasional use of double focus, and the presentation of a series of tableaux which may be the most nearly unique aspect of the poet's style—are all turned to homiletic examples of the evils of pride and the virtues of humble obedience. Where structural imbalance may be charged—for example, the set-pieces are intrusions in the orderly process of a brisk biblical narrative; the skimming rehash of familiar episodes is far too long for the simple function of setting up the lyric elements—the defense need only answer that the *Daniel*-poet structures his material for the poem's purposes and that aesthetic "balance" is not one of those purposes.[1]

As the poet briskly goes about his business, set-pieces notwithstanding, he employs a number of stylistic techniques to maintain his pace, though, as this chapter will describe, his outstanding techniques are employed in changing or arresting that rapid unreeling. For one thing, the sense of brisk movement is conveyed by the starkness of the description, the sparseness of the imagery. The *Daniel*-poet consistently abjures trivial details; at very few points in the narration of episodes is there anything which can profitably be analyzed as imagery. This stylistic peculiarity calls surprised attention to descriptive imagery where it does appear, such as in Nebuchadnezzar's dreams. Another case is the description of the fiery furnace, which is given three times in similar terms; from a poet who is stingy with detail, the audience may expect significance in those few details upon which variations are worked. Thus the pleasant weather inside the furnace, where the light remains while the angel sends flames outside to burn the heathens, is impressed upon the audience with great em-

[1] Besides, one may always suppose for a fragment that the missing parts would redress any imbalance.

phasis.[2] And incidental individual details like the angel's characterization as *wlitesyne wer* (337a) and the description of the writing on the wall as *baswe bocstafas* (723a),[3] which in the work of, say, the *Christ and Satan*-poet would be either ignored or repeated half a dozen times, are here made memorable without any slowing of pace. Another repeated detail is the characterization of Nebuchadnezzar as *wulfheort* (116a, 135a, 246a), but this properly belongs in the discussion of the technique of double focus.

I have remarked the poet's forbearance where other voices might have been quoted directly. Indirect reporting is his characteristic manner, and with the exceptions noted he maintains a distant point of view which can be called panoramic. He keeps shooting (to borrow cinematographic terms again) reel after reel of long shots. Even the four occasions when he signifies his own presence as narrator (*Gefrægn ic* "I have heard" 1a, *geseah ic* "I saw" 22a, *ic* . . . *gefrægn* "I heard" 57a, *ic* . . . *gefrægn* "I heard" 458a) do not bring him any closer to the action. Thus, to take the two most obvious examples of his restraint, the poet simply reports Nebuchadnezzar's temporary conversion by Shadrach, Meschach, and Abednego (444–447) and he simply describes at a distant remove Nebuchadnezzar's dream of the tree (495–522).

The pace is maintained, moreover, by frequent use of the familiar device of telescoping, in which the passage of long periods of time or the occurrence of complex events may be reduced to a single all-embracing image or state-

[2] Mr. Hugh T. Keenan, among other valuable suggestions about *Daniel*, has pointed out to me that the poet's changes from the Vulgate here (and elsewhere) tend to identify the angel as the Holy Spirit: only God could divide the two properties of fire, light and heat, according to Basil, Gregory, *et al.*

[3] The poet omits Belshazzar's offer of a scarlet coat as a reward for accurate handwriting-analysis, but he may simply have transferred the assignment of color to the writing itself. His audience was perhaps somewhat more familiar with red letters than with red robes.

ment. Thus a great deal of ground is covered, particularly in the early part of the poem: the Hebrews' prosperity in Jerusalem since Moses led them from Egypt; the sending of holy spirits who are heeded but briefly; the conquest by the Chaldeans, under God's direction and Nebuchadnezzar's leadership; and the subsequent captivity, occupation, and recruitment of bright young men. All this is covered before l. 87 of the extant 764 lines.[4] Nor is telescoping limited to the early episodes; the poet calls upon the device from time to time throughout, the most notable examples being the disposing of seven years in a verse (638a) and the telescoping of the generation from Nebuchadnezzar to Belshazzar (675–676).[5] It should be observed, however, that telescoping is necessarily common in the Scriptures themselves.

In *Daniel,* telescoping is frequently combined with the technique of double focus, so that ambiguity and allusions are flashed briefly before the audience, giving some semblance of significance and order to the swiftly unreeling narrative. Moreover, there appears frequently the closely related technique of the doubling of motif, that common technique of oral poetry, of edda, and of saga which becomes a staple for late medieval romance. Early occurrences anticipate later ones; later ones echo earlier; and brief repetitions (instead of extended description) keep up the pace. Thus Moses' leading the Hebrews out of bondage in Egypt ironically anticipates Nebuchadnezzar's leading them from Jerusalem to slavery in Babylon, and the capture of Babylon by the Medes and Persians under God's direction echoes the Chaldeans' capture of Jerusalem under God's direction.

[4] Hananiah, Azariah, and Mishael, "chosen of God," are introduced at l. 91, and Daniel, "chosen of the Lord," enters at l. 150. Krapp, p. xxxi, calls Daniel the central character of the poem, but no actor's agent could sell the part as the leading rôle. The star would have to play Nebuchadnezzar. The poem, unlike its source (from which Krapp was no doubt projecting his evaluation), is not formed around a central character but around a central theme.

[5] Krapp, however, supposes "a considerable loss in the MS here," p. 246.

Nebuchadnezzar himself is twice resistant to belief in God, twice converted to belief, and twice subject for Daniel's dream-analyses. This complex figure is finally rewarded abundantly in this world for his newfound righteousness—a prodigal, indeed, to cause rejoicing in heaven. But he is associated at different times with God, Christ, and the Devil (see "wolf-heart" above).

In the fiery furnace scene, the coming of the angel is reported twice, giving rise to much comment and conjecture, but this doubling ought to fit comfortably into an often-repeated pattern with God sending holy spirits (26b, generally interpreted as "prophets"), the Three Children and Daniel being "chosen" (92b, 150b), the holy spirit coming to strengthen Daniel (532–53), the description of the angel going back to heaven (440–442), and the writing of the angel, also called holy spirit (732b), on Belshazzar's wall. The "prophets" are not heeded, Daniel is not heeded, even the writing in red is not heeded. To proceed with a list of the many doublings discovered in *Daniel* would be tedious, but two observations ought to be made. One is the presence of the theme of exile, that ubiquitous element of the Old English canon.[6] The other is that, like almost everything else in the economical scheme of *Daniel,* the doublings are usually employed for exemplum-purposes in association with presentations of pride or humble obedience. For example, the early instance in which the Hebrews are seized by pride *æt winþege* "at the wine-feast" (17b) is an obvious foreshadowing of Belshazzar's feast.

Because there are so many techniques for hurrying things along, the devices that stop action are not only arresting in effect and impression but also suspect in the whole context of the art of *Daniel*. This is not the place to argue the knotty problems of interpolation and the relationship be-

[6] Cf. Stanley B. Greenfield, "The Formulaic Expression of the Theme of Exile in Anglo-Saxon Poetry," *Speculum,* XXX (1955), 200–206, though *Daniel* is mentioned only in a footnote reference to l. 631a (and *Exodus* not at all).

tween *Azarias* and *Daniel*, nor do I have any new solutions to offer. My concern is with the existing text of a poem, and that text shows me two hymns which intrude upon and impede its normal pace. Yet there are two other passages, Daniel's explanation of Nebuchadnezzar's dream (551-592) and the beginning of his angel-handwriting analysis (743-764, the end of the fragment), whose length and effect are so nearly identical to those of the hymns that all four may be grouped as set-pieces. The important difference is that the two hymns are exempla of humble obedience and the two judgments of Daniel are preachments against pride. The latter have never been considered interpolations, and it would seem to be a rather difficult and delicate critical operation to remove one side of a single coin from consideration.

These four passages are the only substantial ones in *Daniel* where the poet zooms in for close-ups of speakers, but they are not the only places where he stops action. In at least six other places, the panoramic sweep of his long-distance camera stops to focus on a still. These remain wide-angle long takes, but in them the action is frozen to give the effect of a tableau, an effect which is solidified in most cases by the presence of a multitude. In fact, the summoning of a multitude seems almost to be a cue to hold everything briefly so that the scene can be taken in. The first tableau can be labeled "idolatry" with the Babylonian masses genuflecting before banner and idol at the sound of the trumpet, an ironic reminder of judgment day (178-184). The second is "the fiery furnace" with the people gathered to see the binding of the Three Children before the flames (226-229). The third is Nebuchadnezzar's "state of the miracle address" to his assembled multitude (469-471; in this case the tableau might give way to a close-up of Nebuchadnezzar speaking, 472-485, but it seems to me that his audience is kept in the picture throughout his pronouncement). The fourth is a diptych, "Nebuchadnezzar questions the assembly" and "Daniel comes to judgment" (526-528, 531). The fifth is Nebuchadnezzar surveying the strength of Babylon, "the city of pride" (599–603; this is the exception to the crowd-scene rule). The sixth and last to be noted here (though there may be other tableaux in the poem) is "Belshazzar's feast," a depiction of Hogarthian dimensions which shows the king dispensing treasures like the leader of a mighty duguth (700–711), but the treasures are plundered sacred vessels and his people are doomed. This too is judgment day (*siðestan dæge* 700b), and the tableau may include an exterior background scene of the invading armies closing in on the festive hall of the Chaldeans (695–699).

Though the rush of incident seems to be the dominant trait of the *Daniel*-poet's style, the occasional arresting of that rush seems to be his outstanding technique. It may be that the inclusion of set-pieces and tableaux was inevitable in the aesthetic scheme of a poet mainly interested in suiting his episodic-narrative material to his thematic-exemplum purposes, that is, if he had any idea of what he was do-ing. The fragment of *Daniel*, though not among the best extant examples of the art of Old English poetry, suggests that Anglo-Saxon poets, even if they composed orally, were neither unconscious redactors nor automatic versifiers but artists aware of the artistic possibilities of their conventions.

EXODUS AND THE ESSENTIAL DIGRESSION

Edward B. Irving, Jr., in his admirable edition, touches on most of the points for critical discussion of *Exo-dus*.[7] This chapter will be limited to analysis of a few structural problems, although the poem deserves eventually to receive a full treatment of its art. Such an undertaking would have to include, among others of course, analyses devoted to the four following techniques and stylistic traits:

[7] *The Old English Exodus* (New Haven, 1953).

(1) the language of heroism—in which the poet aptly renders biblical material into communicable Germanic conventions, including a depiction of Moses as ring-giver and battle-king and the like, the familiar duguth-Lord metaphors, the brilliant metaphors and variations of traditional sea imagery, the Germanic concepts of nobility and kinship, the often-paralleled motifs of exile and death, and the traditional accouterments of battle; (2) the imagery, visual and especially auditory—through which the poet brilliantly conveys the sense of motion throughout, and, perhaps more, the sense of meaningful movement, of purposeful action, of destined direction; (3) the formality of speech, gesture, action, incident, and description—in which suggestions or vestiges of ritual may be seen at every turn;[8] and (4) the use of ambiguity and allusions, what I have termed double focus—in which, for example, Moses as hero fades into God as hero[9] and Pharaoh seems at times to be Satan (*Godes andsaca*).[10]

No matter how many elements of the *Exodus*-poet's art are isolated, there still will remain the task of accounting for the poem's unity; for the unity of *Exodus* has been generally accepted and praised as a rare achievement among longer Old English poems.[11] The time sequence, for example, and its relationship to the sequence of ideas (that is, the integration of dramatic and thematic order) need to be examined. Irving has made a beginning along these lines, especially where, with educated estimates of missing parts at ll. 141 and 446 and with an analysis of arguments for rearrangement of the passage 86–124, he has defended

[8] James W. Bright, "The Relation of the Cædmonian Exodus to the Liturgy," *MLN*, XXVII (1912), 97–103, sees the poem governed by medieval church ritual. Mr. Thomas J. Gasque, in an unpublished paper, has begun an investigation of Germanic ritual in the poem.

[9] Cf. Irving, p. 30.

[10] In this light *gyrdwite* (15b) may be closer to "enmity-bond" than to "punishment with a rod" (Irving).

[11] E.g., Krapp, p. xxvii; Stanley B. Greenfield, *A Critical History of Old English Literature* (New York, 1965), p. 157.

by explanation, not apology, the existing text of the poem.[12] He has also offered a defense for the so-called "Exodus B" passages (a case which I hope to strengthen below). But he finds the end of the poem, 516–590, "confused to the point of incomprehensibility,"[13] and he arranges his text by transposing 516–548 and 549–590.

The "simple transposition" (which needs "no more elaborate reconstruction of the error" than a misplaced leaf in a previous MS),[14] aside from being somewhat inconsistent with Irving's earlier arguments about the text, is unjustified except by a judgment of satisfactory form brought to the poem from outside. What seems anomalous to Irving is the order of things:

> From a scene of violent action the poet passes to what seems to be a reference to the laws of Moses and the book of Deuteronomy, and then into a general moralizing peroration on Judgment Day, which seems to lead to a definite climax in l. 548 (MS). Then he returns to a description in terms of physical action, telling of Moses' speech and the emotions and behavior of the Israelites. In other words, he generalizes on the significance of the scriptures and the meaning of a Christian life and *then* goes on to finish his story.[15]

But with the transposition the "story unfolds logically to its natural end . . . and the poet concludes with appropriate reference to the laws of Moses . . . and a brief homily . . . ."[16] Support is adduced from the facts that the laws of Moses were referred to at the beginning of the poem and that homiletic endings were common in Old English Christian poems.

Krapp's rejection of Gollancz's similar arrangement is

[12] Pp. 4ff.

[13] P. 11.

[14] P. 12. Cf. the arrangement proposed by Gollancz, pp. lxxv–lxxix— after l. 514: (1) 579–589, (2) 548–578, (3) 515–547—with its much more complicated reconstruction of error.

[15] P. 11.

[16] P. 11.

based on his judgment that such an anticlimactic ending would weaken the poem.[17] Arguments from contemporary taste in form must be rejected, but Krapp's conservative instinct is sound on this point. The manuscript arrangement can be accounted for, specifically, in terms of the way the *Exodus*-poet is working. Considerations of symmetry and anticlimax may be set aside (having been employed with equivalent effect on either side), while the manuscript sequence is examined for the transitions and associations that provide for its order.

The passage before the disputed section, which describes the total destruction of the Egyptian host, ends with the graphic understatement, *Hie wið god wunnon!* "They had contended with God!" (515b). Near the end (508–514a), the poet states that no messenger survived to report in the Egyptian towns the defeat of their army. Thus negatively, ironically, he traces the remnant of battle (a familiar device of battle poetry, for example, *Brunanburh*). We naturally expect a subsequent report on the other party to the conflict, the real survivors, the Israelite host (this is the expectation which Irving refers to as a logical unfolding of the story), and the report which fulfills that expectation does come (565–590). But it is delayed for forty-nine lines, and one must answer why. Assuming that all the lines 516–590 are authentic, that is, that the poet of *Exodus* wanted to include all the material of these lines, we can then examine the seams employed to join the various separate elements together. The elements are as follows:

1. Moses preaches to the Israelites   516–519
2. Men may still with benefit study the words of Moses in Scripture   520–521
3. if God permits our souls so to gain knowledge of eternal joy   521–532
4. This [here on earth] is temporary joy, destroyed by sins, granted to exiles   532–534

[17] Krapp, pp. xxx–xxxi.

The threads joining these elements operate so successfully that it is difficult to conceive of a better way to put them *all* together. The first seam joins the first element to the preceding description of the Egyptians in the sea. It is the naturally expected reference to the other party on the shore: *on merehwearfe* (517a). Next, the reference to a single occasion of preachment gives way to general remarks on Moses' preaching (#2). The process of spiraling out from the specific subject continues in remarks on the workings of holy writings in general (#3), concluding with a reference to eternal joy (*lengran lifwynna* 532a). In contrast is *læne dream* "transitory joy" (532b) of this world (#4), granted *wreccum* "to exiles" (533b), who go to hell (#5). The generalized contrast of heaven and hell includes the specific, dramatic, symbolic contrast of Hebrews and Egyptians. The exiled Hebrews are being led home, while the Egyptians who enjoyed earthly splendor have been sent to hell. The day of judgment is coming (#6), when the Lord will lead the blessed into heaven. In other words, the audience is explicitly directed to understand, now, what it has perhaps sensed all along: the Red Sea crossing, with the Egyptians swallowed up and the Hebrews led through to the Promised Land, is a *type* of judgment day when the damned will be swallowed up to hell and the blessed led to heaven. In a sense, then, it is possible to attribute the readily apparent unity of the whole poem to the underlying motif of judgment day and to the wholly effective way in which the details of the exodus cohere as a type of judgment day. The explicit theme of the Hebrews' covenants with God is similarly a symbolic dramatization of Faith. Thus, Irving's objection to shifts from violent action to general moralizing and back to physical action seems unwarranted: the traditional associations of judgment day maintain the violently physical aspect of the action.

Picking up the thread again, the poet re-announces Moses as speaker (#7), returning to the specific instance at the seashore, a gathering of a multitude not unlike the judging of God Himself at the meetingplace (*Drihten sylfa/on þam meðelstede   manegum demeð* 542b–543). His speech (#8) talks of God as the leader of this multitude and of the Promised Land as a reward for keeping the covenants. The promise of *beorselas beorna* "beer-hall of heroes" (564a), where *Bið eower blæd micel* "great glory shall be yours" (564b), is like a typical Anglo-Saxon description of heaven. It is followed by a celebration (#9) which combines imagery of heaven, judgment day, and exodus, beginning with the ambiguous sound of the trumpets and continuing with a reference to the *wuldres beam* which had led the host *on hild godes* (569b)—where heaven may be the *primary* referent. The rest of this element (570–579) and most of the next (#10) deal more specifically with the literal exodus, but the concluding reference to the Egyptians (*Werigend lagon / on deaðstede,   drihtfolca mæst* 589b–590) is a final doubling of the focus where "the place of death" is both the Red Sea and hell. The passage which Irving shifts (549–590), then, would make good sense after l. 515, but it makes better sense where the manuscript has it because the intervening passage has established explicitly the relationship between the exodus and judgment day.

Another argument in favor of the manuscript arrangement of the poem has to do with the structure of the poem as regards dramatic voices. Even more restrictive than the *Daniel*-poet, the *Exodus*-poet allows himself only three direct quotations, but their placement and impact have a great deal to do with the total effect of the poem. The first, occupying a central position (either counting the existing lines or accepting Irving's estimates of the lacunae), is the long speech of Moses to his people (259–275, 278–298). Moses exhorts the Hebrews to fear not, to renew their faith in God, and to observe (as he speaks) the parting of the sea. He contrasts the transitory life of the doomed Egyptians with the eternality of the God of Abraham, the Lord of Life; and he concludes by calling the parted sea *wrætlicu wægfaru oð wolcna hrof* "a wonderful sea-path up to the roof of heavens" (298) which may ambiguously refer not only to the towering walls of the sea but also to the significance of the passageway to the promised land as a figuration of judgment day and the salvation of the blessed. Thus the first climax of the poem, the parting of the sea, is viewed through the direct quotation from Moses. Moreover, the speech includes the reaffirmation of the Hebrews' covenant with God which is the explicit theme throughout this uniquely unified long Old English poem.

The second direct quotation (419–446) is the speech of the voice from heaven (*stefn of heofonum* 417b) to Abraham. It is the climax of the sequence of digressions, which will be discussed shortly; the point to be made here is that the voice establishes the covenant with Abraham that Moses is reaffirming in the other speeches. The third speech is Moses' address to the people after the crossing (554–564). It is the definitive statement of the covenant's fulfillment and therefore the climax of the explicit thematic material. The strategic placement of the speeches at high points of the poem's movement suggests that the final speech belongs where it is, very near the end. It might be argued that the speech is a fitting climax for the action wherein the Egyptian host is destroyed, but I think it rather clearly embodies a thematic rather than dramatic climax. Barring any *positive* evidence for transposed passages, one may assume that the manuscript order accurately carries the structure of *Exodus*.

An even stronger case may be made in defense of the

Noah–Abraham passage (362–446): no interpolation, it is in fact an essential part of the poem. The integrity of the passage has been defended convincingly by Gollancz, Krapp, and Irving,[18] and there seems to be no need to rehearse the arguments at length. Three observations, however, may be in order. First, the transition to Noah is not so abrupt or startling as it has appeared to several commentators. Directly following the description of the Hebrews' progress through the parted sea (which itself continues the elaborate pattern of sea-voyage imagery, one of the most salient features of the poet's remarkable style), the introduction of Noah has the most obvious kind of automatic association with flood, sea, and sea-voyage. The story of Noah also comfortably fits in with the theme of covenants with God. But there is an additional aspect of the Noah passage which confirms the connections of the transition: the preceding passage involves an elaborate treatment of genealogy, kinship, and the protocol of tribal lineage; and the Noah passage echoes and emphasizes the same concerns. Moreover, the transition from Noah to Abraham is accomplished by extending the theme of lineage. And the Akedah itself, the binding of Isaac, is a dramatization of the dominance in the poem of the one theme over the other—the covenant with God over human kinship.[19]

Second, as suggested above, the digression is structured in such a way as to reach a dramatic and thematic climax in the speech of the voice from heaven. This technique may be a key part of the structural pattern of the whole poem; in any case the poem as it stands shows the technique used similarly three times.

Third, the digression has its own digression in the reference to David (389–396). The relevance of this brief passage either to the digression or to the whole poem is difficult to see. The ostensible connection is a geographical one: David

[18] Gollancz, pp. lxxii–lxxiii; Krapp, p. xxviii; Irving, pp. 8–9.

[19] Another theme common to the stories of Noah, Abraham, and Moses, which is variously referred to throughout the poem, is the theme of exile and return.

later built a temple where Abraham led Isaac. But additional point to the digression may be seen in David's temple
as a commemoration of God's covenant with Abraham, as
well as in having the place called *meðelstede* "meetingplace" (397a) in a formula-system which recurs at 543a in
reference to judgment day (and may have connotations of
battlefield and of oath-swearing).[20] The importance of this
suggestion lies in its reminder of the many ways digressions
may operate in *Exodus* (and in Old English poetry in general), making associations of ideas, formulas, motifs, themes,
people, places, or things (images or symbols), but always
with the end of enriching on one or another level the audience's perception of the referent in the immediate context.
The Old English *Exodus* is a poem composed, as Irving
aptly states, by a poet of "rare architectonic ability."[21] That
ability may be seen in the way the techniques listed at the
beginning of this chapter coalesce in formal patterns of
organization.

MALDON AND MAGNETIC ACTION

The *Battle of Maldon* is every bit as interesting a poem
as the extensive bibliography of scholarship on it suggests.[22] Several of the problems it presents are char-

[20] Cf. *Maldon* 199a, *Andreas*, 658a, 697a, *Elene* 554a, *Beowulf* 1082b,
Daniel 145b.

[21] P. 35.

[22] Of particular interest are three recent essays: Edward B. Irving,
Jr., "The Heroic Style in *The Battle of Maldon*," *SP*, LVIII (1961),
457–67; Jess B. Bessinger, "*Maldon* and the *Óláfsdrápa*: An Historical
Caveat," *CL*, XIV (1962), 23–36; Ralph W. V. Elliott, "Byrhtnoth and
Hildebrand: A Study in Heroic Technique," *CL*, XIV (1962), 53–70.
The last two are reprinted in *Studies in Old English Literature in
Honor of Arthur G. Brodeur*, ed. Stanley B. Greenfield (Eugene, Ore.,
1963).

acteristic of poems discussed and approaches employed in the preceding chapters. In the first place, it is a fragment with both beginning and end missing, and no detail of structural analysis has given a firm leading clue as to how much is missing from either part or which part has the greater loss. In the second place, the extant 325 lines offer a poem of sufficient length and complexity to render the isolation of structural principles a difficult and perhaps tenuous practice. Third, the shifting point of view of the poem presents its material in such a way as to invite analysis in terms of cinematographic parallels.[23] Fourth, the use of direct quotations must surely be considered a primary element of the poem's structure, though perhaps the arrangement of the speeches is not based on so simple a rationale as has been supposed.[24] Fifth, the formality or formalization of action, diction, characterization, motivation, and exhortation suggests that an examination of ritual elements might be fruitful.[25] And sixth, of course, analysis of the diction for formulaic content and other stylistic characteristics can lead to useful conclusions about the poem and its structure.[26]

For the present, however, the approach will be limited to one specific aspect of the poem, the focus on movement apart and together, which is significant to its structure (though I think *Maldon* is governed by a combination of several structural principles). I have called it "magnetic

[23] Cf. Elliott, p. 62.

[24] Oversimplification is usually due to the tendency to divide the poem into two parts, first the straightforward narration of Byrhtnoth's fall and then the increasingly symbolic speeches. The best such treatment is Irving's.

[25] For example, the repeated gesture of raising shield or brandishing sword or spear which Magoun has called a "heroic poem theme" in "Some Notes on Anglo-Saxon Poetry," in *Studies in Medieval Literature: In Honor of Professor Albert Croll Baugh*, ed. MacEdward Leach (Philadelphia, 1961). Bessinger's "historical caveat" might well be kept in mind in pursuing this approach.

[26] Both Magoun and Elliott in the articles noted above have provided the beginnings for such an approach.

action" not because of any principle of unlikes attracting
and likes repelling but because the poet's concern with
movements toward and movements away from suggests both
the compelling violence and the inexorability of the laws
of magnetism.

Some of the larger elements in the overall design of the
poem can easily be associated with apartness or togetherness
or movement from one toward the other. The most obvious
is probably the step-by-step progression by which the Danes
and Essexmen draw together in the early part of the poem.
First they are *kept apart* by the river, and the Danes *send* a
messenger *to* the Essexmen (29a) with an offer. If tribute is
paid, they will *stay apart:*

> we willaþ mid þam sceattum   us to scype gangan,
> on flot feran,   and eow friþes healdan
>
> *we'll take ship with the coins, put out to*
> *sea, and keep peace with you.* (40–41)

But Byrhtnoth answers that he and his men *stand together*
unafraid (51); the Danes have *come too close* to be allowed
to *leave with* Essex coins—Danes and Essexmen will be
reconciled (geseman 60b) by weapons and battle (55–61).
The Essexmen *move closer,* but the tide *keeps them apart
from* the Danes (62–71). The tide goes out, but the bridge
or ford or causeway still *separates* them (72–83). At the
Danes' request, Byrhtnoth allows them passage over the
ford (84–95), urging them *gað ricene to us* "come quickly
to us" (93b). The Danes *move closer*—battle *is near (feohte
neh* 103b)—until finally the time *has come (Wæs seo tid
cumen* 104b, with a play on *tid?)* and the fighting actually
starts at l. 108.

Interestingly enough, this pattern is repeated several
times as individuals come together in the battle. After Dun-
nere's speech, all the Essexmen move forward toward the
Danes (*þa hi forð eodon* 260a), and as the Danes advance
(*Brimmen wodon* 295b) Wistan goes to meet them (*Forð þa
eode Wistan* 297b). Æþeric is described as eager and anxious

to get at 'em (*fus and forðgeorn* 281a), and at the end of the fragment, the other—that is, the loyal—Godric is the first of the remaining band as they go forward (*swa he on þam folce fyrmest eode* 323). Earlier in the poem Ælfwine advances after his speech (*þa he forð eode* 225a), Offa in his speech urges everyone forward (*þæt hi forð eodon* 229b), and Leofsunu angrily moves up, disdaining flight, after his speech (*He ful yrre wod* 253b, *fleam he forhogode* 254b). The clearest examples may be seen in the single combat between Byrhtnoth and a viking and the subsequent action involving Wulfmær. The Dane (*Wod* 130a, *stop . . . wið* 131b) and Byrhtnoth (*Eode swa* 132a) come inevitably closer together until the Dane, having wounded Byrhtnoth, is killed. Then when a spear thrown by another Dane gives Byrhtnoth his mortal wound, Wulfmær sends it back and kills the one who, as the poet phrases it, had "reached" Byrhtnoth (*geræhte* 158b).

Throughout this passage frequent reference is made to weapons, sometimes passively—weapons are raised (130b), sent (134a), pushed (136a), let go (140b), guided (141b), and shot (147b)—but often actively in conventional personifications:[27] they spring back (*sprang ongean* 137b), reach life (*feorh geræhte* 142b), stand at heart (*æt heortan stod* 145b), and go back again (*faran eft ongean* 156b). In other words, the togetherness of battle is consummated by the weapons: the poet says that "battle is joined" by having weapons accomplish the joining, particularly in ll. 108–129 where spear, arrow, shield, and sword take part in the opening skirmishes. Later the loyal Godric lets his spear fly or turn toward the enemy (*wælspere windan* 322a), and earlier, before the fighting, the Essexmen feel that they can't wait until they can "bring spears together" (*To lang hit him þuhte / hwænne hi togædere   garas beran* 66b–67).[28]

[27] See Neil D. Isaacs, "The Convention of Personification in *Beowulf*," *Old English Poetry*, ed. Robert P. Creed (Providence, 1967), pp. 215–48.

[28] But cf. *randas beran* formula-system in *Psalm 105* 8, *Exodus* 332b, with variation in *Beowulf* 2653b. It may simply mean "go"; see John

Thus, the *Maldon*-poet infuses a familiar device of Old English heroic poetry with his own pattern of movement. Moreover, he extends the pattern to take in other aspects of his diction, thereby bringing otherwise disparate elements into his organic structure. For instance, Byrhtnoth's dying prayer (173–180) is a request that his soul, when *separated from* his body, be *brought to* heaven, to God and the angels:

> þæ min sawul to ðe   siðian mote
> on þin geweald,   þeoden engla,
> mid friþe ferian.   (177–179a)

Another time the pattern is employed ironically, where the waters which keep the opposing forces *apart* are described in terms of their own *togetherness: flod æfter ebban, | lucon lagustreamas* (65b–66a). Again, Offa's fall is described in terms of his seeking to join or approaching the ground (*grund gesohte* 287b—cf. "bit the dust"), and a particularly violent part of the battle is called a *stið gemot* "fierce meeting," that is, "a formal meeting, a council" (301a). Perhaps the most interesting extension of the pattern comes with its initiation in the opening passage, where there are two juxtaposed images, both of which include moving apart *and* moving together. First, Byrhtnoth orders his men to *separate from* their horses (*hors forlæten* 2b), *drive* them *away* (*feor afysan* 3a), and *advance together toward* the place of battle (*forð gangan* 3b), thinking on hand-to-hand conflict, the ultimate *joining* of battle (*hycgan to handum* 4a). Then Offa's kinsman, when he discovers that Byrhtnoth means business,

> ... let him of handon   leofne fleogan
> hafoc wið þæs holtes   and to þære hilde stop.   (7–8)

He looses his dear hawk from his hand (*hands* link the

D. Tinkler, "A Critical Commentary on the Vocabulary and Syntax of the Old English Version in the *Paris Psalter*" (Stanford University Dissertation, 1964, unpublished, but to be published by Mouton), p. 155.

two passages very closely), *separating* himself *from* peaceful pursuits, and *marches towards* battle.

Extending into diction, dramatic action, and potentially symbolic imagery, the pattern of apart/together also takes on crucial thematic significance when associated with treachery/loyalty, as the poet sets up consistent and extensive equations: apart = treachery, together = loyalty. These equations appear most obviously in two contrasting passages: Byrhtnoth's taking his position with the dearest hearth-companions of his people (23–24) and the defection of the cowardly retainers (185–201). To begin with part of the negative equation: an obvious and trite image of cowardice is running away, and the poet uses such terminology as *Hi bugon þa fram beaduwe* (185a), *on fleame* (186b), *forlet* (187b), *ærndon* (191b), *ac wendon fram þam wige* (193a), and *flugon* (194a) to describe the defectors. Ironically, the same passage also has several suggestions of togetherness and movement toward: *and his broðru mid him begen* (191), *and þone wudu sohton* (193b), *on þæt fæsten* (194a), and *on þæm meþelstede, þa he gemot hæfde* (199). The last quoted line heavily underscores the irony, for it was at the meetingplace, at the coming together of the council, that the retainers made their vows of loyalty— that they would stay with their leader—which they have now treacherously broken.

In the subsequent speeches of the loyal retainers, this negative element is stressed repeatedly as they pledge anew not to leave Byrhtnoth even though he has fallen. Ælfwine won't be reproached

> þæt ic of ðisse fyrde   feran wille,
> eard gesecan,   (221–222a)

that he ever wanted to leave the troops and go home; Leofsunu refuses to flee one footstep (*ic heonon nelle | fleon fotes trym* 246b–247a), won't be reproached that he journeyed home (*ham siðie* 251b) or even left the battle (*wende fram wige* 252a) unless some weapon should take him (252b–253a); Eadweard the tall, too, won't flee back even one foot (*þæt he nolde fleogan fotmæl landes,* / *ofer bæc bugan* 275–276a); Byrhtwold, pledging not to be moved (*fram ic ne wille* 317b), curses those who consider flight (*A mæg gnornian* / *se ðe nu fram þis wigplegan wendan þenceð* 315b–316); and Offa, decrying the flight of Godric (*rad* 239b) and the many who followed (*aflymde* 243b), describes the act of betrayal as splitting the army (*folc totwæmed* 241b). In the action, too, refusal to run is a concise figure for loyalty, as when Wulfstan, Ælfere, and Maccus would not flee from the bridge (*noldon . . . fleam gewyrcan* 81) and, in the final extant verse, the loyal Godric is distinguished from the one who *ða guðe forbeah* (325b).

The speeches display the positive equation, too, as in Leofsunu's pledge to fight on (*wille furðor gan* 247b) and Byrhtwold's to die by Byrhtnoth's side (*ic me be healfe minum hlaforde,* / *be swa leofan men, licgan þence* 318–319). And as the loyal men come forward (*wendon forð* 205a), hastening eagerly (*efston georne* 206b) to gather round their fallen leader, other images and idioms reinforce the equation. A good example is the notion of standing firmly in place (whence the primary modern meaning of "steadfast" as "firm in loyalty") which appears in *stedefæste hælæð* (249b), *stodon fæste* / *wigan on gewinne* (301b–302a), *and þone stede healdan* (19b), *stodon stædfæste* (127a), and *Swa stemnetton* (122a). Perhaps to this list of those who "stand fast" should be added Wulfstan, Ælfere, and Maccus, who "stand together" at the bridge (*stodon mid* 79a).

Two other passages seem to capture fully the sense of the equation, the essence of the whole pattern of movement, and the spirit of *Maldon* as well. The first consists of three lines at the end of the passage describing the death of Byrhtnoth:[29]

and begen þa beornas   þe him big stodon
Ælfnoð and Wulmær   begen lagon,
ða onemn hyra frean   feorh gesealdon.

[29] Note the symbolic action of dropping the sword (166–168a). Where men consistently and conventionally vow to fight as long as their hands may hold their swords, the failure represents final doom.

and both the men who stood by him, Ælfnoth
and Wulmær, both lay dead, who side by side
with their lord gave up life. (182–194)

Here, almost as an afterthought, and almost as a matter of course, two men fulfill their heroic loyalty. The second passage comes after the poet tells that Offa was cut down:

he hæfde ðeah geforþod   þæt he his frean gehet,
swa he beotode ær   wið his beahgifan
þæt hi sceoldon begen   on burh ridan,
hale to hame,   oððe on here crincgan,
on wælstowe   wundum sweltan;
he læg ðegenlice   ðeodne gehende.

he had, however, accomplished what he had promised
his lord, as, earlier, he had boasted to his ring-giver
that they should both ride into town, hale to home, or fall
among the troops, die from wounds on the
battlefield; like a [good] retainer he lay dead near
his chief. (289–294)

The poignant because now impossible image of the two riding home together, the strategic accent on *begen* "both" (as in 182 and 183), and the perfect juxtaposition of *ðegen-* and *ðeodne* render the passage (and with it the whole poem) not bitterly ironic but triumphantly heroic. There is no better place to end a discussion of *Maldon* or, for that matter, of structural principles in Old English poetry.

AFTERWORD ON THE SCANSION
OF OLD ENGLISH POETRY

Scansion of Old English poetry is an extraordinarily complex problem. There have been several contributions toward a solution, but it is not likely that a final solution can ever be agreed upon. The fascination of the problem, however, has led to much conjecture, and it seems quite plausible that working explanations can be made to account for the metrical phenomena of almost all the verse and that an approximation of the rhythm be postulated; it also seems to me important that such explanations be attempted.

Two great contributions toward this pragmatic end are those of Sievers[1] and Pope.[2] Sievers produced a classification of the types of verses according to distribution of stresses which has been of enormous value, so valuable in fact that most subsequent approaches to Old English scansion, however divergent, have been able to use Sievers' five types. But as Sievers himself suspected, the classification has nothing to do with the rhythm of the poetry. John Collins Pope, using Sievers' types as a basis for classification, has produced an account of the rhythm of the poetry based on principles of isochronous measures and a kind of regular harp accompaniment. Pope's basic arguments are quite convincing and the influence of his system has been correspond-

[1] Edouard Sievers, "Zur Rhythmik des germanischen Alliterationsverses," *PBB*, X (1885), 209–314; *Altgermanische Metrik* (1893).

[2] John Collins Pope, *The Rhythm of Beowulf* (New Haven, 1942, revised ed., 1966).

ingly great; but he has been challenged in two directions, from those who do not agree with his theory of composition (despite the subsequent discoveries of Magoun and other followers of Parry and Lord) and from those who find his classifications overly complicated and impractical. No new system will be presented here. Sievers' classifications will be used as labels (A, B, C, Da, Db, E, and A3, though a handy additional one will be suggested—E3), and Pope's thesis of roughly isochronous measures accompanied by a regular harp-beat with occasional initial rests is the framework within which a few modifications will be offered. Of the writers since Pope, occasional reference will be made to Baum, Le Page, Bliss, and Taglicht, and substantial reference to an important recent article by Robert P. Creed.[3] The results of my investigations may be codified into ten— not commandments but—amendments, a kind of bill of rights (and wrongs) for a pragmatic approach to scanning Old English poetry (not including expanded verses).

I am going to follow the unusual procedure of starting with a presentation of the amendments, while my few comments on the body of the constitution as presented by Pope will follow remarks on the modifications presented by Creed.

I. Stress and time being nowhere *necessarily* correlative, syllable length (physiological, etymological, positional, or whatever) may be discounted in rhythmic analysis. Unlike classical Latin meters, Old English poetry determines stress by alliteration, natural accent, rhetorical emphasis, and syntactical priority (in that order); and though stress often coincides with long syllables and sometimes in practice re-

[3] Paull F. Baum, "The Meter of the 'Beowulf'," *MP*, XLVI (1948–49), 73–91, 145–62; R. B. Le Page, "A Rhythmical Framework for the Five Types," *English and Germanic Studies*, VI (1957), 92–103; A. J. Bliss, *The Metre of Beowulf* (Oxford, 1958); Josef Taglicht, "*Beowulf* and Old English Verse Rhythm," *RES*, n.s. XII (1961), 341–51; Robert P. Creed, "A New Approach to the Rhythm of *Beowulf*," *PMLA*, LXXXI (1966), 23–33.

sults in a lengthening of syllables, the length cannot be used to determine stress. Any attempt to use length to determine stress (and as a corollary any attempt to impose chronometric rhythm) confuses the issues, becomes hopelessly involved with extraneous matters, and is foredoomed to failure.[4]

II. Old English poetry is formed when words (which fall generally into certain basic patterns of stressed and unstressed syllables—Sievers' types) are linked together—truly bound—by alliteration or initial rhyme. Thus the basic unit of the poetry, the cell of the organism, is the line.[5] An analysis of the workings of nuclei, protons, etc.—the verses and measures—may contribute to an understanding of the poetry, but the line, with whatever relationships among its parts may be discovered, must be seen whole.

III. The alliteration that counts, then, is what holds the line together, and the alliterating syllable in each verse occupies the primary stress. It is the *pair* of alliterating syllables around which the rest of the line forms. Other alliterations, when they occur (and they sometimes occur in profusion), should not be allowed to influence or alter the

[4] This amendment was anticipated by Baum, p. 73, and Bliss, p. 24 (see also the latter's remarks, p. 108, about the relation of stress, duration, and length). Bliss's discussion is particularly interesting when brought to bear on Taglicht's listing among "basic facts" the necessity for distinguishing length in scansion (p. 345). Taglicht is led from this "fact" to a conclusion of a chronometric system of great simplicity, but when applied to the poetry it results in what Pope calls (p. xii, 1966 edition) "a loosely patterned prose." Yet Bliss has himself insisted on distinctions of length under certain conditions (e.g., pp. 27–35; cf. Creed, 28n).

[5] Cf. Le Page, p. 101, though he suggests, p. 97, the possible rhythmic effects of larger units. This amendment voices the major objection to Creed, as discussed below. But Bliss's entire system of classification is based on the location of the caesura in each verse, a dubious subjective process which is rendered insignificant by the recognition of the line as basic unit with caesura regularly occurring between half-lines. Bliss's statistical information, then, is not the objective collection of data it seems to be, but rather the presentation of often doubtful judgments.

natural and necessary rhythmic structure. They are incidental or accidental. Naturally, in a poetic form geared to
the effects of alliteration, the effects will be cultivated, and
the alliterations will proliferate. Naturally, too, the most
common and obvious proliferation will occur in the position of the second accent in an A-type verse. Moreover, the
oral-formulaic nature of the poetry will tend to perpetuate
the effects so produced. But the basic rhythm depends on
the linking alliterative pair, not on any additional effect,
however obvious or subtle. Sub-types of basic rhyme schemes
are never categorized according to internal rhymes or internal assonance and consonance, no matter how profuse the
sound-effects.[6]

IV. Where alternate readings for a verse are possible, particularly where it is hard to tell *which* of the alliterating syllables matters, formulaic evidence may be called to account.
Since one of the requirements for identifying formulas is
the identity of metrical conditions, it is possible to work
backwards from an established formula-system to see (or
hear) the metrical conditions of a particular verse that
forms part of the system.[7]

V. The resolution of syllables is a common feature of
major attempts to reckon the meter and rhythm of Old

[6] Interesting comments on alliteration may be found in Baum, pp. 73,
145, 149, 153, and Bliss, p. 110, both of whose warnings against non-
functional alliteration echo occasional practices of Pope and Creed.
But when Bliss say that "the first alliterating word of the *a*-verse is
the most important, since it gives the first clue to the alliteration of
the line," he is making the illogical assumption that alliteration can
be anticipated before it occurs. One would have to hear (or see!) the
alliterating partner before the "first alliterating word" is recognized as
such—unless, of course, that word is always signalled somehow, by the
first simultaneous harp-stroke, for instance. The priorities of D. Slay,
summarized by Creed, p. 25, are helpful guidelines. They could probably be broken down further, on a statistical basis; but it is important to
remember that they are tables of usual practice, not rules of procedure.

[7] The application of this amendment will point the way to many of
the exceptions I take to Pope's readings.

English poetry. Allowance for resolving syllables is necessary, not so that verses can be fitted neatly into systems of scansion, but because scops could, often did, and in practice had to pronounce syllables in close juncture together. There are no regular rules for resolution.[8] Syllables are resolved *when they can be* (when they can be elided, contracted, or slurred with others) *if they must be* because the rhythmic pattern calls for it. The ability to pronounce the sounds in accordance with the rhythm is the only criterion. Apt parallels and demonstrations of this procedure are found when Calypso and other folk singers—either extemporaneously or perpetuating or approximating an extemporaneous situation—employ variations of syllabification and pronunciation in a set rhythmic (or melodic) pattern. It is even possible to substitute "Uncle Aloysius" for "Billy" in "Happy Birthday to You." Priorities for resolution might be established as guide-lines for students, with final -*e*'s[9] and other vowels getting precedence in accordance with nearly universal lyric, rhythmic, and musical practice.

VI. Anacrusis represents a failure of a system of scansion to account for all syllables. Allowance for anacrusis is especially necessary when the system insists that each line, verse, and even measure begin with an accented syllable (the basic trochaic pattern, the lift-dip theory, the downbeat equation).[10] In fact, a comparatively high percentage of lines and verses in Old English begin with unaccented syllables. Pope's musical notation should have resolved this problem, since the key to his system is the initial rest in all B- and C-type verses, with the harp occupying a central rôle in the rhythm. Besides, with a regular harp-beat and four isochronous measures per line, anacrusis would mean an

---

[8] Cf. Creed, p. 25.

[9] Incidentally, it might be instructive on this matter to look at the syllable-counting metrical practices of Chaucer: where needed final -*e* is pronounced, when not needed it is not pronounced (including, surely, most final -*e*'s at the end of lines).

[10] Cf. Le Page, p. 94, on "this dogma of no rising measures."

extra measure or part of measure *between* lines and would break the continuous rhythm which the basis of the system postulates. Yet Pope allows for sixty-three sub-types with anacrusis in the first half-line. Creed's analysis of anacrusis perpetuates Pope's anomaly, but willy-nilly Creed has demonstrated therein the need for treating the *line* as the basic unit. Here are his first two examples, *Beowulf* 93 and 2247:[11]

> ╱ ╲ x ╱   x ╱ x ╱ x
> | wlite-beorhtne | wang, swá | wæter be- | búgeþ

> ╱   x   ╱ x   ╱ x ╱ x
> | Heald þú nú, | hrúse, nú | hæleþ ne | móston.

Such scansion does not "locate" anacrusis, it *eliminates* it. We now have, by Creed's labels, lines of gamma-alpha-alpha-alpha and alpha-alpha-alpha-alpha measures, or four A-type verses. After all, oral poetry, if recited anything like the way Creed (or Pope) says, would include *swa* and *nu* in the first half-line of 93 and 2247, and a scribe-recorder would have put it so if he wrote poetry the way we do. Only when the on-verse is B-type, then, can anacrusis occur in the off-verse. Any other construction can accept an additional unaccented syllable or two (E-types thereby becoming A-types). And with continuous recitation from line to line, the same would apply to on-verses and preceding off-verses. If musical notation and its implications (isochrony, harp accompaniment) are to be accepted, then many, if possible all, anacruses should be eliminated. Judicious application of Amendments II, III, IV, and V will remove many, VII and VIII most of the rest.

VII. There may be initial rests in A3-type verses. This possibility solves many of the problems concerning the several kinds of verses grouped under this heading. Pope has allowed for initial rests in many A3-type verses from *Beowulf*[12] but has found anacrusis in thirty-one others, retaining stress on a syllable before the heavy alliterating syllable for a variety of reasons (length, rhetorical emphasis, syn-

---

[11] P. 32.   [12] Pp. 264ff.

tactical priority). Thus even 2258a "with heavy secondary stress at end" is scanned

gē swylce sēo herepād,

𝄿| 𝅘𝅥 𝅘𝅥𝅮 𝅘𝅥𝅮| 𝅘𝅥𝅮𝅘𝅥𝅮 𝅘𝅥 |

though Pope concedes, "This might be read with initial rest, like [1521a: *þæt hire on hafelan*]."[13] In all thirty-one cases the syllables before the alliteration could be accommodated in the first measure, either with an initial rest or with resolved non-alliterative stress (as in Creed's doublets and triplets).

VIII. On the analogy of A3-type verses I suggest the possibility of E3-types, replacing the final unaccented syllable(s) with a rest, but alliterating only on the second stress. The only clear example in *Beowulf* is 2615a: *brunfagne helm   hringde byrnan* (Pope calls it "transverse alliteration" but says that it "is of course a very questionable example, because it would be easy to transpose the second half of the line and so produce crossed alliteration"[14]), but there are other cases, including *Seafarer* 9a: *wæron mine fet* and 56a: *esteadig secg, Widsith* 108a: *þæt hi næfre song, Azarias* 23a: *wæs ure lif,* and the first verse of *Fates of the Apostles: Hwæt! Ic þysne sang.* The only reason for trying to account for these verses another way is their rarity. They violate no principles except one prohibiting them (presumably because of their rarity). But in practice it might be that many A3-types are read as "E3" by resolving light final syllables for effect, e.g., *Beowulf* 22a, 1142a, 1197a, 1933a, 2000a, 2976a.

IX. Syncopation forms an essential part of the rhythm of Old English poetry. It seems impossible to conceive of sustained rhythmic performance or sustained isochrony or of a regularly music-based or musically accompanied beat with-

[13] P. 271.   [14] P. 315.

out syncopation. But syncopation is suggested more forcefully by the many B-, C-, and D-type verses that have more
than one candidate for secondary stress; it is required when
those candidates have equivalent claims. Syncopation as
used here means the displacement of the regular rhythmic
beat so that one syllable or note crosses the bar-division
between measures and shares some of the time of both
measures (e.g., a regular | bum diddy | bum diddy | may be
syncopated to | bum di bum|m diddy|). It is possible that
syncopation regularly occurred in B- and C-types, but it
seems to be required only in those cases where there is a
choice between a B or C scansion.[15] A common case is the
choice between the second element of a compound noun or
name and a following verb or pronoun, as in *Ðone siðfæt
him* 202a and *þær Hroðgar sæt* 356b. Either verse could be
read as B or C, but if *sið-* and *Hroð-* are syncopated, accom-
modation has been made for both the other elements to
receive secondary stress. Similarly, in D-types, where there
is a question as between Da and Db, syncopation of the
second primary stress allows for both aspirants to receive
some secondary stress. Again, it may be that D-type verses
regularly were syncopated.[16] Questions as between A3 and

---

[15] Baum insists on a great latitude of choice (see, e.g., pp. 79 and
147), but his permissive approach goes too far. If Pope's system makes
scansion difficult, Baum's non-system makes agreement about scansion
impossible—a more serious form of self-defeating scholarship.

[16] Le Page makes similar suggestions, pp. 98–99. The difficulty with
Le Page's "rhythmical framework" is that it is not a framework at all
but an elastic band capable of accommodating rather extreme variations of stylization, syncopation, expansion and contraction of measures,
and shifting time signature. While I would agree with Le Page (and
Baum) that we cannot confidently assign to the Anglo-Saxon scop a
particular *kind* or *style* of or *taste* in music, I would also suggest that
we might make an evaluation of the degree of subtlety in the basic
format of his traditional music. Le Page, as his analogies indicate,
appeals to the sophistication and subtlety of modern music and poetry.
I cannot doubt (not with the bulk of this book behind me) that Old
English poets could employ great sophistication and subtlety metrically and otherwise; but that these special excellences were part of the
traditional rhythmical framework I cannot believe.

C, e.g. *þonne iu hongade,* may also be included here.

All of this raises questions concerning the use of the harp. As Jess B. Bessinger ably demonstrated in the Old English group meeting at MLA in 1960, playing on a harp reconstructed according to the specifications of Sutton Hoo fragments, a great latitude of accompanying procedures may have been open to Old English scops. Basically there has been an assumption of a one-strum-per-measure arrangement, but any number of pickin' and frailin' designs are possible; and a four-measure line can easily accommodate six strums for two pairs of syncopated bars.

X. In the use of exclamatory *Hwæt* there is ample evidence for one specific variation in the use of the harp. I have examined the sixty-seven occurrences of the word (not including those in the *Paris Psalter* where a pedestrian versifier, with probably very little knowledge of metrics and no sense of rhythm, used *Hwæt* sometimes to translate *etenim* and *nonne* but mainly as a filler). Eight times *Hwæt* begins a poem, once a poem within a poem, and nine times a speech within a poem—more than a third of the occurrences if the fifteen in the *Meters of Boethius* are set aside. Though it is an interjection designed to call attention to what is to follow, it never forms part of the essential alliteration (although thirteen of the sixty-seven have *h*-alliteration, including eight occurrences of a formula-system which appears basically as *Hwæt, we þæt hyrdon   þurh halige bec*— *Elene* 364, 852, *Fates of the Apostles* 63, cf. *Christ* 586, *Juliana* 1, *Guthlac* 108, *Fates of the Apostles* 23, *Genesis* 939), never receives even secondary accent, and thus never is accompanied by a harp-stroke. How can *Hwæt* then call attention to anything (but its own lack of power)? Moreover, in every case of its occurrence, its presence or absence has no influence whatsoever on the metrical classification of the verse.

I suggest that initial exclamatory *Hwæt* stands outside the regular rhythmic framework and bears its own harp-stroke. Does it form an expanded verse then? Probably not:

Christ 1423b is the sole occurrence in an expanded-verse context, but the verse remains hypermetric without *Hwæt*. Perhaps there was conventionally an introduction with a harp, ending in a stroke and a simultaneous *Hwæt* signaling the rise of the curtain so to speak—perhaps not so elementary a fanfare as bumbum pabum bum bum STRUM, but on the same idea. Such a convention could be transported for its obvious effects to other parts of a poem (*Order of the World* 38 is the best example; see also *Solomon and Saturn* 391 and *Maldon* 231), but it could also be abused (see the three occurrences in *Menologium*: 48, 122, 176).

Robert P. Creed has offered a new system designed to provide a practical approach to an understanding of the rhythmic workings of Old English poetry. Based in part on the monumental work of John Collins Pope, now happily available in a paperback edition, Creed's system provides a simplification of Pope calculated to render the poetry "scannable" by students and by readers with no great technical skill. Creed's system works. It accounts for every line of Old English poetry which has been tested so far. (Whether the accounting accords with every reading is quite another question, since matters of judgment, taste, *stress*, etc., must inevitably produce rhythmic variations; but the fact is that it accords with Creed's readings,[17] and many who have heard them will feel that that is enough to warrant acceptance of his system.)

Some of Creed's modifications of Pope readily provide relief from some of the complexities and densities of *The Rhythm of Beowulf*, but some may have taken us in the wrong direction. I want briefly to analyze his rules and procedures, and especially some of his results, before going on to an analysis of a large portion of Pope's readings (which should show how my amendments can account for

[17] Folkways recording FL 9858 (1964).

the questionable notations). I have not been wrestling with these problems as long as Creed, but the difficulty of getting a grip on the poetry through Pope's multiplicity of holds is attested to by the number of students thrown thereby.

Like Creed, I too am convinced by Pope's analysis, argument, and poetic appreciation that Old English poetry consists mostly of lines containing four measures of roughly equivalent length though varying in the number of syllables they contain and in their stress-patterns. (I take exception, however, to the assertion that "The stress-patterns are imposed on these isochronous measures."[18] If there is any *imposing*, it is the isochronous measures upon the stress-patterns; i.e., the musical accompaniment follows the words of the poetry. I would prefer to say that there is a working together of stress-patterns and isochrony.) But I too am put off by the extravagant proliferation of types and sub-types in Pope's applications.

It is easy to see why Creed's simplification works, i.e., why it simplifies. First he reduces the number of significantly different patterns of stress (per measure) to six and then argues (post hoc propter hoc) that the *measure* is the way at an appreciation of Old English metrics. This indeed is a great oversimplification. Theoretically there will still be only thirty-six types of verses, i.e., combinations of measure. But if, as Amendment II asserts, the *line* is the significant and basic unit of Old English poetry, then there are theoretically 1,296 types of rhythmic variation per line (if the couplet were the unit, the types would number 1,679,616). And all of these figures are minimal since Creed has resorted to many devices in order to keep the measure-types down to six (though he hedges a little finally by talking about "Epsilons as Alphas," i.e., "alpha minuses"). But he has missed another great opportunity for simplification by failing to eliminate a great number of anacruses (see Amendment VI). Both Pope's and Creed's allowances for resolved stress are

[18] P. 24.

acceptable and necessary, but Creed's rules are sophisticated beyond need and overly prescriptive (see Amendments I, V). His Rule V should be permissive, not dogmatic.

Creed is surely right for all practical purposes in reducing Pope's five degrees of stress to three. This will leave some room for optional readings and certain problems in judgment. Part of the following discussion will attempt to face up to a class of these problems.

Creed's warning about non-significant alliteration needs to be greatly expanded. Extra alliteration accounts for most of the errors, unnatural readings, and gratuitous complications in the study of Old English metrics. For the first half-lines in *Beowulf,* Pope lists 348 types and sub-types. Of these I count 210 which exist in the schematization *only* because of extra alliteration ("double," "crossed," or "transverse"). See Amendments III and IV.

Of Creed's first four rules, I is certainly valid and III demonstrably true. Rule II—"A primary stress *always* begins a measure"—is valid; but notice that there need not be a primary stress in every measure. The parenthetical addition —"There can thus be only *one* primary stress in each measure"—however, needs to be qualified to allow for syncopation in D-type verses, where a primary stress will sometimes begin at the end of the first measure and continue into the beginning of the second measure. Rule IV could be revised to include A3 types. Pope is right in saying that the syllables preceding the alliterating stress in A3 verses sometimes fill the whole first measure and sometimes do not (see Amendment VII). Additional aspects of Creed's system which ought to be accepted are his allowance for doublets and triplets (though I balk at *requiring* their occurrence) and his approval of John Nist's reminder[19] that internal rests may occur as well as initial rests.

Some of the examples employed in Creed's article require comment:

---

[19] *The Structure and Texture of Beowulf* (São Paulo, 1959), pp. 93–110.

B (2289b) | (∕)   \ | ∕∕   \\ |
           | hē   tō | forð gestŏp |

D (210a) | ∕∕   (\) | ∕∕   \\ |
          | Fyrst | forð gewāt |

Line 210a may just be a variation of the formula-system of 2289b, a B-type with *forð* getting the primary stress and carrying the alliteration, the root syllable of the verb getting secondary stress, and the subject (whether or not it carries additional—incidental or accidental—alliteration) at most a secondary stress.

C (3a) | (∕)   \   ð | ∕∕ \\ |
        | hū   ðá | æþelingas |

D (906a) | ∕∕ \ | ∕∕ \\ |
          | eallum | æþelingum |

Line 906a looks like a variation of the C-type formula-system of 3a. The additional vowel-alliteration on *eallum* should be discounted; *æþel-* carries the alliteration as also in 33, etc.

Two of Creed's examples of anacruisis were examined above. These and the problem need further discussion. I suggested that Creed's scansion

$$/ \quad \backslash \quad \times \quad / \quad \times \quad / \quad \times \quad / \times$$
| wlíte-beorhtne | wang,   swá | wǽter be- | búgeþ

$$/ \quad \underline{\times} \quad / \quad \underline{\times} \quad / \times \quad / \times$$
| Heald þú nú, | hrúse,   nú | hǽleþ ne | móston.

removed the anacrusis, but both of these verses allow of
other readings, *swá wǽter bebúgeþ* as a B resolving (con-
tracting) the *-eþ* (which may prefigure the eventual process
by which such endings were lost or replaced by *-s*) and *nú
hǽleþ ne móston* as B resolving *-on* (*móst'n*, cf. "the *cap'm*
he got drunk" and "walk all over God's *heb'm*") or possibly
C resolving *hǽleþ* as indicated and reading

$$\underline{\quad \backslash \quad} \times$$
n'moston.

The second group of anacruses used as examples by Creed
(anacrusis before the *secondary* stress which introduces an
alpha minus measure) presents a much more complex problem. His sixth example (1585b) belongs with the two listed
above. It is B-type and can be scanned

$$\underline{\quad \backslash \quad \quad \times} \quad / \quad \underline{\times} \quad \backslash$$
| to-þæs-þe hé on | rǽste ᵹeseah |

according to Creed's notation. I would simply say that there
are five quick unaccented syllables in the first measure. The
example 2528a also easily dispenses with anacrusis: *þæt ić
wiþ þone gúþ-flogan* is a C-type verse with four (or five
counting the final *-e* in *þone*) quick unaccented syllables in
the first measure (as in 2185, 677, 862, 1686, 2867). The
other four examples (47a, 1011a, 675a, 1322a) are Sievers'
A3-type verses, though it is possible in performance to
resolve the final syllable of each (see Amendment VIII). To
repeat the suggestion of Amendment VII, the first measure
of an A3-type (or E3-type) verse need not have a primary
stress. In fact most can be read as having either secondary
stress, resolved secondary stress (675a, 1322a, 1011a), or no

stress (47a) and therefore preceded as in B- and C-types by the harp-stroke. Again, it is only primary alliterating stress that counts; the rest of the line falls into place around these two syllables.

In Creed's sample notation of twenty-five lines, I would dispute the scansion of only two verses, one of which is the special case of *Hwæt wé Gár-Dena* 1a (see Amendment X). The other, *framum feoh-ʒiftum* 21a, is scanned as a Da with resolution of *-um* in *framum* and double alliteration. I call it a C-type (not requiring the resolution but allowing it), with incidental alliteration on *framum*.

In Creed's conclusion, he lists four accomplishments of his new approach. All four are valid and valuable (though not always right, for reasons set forth above). Of greatest importance is his fourth accomplishment: "we have . . . gained an insight into the ways of the Anglo-Saxon singer, for the simple scheme of replacements sketched out here . . . must, after all, be *his* scheme, however much or little he might have been aware of the simplicity that underlies the beautiful complexity of his verse." This is a fitting and proper and significant aim of metrical analysis, and I think that Creed's system does contribute insights into the scop's method. Pehaps the ten amendments offered above will also help achieve this aim. My major point of contention with Creed is that where he goes measure for measure (as opposed to Baum, as you like it), I would insist that the line's the thing wherein to catch the rhythm of the verse.

I have tested Pope's scansion of the first 498 lines of *Beowulf,* stopping just before Unferth begins the flyting, and found that I could offer alternate readings of 237 verses. In many cases, no application of amendments would convince me finally to disagree with Pope, whose authority in these matters in general is worthy of the greatest respect. But the fact that there is a plausible case for alternate readings of such a high proportion of verses suggested that an analysis of the options might prove interesting, and the results seem to bear out that suggestion.

The largest category (containing over a third) of doubtful readings involves a choice between A and D, A and E, or A and A3. Frequently the matter is simply a question of which syllable to resolve or the location of secondary stress (or both). For example, for the familiar formula *Hroðgar maþelode* 371a (and the twenty-five identical on-verse occurrences) Pope reads Da, minimizing the second elements of the speaker-subject, resolving the second stress (*ma͡þe-*), and giving secondary stress to -*lod*-. Five verses later, *Ecgþeo haten* 373b is read as A. In these cases, the second element of the name, a noun-noun compound, could be given an emphasis at least equivalent to a primary or *secondary* element in a verb, shifting the stress pattern to A and D respectively. Pope's rhythm is surely correct for 373b, but 371a is further complicated by the moot question of whether to resolve *ma͡þe*- or -*lo͡de* (Da or Db). My approximation of the rhythm would be very close to Pope's, but I would classify the verse as A, finding little to stress in the secondary syllables of the verb.

In these examples, Pope has declined to give secondary stress to second elements in noun-compound proper names, but this is no consistent principle, as may be seen in his scansion of *sunu Ecglafes* 590b, 980b and *sele Hroðgares* 826b where the second elements do get secondary stress in Da readings. Even less syntactically significant elements in proper names may be stressed, as in *wine Scyldinga* 30b (Da). But compare the reading Db for *Frescyning[e]* 2503b. A similar distinction is drawn between the readings of *selerædende* 51b and *umborwesende* 46b; in both Pope resolves the light second syllable of the first element, but where the -*end*- gets the secondary stress in the former (Da), it is the final -*e* (-*de?*) which is lightly stressed to form a Db-type in the latter. Again, whereas Pope's transcription of the rhythm is nearly always unexceptionable, I might suggest that the classification of type has been forced by influences of secondary stress and syllable length where such considerations are irrelevant.

In other cases, even the preterite ending of a weak verb is given secondary stress to justify a Da reading (requiring as well resolution of a weak syllable in the first measure), e.g., *Sele hlifade* 81b. On the other hand, fairly important syllables of nouns (and adjectives) are frequently unstressed in order to get A-types instead of D's, e.g., *magodriht micel* 67a. Often the additional alliteration is the key influence in such readings, but not always (e.g., *heaðorof cyning* 2191a). And there seems to be the additional possibility for reading many of these verses as E-types, such as *morðbeala mare* 136a and *feorhbealo feorran* 156a. The resolution of the light final syllables in these verses seems to me as easy as (and the rhythm identical with) *healðegnes hete* 142a, which *is* read as E.

But if I would have syncopation in my readings of 136a, 142a, and 156a, classifying all three as Db-types (with incidental internal alliteration) while Pope reads them as A or E, it must be remembered that the differences are based on the location of *second* stress or the decision to resolve a resolvable syllable and that such decisions are what are known as "judgment calls" in baseball—where the decisions, however much they may be disputed, are not subject to formal protest. And such is the case with this entire category (including my A3 vs. A quibble—e.g., *hwile wið Hroþgar* 152a—where I suspect that the *first* alliterating syllable is incidental); but I want to consider two more examples, both in line 236—

mægenwudu mundum, meþelwordum frægn—

where Pope reads A, E. I feel that the rhythm of these verses is identical, and whether we label it A, E, or D (I lean to the last, with syncopation), the rhetorical effect demands the repetition of the pattern, superseding the relatively unimportant questions of resolution and additional alliteration.

The next largest category of questionable readings, as between E and Db, involving well over a quarter of the cases, is closely related to the first. It regularly involves a judgment between syllables for second stress and secondary stress. For example, in 494b Pope scans *þegn nytte beheold* as Db, giving *nytt-* the second stress and *-heold* secondary stress; while in 161b, he reads *sinnihte heold* as E, giving *-niht-* secondary stress and *heold* the second stress. To complicate matters further, the formula-system of 494b is repeated in 667b *(sundor-nytte beheold)* and 3118b *(sceaft nytte heold)*, and Pope reads them as E and Db respectively. All four of these verses may be rhythmically identical, though (like Pope, apparently) I would have great difficulty separating second from secondary stress. Application of Amendment IX (with IV and V to help) renders such separation unnecessary. That is, the syllables in question may be given roughly equivalent stress (and time) with a syncopated rhythm.

Similarly, it is difficult to distinguish the rhythms of *þanon eft gewat* 123b (which Pope scans Db) and *lif eac gesceop* 97b (which Pope scans E). Formulaic evidence complicates the issues here: *niðer eft gewat* 3044b alliterates on *n-* and must be D or E, but *þanon eft gewiton* 853a and *and him eft gewat* 2387a alliterate with vowels and must be B-types.[20] Perhaps two different formula-systems are involved, perhaps more, and additional alliteration may add to the confusion (see discussion of *Fyrst forð gewat* 210a above).

"Double alliteration" is what leads Pope to classify *yðde eotena cyn* 421a and *wræc Wedera nið* 423a as Db-types. My decision would rest between B and E, depending on which syllable carries the alliteration (though in either case syncopation is possible to give the two secondary stresses approximate equivalence). My inclination was to scan both as B *(eotena cynnes* 883b suggests the location of the primary

---

[20] Here, on *and* in 2387a, Pope quite properly ignores incidental or accidental alliteration, as he does in several places crucial to the rhythm: C-types—*hwyder helrunan* 163a, *ond þe þa ondsware* 354a, *min mondrihten* 436a, *ond for arstafum* 458a, *ofer ealowæge* 481a (or B?); B-types—*Him þa hildedeor* 312a, *þæt hie, þeoden min* 365a.

stresses), but the discovery of *wrecað ealdne nið* in *Juliana* 623b suggests the possibility of an E-type formula-system. The choice between Db and E occurs also with *word æfter cwæð* 315b, *word æfter spræc* 341b, and *word inne abead* 390b. Pope reads all three as D, but it is hard to be so unequivocal about stressing the adverb over the verb; perhaps equivocation has a rhythmic counterpart in the kind of syncopation suggested. In many cases there is a very fine line between second stress and secondary stress in types E and Db, and most of them must remain judgment calls. I do not imagine that complete consistency is possible or even desirable, but I would urge reasonable application of procedures, priorities, and, particularly, practical rhetorical-rhythmic performances.

Over 10 percent of the questionable readings in the portion of *Beowulf* chosen for examination are read by Pope as D-types with double alliteration. These readings may be questioned wherever it seems possible that the first alliteration is not the one that binds the on-verse to the off-verse, and formulaic evidence from *Beowulf* may be brought to bear on most of the cases. Pope's reading for *heah Healfdene* 57a is supported by *maga Healf-Denes* 189a, *sunu Healf-denes* 268a, *bearn Healfdenes* 469a, and *mago Healfdenes* 187a, all of which alliterate on the first consonant of the verse. But the syntax is not parallel, and the possibility of reading 57a as C remains by analogy with *fore Healfdenes* 1064a. No help is *hæleð Healfdena* 1069a, which could be A, D, or C. Other compounds in *-dena* shift the probability only slightly away from D to C. Whereas *aldor Eastdena* 392a, *ærest East-Dena* 616a, and *brego Beorhtdena* 427a, 609a are potentially D (or A), *Hæfde Eastdenum* 828b and *Hwæt we Gardena* 1a are definitely C.

No conclusions can be drawn, either, about *atol angenga* 165a and *eteþ an-genga* 449a, or, for that matter, about *heall heorudreore* 487a (because *heoru-dreore weoll* 849b does not apply). Nor am I convinced about *mære mearcstapa* 103a (and *micele mearc-stapan* 1348a) by an analogy with *ðeah þe*

hæð-stapa 1368a or with *Swa cwæð eardstapa* (*Wanderer* 6a).
Positive evidence can be found, however, for reading some
of the verses in this category as C-types. Line 94a, *gesette
sigehrepig*, looks suspicious as a D (despite its counterpart
Geseah ða sigehreðig 2756a) because it requires anacrusis;
but *þæt he sigehreðig* 1597a suggests a — — — *sigehreðig*
C-type formula-system. Rhythmically similar, if not identical, is *gesægd soðlice* 141a: the supporting evidence is the
C-type system of *swa we soplice* 273a (despite the internal
alliteration in *swa*) and *ac he soðlice* 2899a. Also *side
sænæssas* 223a has *þæt ic sæ-næssas* 571a for support as a C,
and *framum feohgiftum* 21a (see discussion above, p. 181)
has both *no he þære feohgyfte* 1025b and *ond æt feohgyftum*
1089a for similar support.

Rather mixed evidence exists for *Hwearf þa hrædlice*
356a. There is no close parallel, but an A3-type formula-
system occurs in *hwearf þa be bence* 1188a and *hwearf þa be
wealle* 157a. Moreover, *Gehwearf þa in Francna fæþm* 1210a,
a B-type verse, adds to the suggestion that *hwearf* at the
beginning of a verse is regularly unstressed.

Two verses in this category, *þara ymbsittendra* 9b and *þa
secg wisode* 402b, depend on emendation for D-type readings
without difficult anacrusis, by analogy with *ymbesittendra*
2734a (and *ymbsittendra—Elene* 33a) and *secg wisade* 208b.
But as they stand both verses can easily be accommodated in
C-type patterns.

Of the eleven other verses in this category little can be
said. In several, the key words are hapax legomena (e.g.,
morhopu 450a, *wælsceaftas* 398a). For others, the meager
evidence is inconclusive: *scencte scir wered* 496a has *scean
scir werod* (*Exodus* 125a) to support the D reading, while
rondas regnhearde 326a has *swa nu regnþeofas* (*Exodus*
539a) to support a C reading. In one case, *heard her cumen*
376a, at least equal is the possibility of A, with the *second*
alliteration relegated to insignificant and unaccented position. One final observation on most of the verses in this category: whether they are scanned as D or C, if the second

alliterating syllable is seen as the key to the verse (with two other roughly equivalent secondary stresses) then an effective emphasis may be achieved by syncopating this syllable, which musical notation can indicate by starting it at the end of the first measure and continuing it into the second.[21]

The next category consists of potential B-type verses which Pope has designated A, C, or D. The nine verses called D in this category all depend on double alliteration, although it seems possible to consider the second alliterating syllable as the primary stress. Three of these have been discussed under other possibilities above: *yðde eotena cyn* 421a, *heall heorudreore* 487a, and *wræc Wedera nið* 423a. For the last it was suggested that *wrecað ealdne nið* in *Juliana* 623b might influence an E reading, but the presence in this category of *wlanc Wedera leod* 341a supports a B reading for both. Another potential E listed here is *Byreð blodig wæl* 448a. Though I can find no formulaic support, I suspect that the priority of emphasis belongs with alliterating adjective rather than alliterating verb, hence scansion as B.

Three of the verses in this group include compound nouns, of which the first two are hapax legomena: *micel morgensweg* 129a, *wudu wundenhals* 298a, and *seon sibbegedriht* 387a. In support of the first are the several compounds with *morgen-* which appear in B-type verses (e.g., *Beowulf* 484b, 518b, 604b, 917b), but compounds with *wunden-* regularly appear with *w*-alliterating nouns or alone in A-type verses. Parallels for the third are *Exodus* 214a: *eall seo sibgedriht* and *Guthlac* 1372a: *mid þa sibgedryht*. Perhaps *Phoenix* 618a: *Swinsað sibgedryht* and *Beowulf* 729a: *swefan sibbegedriht* should also be read as B's. A reading of B for *þryðlic þegna heap* 400a is supported by B-type verses alliterating with *þegna* in *Christ* 457b, 943b, and *Elene* 549b, especially the last (*þa cwom þegna heap*), and also by *Andreas* 696b (*þegna heape*) and *Elene* 157a

---

[21] In my practice, of course, they would all be labeled C when the second alliterating syllable is seen as the binding one.

(*þegna þreate*), in which the noun following the genitive plural *þegna* gets the second stress in A-type verses.

Double alliteration is an issue, too, in four of the seven potential B's listed as A's by Pope, but anacrusis is also crucial in four cases. The seven are as follows:

in mægþa gehwære	25a
swa wæter bebugeð	93b
in Caines cynne	107a
ne gefeah he þære fæhðe	109a
æscholt ufan græg	330a
manna mægencræft	380a
Ðonne wæs þeos medoheal	484a.

I have discussed above (p. 180) the second of these seven, but the issues are similar for the first four. Is it easier, more natural, to recite with anacrusis or with resolution of light final syllables? Should a regular rhythm be sacrificed to accommodate primary stress for additional alliterations? Practical considerations favor B readings for all of these verses (though 109a is difficult in any case), but there is ample support for the first in *Cædmon's Hymn* 3b, *Beowulf* 2033a (both called B by Pope), 1420a, and 2527a (though Pope scans these two as Db because of the incidental "double" alliteration). The issues are not so clear-cut for the other three. For 380a, one may cite *forþan hie mægenes cræft* 418a, but a Db reading seems equally acceptable. I would probably syncopate *mægen-*. For 484a, see 638a, *Wanderer* 27a, *Elene* 1258a, *Widsith* 55b, and *Gifts of Men* 69a, in all of which *meoduhealle* carries the primary alliterating stress and the secondary stress in B- or C-type verses (depending on whether the medial or the final vowel is resolved).[22] For 330a, it may be a matter of locating stress according to

---

[22] Great assistance in checking out formulas in *Beowulf* comes from Creed's unpublished dissertation (Harvard, 1955): "Studies in the Techniques of Composition of the *Beowulf* Poetry in British Museum MS. Cotton Vitellius A. XV." In this case, for 484a, Creed cites only 3051a, 1745a, and 2063a, all A3-types verses with *þonne wæs* or *þonne bið* openings.

desired rhetorical effect, and perhaps E is the best reading. The largest group in this category contains eighteen potential B's scanned as C's by Pope. In every case, the issue is whether to resolve a medial or a final syllable, and again I suggest that in practice it is generally easier to contract, slur, or drop a final syllable. Little formulaic evidence is helpful here, since the parallel verses usually offer the identical problem. Possible exceptions are *se pæm heaðorincum* 370a, for which *no ðy ær he pone heaðorinc* 2466a (though Pope scans it A3) supports the B reading, and *pa hie to sele furðum* 323b, for which *to (in) sele pam hean* 919b, 713b may suggest the B reading. A check on *ongytan mihtan* 308b and *agifan penceð* 355b turns up a different sort of evidence: apparently there are elementary A-type formula-systems consisting of infinitive plus *penceð* or *mihte* (448b, 1535b, 541a, 739b, 800b, 964b, 1911b, 1496b, 2770b, 207a). These verses and others like them, then, should be read as A with anacrusis. In every case, however, the anacrusis is illusory since the extraneous syllable is pronounced without difficulty in the preceding measure, and since every occurrence in *Beowulf* of the apparent anacrusis is in the off-verse (see Amendment VI).

In the final (and smallest) category are grouped potential C's labeled A (e.g., 431a) or B (e.g., 202a) and potential A's labeled C (e.g., 296b). The issues here are the familiar ones —choice of primary alliteration, choice of resolvable syllable, choice of secondary stress, choice between anacrusis and alternate readings—but here, for the most part, formulaic evidence supports Pope's scansion. For example, I suspected the choice of secondary stress in reading *pær Hroðgar sæt* 356b as B (see above, p. 174), but *pær on wicge sæt* 286b and *pær se goda sæt* 1190b seem to clinch the matter (see Amendment IX above).

Two special cases remain for discussion, from this sample of slightly less than a sixth of *Beowulf: under heofenes hador* 414a and *swutol sang scopes* 90a. The first is called "F" by Pope, i.e., one of the "unclassified remainder." Two aspects of this verse raise problems for Pope: the double alliteration and the long vowel in *hador*. The emendation *haðor*, which Pope supports with new evidence, eases matters somewhat. Application of Amendments I and III suggests that these problems do not exist, but it takes judicious application of Amendment V to read the verse as a rhythmically regular B-type (emendation or not), parallel to *under heofenes hwealf* 576a, 2015a and *under Heorotes hrof* 403a.

The other verse, catalogued "D 11 (?)" by Pope in 1942, is discussed along with *beorht beacen Godes* 570a in the Preface to the 1966 Edition, pp. xxi ff. The awkwardness of the D reading is acknowledged, discussed, and finally corrected by a "three-stress variation" of a short A-type with "the alliterative pattern" of a D. Pope's three stresses here come close to the syncopation that might be suggested for these verses; but it is the additional alliteration in initial position that has distorted the scansion. They may be read as C-types, similar rhythmically to *druncon win weras* 1233a, *oððe gripe meces* 1765a, *ne gemet mannes* 2533a, *on bearm scipes* 35b, and *scop him Heort naman* 78b.

The purpose of this examination has been not to challenge a number of Pope's readings but to look for ways of handling some of the common problems of scansion. Those ways may be found in the ten statements of policy or Amendments with which I began.

INDEX

The index is arranged in four sections: (1) an index of Anglo-Saxon works and authors (italic figures refer to pages on which the poems are treated extensively); (2) an index of scholars and critics mentioned (instead of a straight bibliographical listing); (3) an index of other points of reference and comparison; and (4) an index of techniques and devices discovered in the poems and treated in the book. The first three sections are intended to be complete, but the fourth is quite selective. It omits references to sound effects and metrical terms, e.g., assonance and syncopation, and thus does not refer to the Afterword at all; to mental processes, e.g., rationalization; to the ubiquitous terminology of Old English poetic analysis, such as formula, formula-system, theme, motif, and topic; to general terms, e.g., structure and strategy; and to terms of *mere* arrangement of material, such as parataxis, juxtaposition, dichotomy, dialectic, balance, symmetry, and parallel. The first three sections are arranged in the usual alphabetical order, but an attempt has been made to arrange the fourth section schematically, so that a quick glance will show the reader what topics are discussed. For convenience in indexing throughout, the footnotes have been treated as part of the text.

III. Miscellaneous points of reference and comparison

IV. Techniques and devices

Structural Principles in Old English Poetry was set on the Linotype in Baskerville, a revival of a typeface designed by John Baskerville in the eighteenth century for use at his press in Birmingham, England. Display lines and initial letters were set in Weiss Initials Series II, modeled on the uncial handwriting in which Old English poetry was first recorded.

Hugh Bailey designed the book; it was composed, printed on paper manufactured by the S. D. Warren Company, and bound using a cloth made by Arkwright-Interlaken, Inc., by the George Banta Company, Inc., Menasha, Wisconsin.

THE UNIVERSITY OF TENNESSEE PRESS